Behind Closed Doors

HOOVER ARCHIVAL DOCUMENTARIES

General editor: *Milorad M. Drachkovitch*

The original documents reproduced in this series (unless otherwise indicated) are deposited in the archives of the Hoover Institution on War, Revolution and Peace at Stanford University. The purpose of their publication is to shed new light on some important events concerning the United States or the general history of the twentieth century.

Behind Closed Doors

Secret Papers on the Failure of
Romanian-Soviet Negotiations,
1931–1932

translated, with an introductory essay, by

Walter M. Bacon, Jr.

HOOVER INSTITUTION PRESS
Stanford University   Stanford, California 94305

Hoover Institution Publication 180

© 1979 by the Board of Trustees of the
    Leland Stanford Junior University
All rights reserved
International Standard Book Number: 0−8179−6801−6
Library of Congress Catalog Card Number: 77−78050
Printed in the United States of America

for Lynne

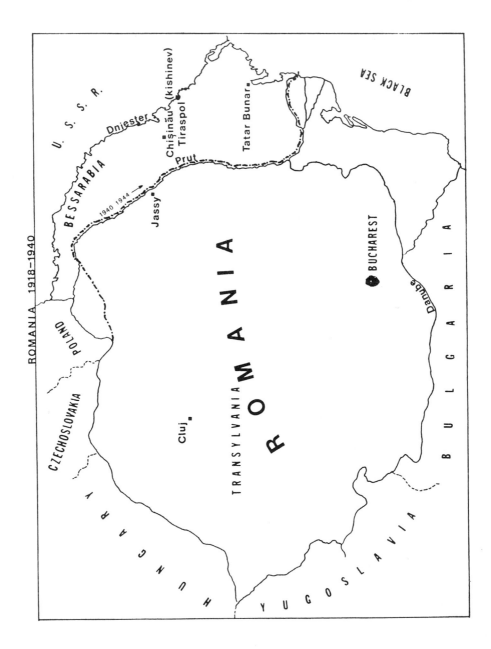

Contents

List of Documents

Preface

This volume is composed primarily of translated documents drawn from the Nicolae Titulescu Collection deposited in the archives of the Hoover Institution on War, Revolution and Peace at Stanford, California. Of the 440 documents found under the heading "USSR Peace Negotiations 1931–1932," only the most important 103 have been translated from the original Romanian or French. Together with the introductory essay, these documents provide a detailed account of Romanian-Soviet negotiations for a pact of nonaggression in 1931 and 1932. The documents are all copies of telegrams, dispatches, and intradepartmental memos of the Royal Romanian Ministry of Foreign Affairs.[1] They were originally used by Nicolae Titulescu, the eminent Romanian minister of foreign affairs and one of the chief protagonists of the episode, in his defense before the Romanian parliament on November 23 and 24, 1932, of his decision to terminate the negotiations.[2]

The documents are of both contemporary and historical importance. Contemporary Romania's independent foreign policy includes unequivocally nationalist premises. When translated, however tacitly, into action, these premises exclude any justification for the Soviet Union's annexation of Bessarabia in June 1940.[3] The nationalist element in Romanian policy had precedents in the late 1950s and early 1960s, but the statement in April 1964, of the Romanian Workers' [Communist] Party marked a clear departure from strict Soviet control.[4] In this statement, the party's Central Committee proclaimed each state's right to formulate policy in accordance with its own national interests.

One of the first manifestations of Romania's un-Soviet, though not necessarily anti-Soviet, policy was the appearance of four previously unpublished articles on Romania by Karl Marx, edited by the respected Romanian historian Andrei Oțetea. In these articles Marx polemicized against Russian imperialism, using the Russian annexation of Bessarabia as a case particularly warranting condemnation. Oțetea let Marx's statements stand by themselves. Thus the "Romanianness" of Bessarabia was legitimized by the most irrefutable source.[5]

The changing Romanian historiography on Bessarabia did not go un-noticed in either the West or the Soviet Union.[6] President Nicolae Ceauşescu himself has esoterically criticized the Comintern's, and thus the Soviet Union's, policy that directed the Romanian Communist Party to agitate in favor of the "return" of Bessarabia to the Soviet Union.[7] However, neither the Soviets nor the Romanians were prepared to permit the disagreement on Bessarabia to reach the level of open political debate. As a result, "Moldavian" and Romanian historians have been assigned the task of carrying on the debate, cloaking the under-lying issue in scholarship. Ion Oprea, a Russian-trained Romanian his-torian of high scholarly and intellectual talent and biographer of Nicolae Titulescu, found himself at the center of the controversy.[8] The occasion was his *A Fruitful Stage in the History of Romanian-Soviet Diplomatic Rela-tions 1928–1936*, published in 1967.[9] The casual reader of this amply documented work would not have noticed the implications of Oprea's presentation of the 1933 Definition of Aggression or the establishment of diplomatic relations in 1934. The Moldavian leaders in Kishinev, however, did notice, and rebutted the inference that these and other exchanges between Nicolae Titulescu and Maxim Litvinov concerned the Bessarabian question.[10] It was not until 1971 that I. M. Kopanskiĭ and I. E. Levit, attempting to refute Oprea's thesis in detail, published *Soviet-Romanian Relations 1929–1934 (From the Signing of the Moscow Protocol to the Establishment of Diplomatic Relations).*[11]

In terms of documentation the Soviets have the decided advantage, having already published the series *Documents on the Foreign Policy of the U.S.S.R.*[12] The Romanians, on the other hand, have been reluctant to publish many documents on interwar Romanian-Soviet relations, since the question of Bessarabia would be mentioned openly in almost every exchange. The present volume of Romanian documents is also of historical interest because the contents shed more light on both the Romanian and the Soviet policies of 1931–1932. On the Soviet side the reader will observe not the jovial, almost fatherly Litvinov Americans admired during the Second World War, but a sober, calculating diplo-mat of great ability and still greater disingenuousness. The domestic trauma of the First Five Year Plan and the ominous presence of an expanding Japan in the Far East demanded a substantial reduction in tension along Soviet Russia's western border. The reader will observe the uncertain transition of Soviet foreign policy in the years 1931–32, a policy formulated to accomplish just such a reduction.

On the Romanian side the reader will become acquainted with the policies and techniques of Nicolae Titulescu, one of the great diplomats of his time. Titulescu bore the responsibility for the Romanian-Soviet rapprochement of 1933–1936, which almost led to outright military alliance.[13] In the period 1931–32 Romania had only the wit and ability of her diplomats to defend her disputed possession of Bessarabia. The translated documents show the means by which a small state, deserted by her friends and pressed by her enemy, contrived to defend her national patrimony. The documents will also enlighten the reader about the policies of Poland and France, particularly as represented by Josef Beck and Edouard Herriot. Together with published French, Russian, and Polish documents, the contents of this volume offer a richly detailed account of an important interwar diplomatic episode, the Romanian-Soviet negotiations for a pact of nonaggression in 1931 and 1932.

I wish to thank Dr. Milorad M. Drachkovitch, director of the Archives and senior fellow of the Hoover Institution on War, Revolution and Peace, for his encouragement and sponsorship of this project. This volume would not have been written if it were not for the advice and friendship of Professor Josef Korbel, Dr. Ion M. Oprea, and Mr. Georges Anastasiu. I also wish to acknowledge the invaluable technical assistance of Mr. John Bryan, Mr. George Duca, and Miss Ludmila Sidoroff in preparing the essay and translations. Mr. J. M. B. Edward's editing of the volume was professional, insightful, and deeply appreciated. Above all, I wish to thank my wife, Lynne, who helped me translate, edit, and type the draft for this volume. The final manuscript draft was typed by A and D Copy and Typing Service of Denver, Colorado, and the map was drawn by Sam Cohen of the same firm.

WALTER M. BACON, JR.

Introductory Essay

Introduction

The development of Romanian-Russian relations during the last two hundred years has been dominated by two conflicting movements: Romanian nationalism and Russian expansionism. The former differed little from other East European nationalisms. Its first important manifestation was the union of the Romanian principalities of Wallachia and Moldavia in 1859. The termination of Turkish suzerainty in 1877 made independent statehood possible. Finally, as a result of World War I, an ethnically defined Greater Romania came into being. Russian expansionism, fueled by the pan-Slavic and pan-Orthodox ideologies of tsarism, sought to extend Russian "protection" to orthodox Christians under Turkish rule and to the Balkan Slavs. To accomplish either end, Russia needed access to the populations in question. Without directly encountering the interests of other great powers, Russia's only route to the Balkans was through the Romanian lands. It was therefore inevitable that Romanian nationalism and Russian expansionism would come into conflict.

ROMANIAN-RUSSIAN RELATIONS TO 1931

In an era dominated by great powers who had not yet acknowledged the right of nations to self-determination, the interests of Russian imperialism generally held sway. Other great powers, preoccupied with the defeat of Napoleonic France, acquiesced to the Turkish cession of Bessarabia to Russia in 1812. These same conservative powers did not hinder Russian occupation of the principalities from 1828 to 1834, and approved Russia's crushing of the nationalist revolution in 1848. The Congress of Berlin allowed Russia to reannex southern Bessarabia in 1878. Similarly, the dominant powers, first Germany and then the Allies, endorsed the annexation of Bessarabia in 1940 and its legitimization by the peace treaty of 1946.

These events point to one conclusion: only when Russian interests conflicted with those of a more powerful coalition of powers were the manifestations of Romanian nationalism allowed to appear. The restoration of southern Bessarabia to Moldavia and the union of 1859 were outgrowths of Russia's defeat in the Crimean War; independence was acknowledged by the Congress of Berlin in return for Romania's forced cession of southern Bessarabia; and the inclusion of Bessarabia in Greater Romania was made possible by Russia's defeat in World War I and the Allies' fear of Bolshevism.

Nationalism, or more properly irredentism, was the operative factor in Romania's decision, in August 1916, to enter World War I on the side of the Entente. The Central Powers, with whom King Carol I (ruled 1866–1914) had secretly aligned his country in 1883, offered Bessarabia as Romania's reward for belligerency against the Allies. King Ferdinand's (ruled 1914–1927) government, however, accepted the counteroffer of Transylvania made by the Entente. The war was difficult for Romania. One of the principal reasons for the Romanian defeat was the collapse of Russia from battlefield catastrophes and domestic revolution. Despite two significant Romanian victories during the summer of 1917, the Russian debacle exposed the Romanian right flank and forced the government to sue for peace. The dictated Treaty of Bucharest (May 7, 1918) was never ratified, and Romania reentered the war. The Paris Peace Conference, which Romania attended as a victorious power, legitimized the union of Transylvania with the Old Kingdom.

During the time of her most trying battlefield experiences, in 1917 and 1918, and as a direct result of the Russian revolutions of March and November, 1917, Romania also came into de facto possession of Bessarabia. There, as elsewhere in the non-Russian lands of the former tsarist empire, nationalism and social revolution combined in creating vehicles for expressing popular will. Initially the Bessarabian revolution demanded only autonomy within the new democratic and federated Russian state: first through the voice of a Moldavian National Party (March, 1917); then of a soldiers' congress (October, 1917); and finally of the Sfatul Țării, or State Council, in the form of the Moldavian Federated Democratic Republic (December, 1917). The newly formed Soviet government in Petrograd, perhaps in the spirit of revolution but more likely in that of Russian nationalism, refused to accept its lack of direct control in Bessarabia and fomented violence. By January 1918 the province had been brought to a state of chaos that endangered the provisioning of what was left of the Romanian army and government (both had fled to Jassy). In order to insure its own survival, and in response to the urgent requests of Moldavian deputies of the Sfatul Țării, which had been disbanded by the Bolsheviks, the Romanian army entered Bessarabia. It quickly occupied most of the province despite spirited Bolshevik resistance. Under pressure from both the Bolsheviks and the Allies, the Romanian prime minister, Alexander Averescu, himself a Bessarabian, agreed to evacuate Bessarabia gradually and not to interfere in its internal affairs.

Simultaneously with Bolshevik acceptance of this pledge, however, the new Germanophile government of Alexander Marghiloman signed a preliminary peace with the Central Powers. The latter agreed to invite Bessarabian delegates to the peace negotiations in Bucharest. The Bessarabian revolutionaries distrusted Marghiloman's marked conservatism. Nevertheless, with the blessing of the Allied ministers in Jassy, the reconvened Sfatul Țării declared for union with Romania on April 9, 1918. The vote was eighty-six to three with thirty-six abstentions and thirteen absent, the last three groups representing various non-Romanian minorities.[1]

Despite a second unconditional affirmation of the act of union by the Sfatul Țării (December 8, 1918), the Bolsheviks continued to machinate against Romanian sovereignty in Bessarabia. In this effort they were joined during the Paris Peace Conference by Russian Whites of varying political persuasions.[2] The Allies' anti-Bolshevism, fueled by the excesses of Bela Kun's abortive Hungarian Soviet Republic and Romania's successful intervention against it, combined with the substantial arguments presented by the Romanian delegation to negate all the Russian depositions. The conference's commission on Yugoslav and Romanian affairs, chaired by André Tardieu, accepted the recommendation of the French delegate Jules Laroche supporting the justice of Romania's claim. On October 28, 1920, the British Empire, France, Italy, Japan, and Romania signed a convention recognizing Romanian sovereignty in Bessarabia. Romania was obligated to guarantee minority rights and to assume a fraction (one to one and one-half percent) of the tsarist debt. The convention also stipulated that, upon Russian request, the Council of the League of Nations could be empowered to arbitrate the dispute.[3] The Soviet government, which had not participated in any of these decisions, never recognized their validity and continued to insist that Romania was illegally occupying Bessarabia.

While an international solution to the Bessarabian question was being discussed, a series of sporadic face-to-face meetings between Romanian and Soviet representatives began to get under way. On the urging of Lloyd George, Romanian Prime Minister Alexander Vaida-Voevod sent Dimitrie N. Ciotori to Copenhagen to discuss Romanian-Russian prisoner exchange with the Soviet diplomatic agent Maxim M. Litvinov. Although no substantive progress was made, the Copenhagen talks led to

formal negotiations in Warsaw.[4] Moscow agreed to all Vaida's conditions
for the negotiations except the principle of the return of the Romanian
treasure, which had been sent to Moscow during the war to preclude its
falling into German hands. After the conclusion of the Russo-Polish
War, in which Romania remained strictly neutral, the Warsaw negotiations were convened in September 1920. The Soviet delegate, L. M.
Karakhan, suggested what amounted to an exchange of Bessarabia for
the treasure.[5] Although the new Romanian prime minister, General
Averescu, was in favor of accepting the proposal, Foreign Minister Take
Ionescu opposed it; the above-mentioned Bessarabian Convention had
intervened, and France feared a Romanian-Russian accommodation.
The Warsaw talks, perhaps the best and last opportunity to settle the
dispute amicably, were adjourned.

Romanian-Soviet relations during the next three years ranged from
correct to chaotic. There were intermittent diplomatic contacts (at
international conferences and in Warsaw), mutual assurances of good
will, numerous insurrectionary incidents in Bessarabia (which Bucharest
claimed were instigated by Communist agents), press recriminations,
and official protests. After prolonged preliminary meetings, low-level
Soviet and Romanian diplomats did agree on the establishment of mixed
commissions to deal with incidents on the Dniester (November 20,
1923). In early 1924 the Soviet government agreed to a Romanian
proposal for a conference to review all Romanian-Soviet questions,
including the establishment of diplomatic relations. Hopes for success
were diminished by France's ratification of the 1920 Bessarabian Convention just two weeks before the opening of the conference. Because
any Soviet concessions would have been interpreted as acquiescence in
the status quo, the Chief Soviet delegate, N. N. Krestinsky, was compelled to restate Russia's position and to demand a plebiscite. The
Romanians, who had wished to avoid such a public restatement of the
dispute, refused to discuss the issue and the Vienna Conference ended
in failure.[6]

The press exposure of the Romanian-Soviet controversy in Vienna
could only harm Romania since she refused to acknowledge the existence of a "Bessarabian question." Succeeding Romanian governments
resolved never again to allow the Soviets a similar opportunity to openly
air their Bessarabian pretensions. The press polemic continued. C. G.
Rakovsky, the Soviet ambassador in Paris, who was a Bolshevik of
Bulgarian descent and a former Romanian citizen, became the primary
spokesman for the Soviet cause, while Nicolae Titulescu, Romania's
minister in London and chief delegate to the League of Nations, wrote
extensively on the Romanian position.[7]

In September 1924 the most serious Bessarabian disturbance to date broke out in the predominantly non-Romanian southeastern part of the province around the town of Tatar Bunar. The government quickly crushed the insurrection, but not before it had resulted in considerable destruction, heavy casualties, and mass arrests. Soviet reaction to the "Tatar Bunar affair" gave rise to the creation of the so-called Moldavian Autonomous Soviet Socialist Republic (MASSR) within the Ukrainian SSR; it consisted of those districts north and east of the Dniester with concentrated Moldavian (i.e., Romanian) populations. Until 1940 the MASSR acted as an irredentist magnet for the dissatisfied inhabitants of Bessarabia and as the center for Soviet subversion of Romanian territorial integrity.

Postwar Romanian foreign policy was based on a system of three alliances, all of which were established to protect member-states against revision of the settlements of 1919 and 1920. The Little Entente of Romania, Czechoslovakia, and Yugoslavia was directed against Hungarian and Bulgarian revisionism; the Polish-Romanian alliance provided for a common defense against Soviet aggression; and the French alliance (with the League of Nations guarantees) was aimed at thwarting revision on a continental and global scale. Upon signing of the Franco-Romanian Treaty of Friendship (June 10, 1926), France required Romania to formally restate her permanent pledge of nonaggression vis-à-vis Russia. Despite the treaty's nebulous provisions, Rakovsky, the Soviet ambassador in Paris, protested France's implicit guarantee of Romanian territorial integrity.[8]

Romanian-Soviet relations remained stable—uniformly bad—from 1925 to 1929. In loyalty to her ally, Poland insisted that Soviet Russia invite Romania to sign the Litvinov (or Moscow) Protocol of February 9, 1929, which stipulated the early coming into force of the Kellogg-Briand Pact (Pact of Paris) renouncing war. The Soviets unwillingly consented.[9] While Litvinov recognized that the Soviet signature eliminated the legal possibility of resolving the Bessarabian dispute by force, he explicitly stated that neither the pact nor the protocol prejudiced Soviet claims in any way.[10] These new promises of nonaggression did not significantly improve Romanian-Soviet relations, which continued in their previous pattern until May 1931.

PRELIMINARIES TO NEGOTIATIONS, MAY–DECEMBER 1931

The new direction in Romanian-Soviet relations was the product of events tangential to them. The change originated neither in Bucharest

nor in Moscow. The latter continued to proclaim the illegality of the
Romanian "occupation" of Bessarabia.[11] At the same time, the new
(April 1931) Romanian government of Professor Nicolae Iorga was
just as nationalist and anti-Communist as any of its predecessors. As
in 1929, it was the Poles who initiated the attempt at Romanian-Soviet
rapprochement.

On several occasions since 1926, Soviet and Polish diplomats had
discussed the possibility of a bilateral pact of nonaggression.[12] Mid-1931
was a propitious period in which to resume such discussions, for three
reasons. First, the Soviets were apprehensive about Japanese aggression
in Manchuria. Moreover, the greatest measure of Soviet energy was
committed to overcoming the traumas of the First Five Year Plan.
Untroubled western borders were therefore a necessity for the USSR.
Second, increasingly strident German revisionism coupled with manifest
French faintheartedness made the Poles more amenable to reaching an
agreement with Soviet Russia.[13] Third, in May 1931, France, tied to
Poland by a pact of mutual assistance, had agreed to start negotiations
between Phillipe Berthelot, secretary-general of the Quai d'Orsay, and
V. S. Dovgalevsky, the Soviet ambassador in Paris, for pacts of commerce
and nonaggression.[14] As France was obligated toward Poland, so too
Poland was obligated toward the Baltic States and Romania. When the
Polish Foreign Ministry drafted a pact of nonaggression with the USSR,
one of the stipulations—not unexpectedly—was that Romania, Latvia,
Estonia, and Finland conclude analogous pacts with the Soviet Union.

The Polish Initiative

In mid-May Count Ian Szembek, the Polish minister in Bucharest,
informed the Romanian Foreign Ministry about Poland's plans and
asked the Romanian government three questions: (1) Was Romania inclined to conclude a bilateral pact of nonaggression with the USSR? (2)
If so, would Romania agree to have Poland act as intermediary? (3) What
was the Romanian opinion of the Polish draft? The Romanian government was less than enthusiastic about the utility and chances for success
of the initiative, but replied positively to the first two questions in order
to please its Polish allies. It then proposed various modifications of the
Polish draft. These were designed to avoid giving the Soviets a pretext
for raising the Bessarabian issue, and to augment the guarantees of the
Kellogg-Briand Pact and the Litvinov Protocol (see documents 1 and 2,
below). The Poles accepted most of the Romanian changes, but rejected
Romania's desire to use the proposed Romanian-Soviet treaty as a
vehicle for de facto Soviet recognition of the Dniester frontier. At the

same time Count Szembek assured Bucharest that the treaties' provisions would strengthen, not weaken, the provisions of the Kellogg-Briand Pact and would enhance solidarity among the Soviet Union's western neighbors (documents 3 and 4).

On August 25, 1931, the draft of a Romanian-Soviet treaty of nonaggression was presented to Count Szembek (document 5). The following day Szembek urgently requested an audience with Foreign Minister Dimitri Ghika. He told Ghika that some discrepancies between the Romanian and Polish texts required clarification before he forwarded the draft to Warsaw. Szembek feared that the specific Romanian exclusion of territorial questions from conflicts subject to arbitration (see document 1) would imperil the success of eventual Soviet-Romanian negotiations carried out through Poland's good offices. While assuring Szembek that the Romanian wording was negotiable, Ghika insisted on a textual guarantee against a legal opportunity for the Soviets to bring Romanian sovereignty in Bessarabia before an arbitration tribunal. Szembek carried the Romanian draft to Poland where Polish Foreign Minister Auguste Zaleski concluded that the Romanian position on arbitration did not constitute an insurmountable difficulty (document 6).

The Polish-Romanian exchange may have been premature. There is some evidence that the Soviets suggested a resumption of Polish-Soviet discussions as early as October, 1930.[15] Despite this, Commissar for Foreign Affairs M. M. Litvinov repeatedly denied that Franco-Soviet negotiations preordained similar talks with Poland.[16] On August 4, Stanislas Patek, the Polish minister in Moscow, broached the question of Polish-Soviet negotiations for a pact of nonaggression to L. M. Karakhan (the USSR's expert on nonaggression, B. S. Stomonyakov, was absent). Among the four unresolved problems discussed was "the question of Romania."[17] Patek presented the Polish draft to Karakhan on August 23, some days after the secret initialing of the Franco-Soviet pact.[18] At first the Soviets refused to proceed with negotiations, citing Poland's insistence on the conclusion of similar treaties with the USSR's other western neighbors (see document 2, articles V and VI).[19] However, as the Japanese advance in Manchuria became more menacing, Litvinov became more amenable. In October he restarted discussions.[20] These led to the crucial Patek-Litvinov meeting of November 14, 1931.

Returning to Moscow after consultations in Warsaw, Patek was received by Litvinov. The commissar for foreign affairs, while willing to begin negotiations with Poland, rejected the Polish draft because of Poland's pretension of negotiating for the Baltic States and Romania. Litvinov insisted on direct negotiations with each state. He also pointed out the difficulties of negotiating with Romania, a country with which the USSR

did not enjoy normal relations and with which it had a territorial
conflict. Patek proposed that the question of Bessarabia be "left open"
(*laissé ouvert* in French, *ostavlennyĭ otkrytym* in Russian) in any Soviet-
Romanian discussion.[21] Litvinov also suggested that the Polish-Soviet
talks be conducted on the basis of the Franco-Soviet text.[22] Most
importantly, the Soviet commissar refused to invite Romania to negotiate, insisting that the initiative come from Bucharest. Litvinov's proposals were duly reported to the Romanian minister in Warsaw, Grigore
Bilciurescu (document 7).

Faced with Litvinov's demands and Poland's less-than-welcome pressure, the Romanian government reluctantly proposed negotiations to
the Soviet Union, but only on the clear understanding that the Bessarabian question would not arise during the discussions (documents 8, 14,
15, and 19). In response to Romania's inquiry, the Quai d'Orsay stated
that France did not object to direct Romanian-Soviet talks, and that in
case of their failure France's commitments to Romania would remain
intact.[23] Consequently, Bilciurescu was instructed to broach the question
to Soviet Minister in Poland V. A. Antonov-Ovseyenko in as unobtrusive
and unofficial manner as possible (document 9). The resulting meeting
took place on December 4. The Soviet Minister confirmed Litvinov's
statements to Patek and promised to ask Moscow for instructions
(document 10). Simultaneously, Romanian Minister Ion Carp in Ankara
(document 12) and Chargé d'Affaires Sturdza in Riga made similar
contacts with their Soviet counterparts.[24] With French prodding (documents 14 and 17) Ghika negotiated through Carp with Y. Z. Surits, the
Soviet ambassador to Turkey, in an effort to find a mutually acceptable
location for the talks. Romania proposed Warsaw (document 13), while
the Soviets countered with Ankara (document 15). After the Romanians
had rejected Moscow (documents 17 and 18), the two sides agreed on
Riga (documents 20 and 21).

Bucharest's lack of enthusiasm for the entire project did not abate.
Ghika was apparently disinclined to tell Szembek frankly that Romania
did not want an extraneous treaty of nonaggression with the USSR, did
not want to negotiate such a treaty, and, most certainly, did not wish to
initiate such negotiations.[25] Instead, he and (by his order) other Romanian diplomats told French representatives that the dangers of entering
into discussions with the Soviets far outweighed any advantages that
might result (documents 11 and 17). Litvinov, as he is revealed in Soviet
documents, appears to have been no more enthusiastic.

Prince Dimitri Ghika was a capable diplomat with a good record as
Romania's minister to Italy, but his diplomatic expertise had not
prepared him for the conspiratorial intricacies of Romanian domestic

politics. Several times during his tenure as foreign minister (April 1931–May 1932) Ghika threatened to resign over relatively insignificant incidents.[26] His frustration was complicated by Prime Minister Iorga's suspicion that Nicolae Titulescu, who had failed to form a government in April 1931 when Iorga had succeeded, was conspiring to overturn his cabinet. Titulescu, although not foreign minister, was accustomed to being consulted on all major foreign policy matters.[27] Ghika found this practice demeaning and annoying. Titulescu belatedly learned of the government's contacts with the Soviet Union not from Ghika but from his friend Auguste Zaleski. From his legation in London, Titulescu warned against the possible effect on Romania's status in Bessarabia of a nonaggression pact that included provisions for arbitration and conciliation (document 16). In the phrasing of his dispatch Titulescu clearly indicated his refusal to be left out of the process of Romanian-Soviet negotiations, an intimation that he frequently reiterated during the following months.

THE RIGA NEGOTIATIONS, JANUARY 1932

Soviet-Romanian contact was established in Riga on January 6, 1932, when Romanian Chargé d'Affaires Mihai R. Sturdza and Soviet Delegate B. S. Stomonyakov exchanged their governments' draft treaties of nonaggression. Mihai Sturdza had witnessed the Vienna debacle in 1924 as a junior diplomat at the Romanian legation. After serving in Washington, Sturdza was assigned to the Riga legation in 1929. He was a man of set opinions and dubious ability whose anti-Sovietism did not augur well for his mission. In his memoirs he remarked of this period that "Rumania was in the happy situation of not having diplomatic (nor any other) relations with the Soviet Union."[28] Perhaps because of his junior status among Romanian diplomats, Sturdza was surprised when he was designated as the Romanian negotiator.[29] Boris Stomonyakov, a member of the Collegium of the People's Commissariat of Foreign Affairs and an expert on the Baltic States, Poland, and Romania, was an experienced diplomat of Bulgarian origin with expertise in nonaggression negotiations.[30] He was charged with negotiating with Romania, Latvia, and Estonia.[31] The match was uneven.

In his instructions to Sturdza of December 31, 1931, Ghika clearly indicated the pessimism and resignation with which the Romanian government entered into negotiations. Above all, Sturdza was not to allow mention of Bessarabia. Ghika also stressed the importance of defining the territory against which aggression could not be committed.

Sturdza was instructed to be dispassionate and admiring of Soviet achievements (document 22). The Romanian text was based on the Polish draft. The key phrase in article I, paragraph 2 stipulated: "Acts considered as contrary [to nonaggression] will be any act of violence impairing the *integrity* and the *inviolability* of the territory which is presently under the *sovereignty* of the other Contracting Party" (author's emphasis, document 23). This passage implied a de facto Soviet recognition that Bessarabia was under Romanian sovereignty and represented Romania's first negotiating priority. On the other hand, the Soviet preamble stated that "the establishment of such relations does not bring any prejudice to the existing litigation between the two Contracting Parties about Bessarabia" (documents 26 and 27). This phrasing was a clear violation of the Romanian interpretation of the "assurances" which Litvinov had given to Patek on November 14 and subsequently to others (see document 42). If these two positions were maintained, the Riga talks would be doomed to failure.

While Sturdza was waiting to begin negotiations in Riga, Ghika was preparing the Romanian government and public opinion. On January 5, he reported to King Carol II and to the cabinet on the considerations that had induced Romania to begin negotiations that she did not want and that, he stressed, were undertaken only because of French and Polish pressure (document 24).[32] Romanian public opinion was dismayed (document 25).[33]

The first formal negotiating session in Riga (January 7) set the tone for the five others that were to follow. Stomonyakov chided Sturdza for negotiating *ad referendum* (i.e., he had to receive the consent of his superiors in Bucharest for all major decisions). Sturdza rebuked Stomonyakov for inserting mention of Bessarabia into the preamble, while the Soviet delegate countered with an attack on the stipulations of article I, paragraph 2 of the Romanian draft. In accordance with a preconceived strategy (document 26), Sturdza suggested that rather than terminate the discussion then and there, the two diplomats might bypass consideration of the preamble and proceed to the articles of both drafts. Stomonyakov replied that he would have to consult his government (document 28).[34] In compliance with Litvinov's replies, at the second meeting (January 11) Stomonyakov told Sturdza that the USSR could not sign a pact that did not formally state that the Bessarabian question remained open.[35] Sturdza refused to sign a procès-verbal and to acknowledge a Soviet note mentioning Bessarabia.[36] Both negotiators then agreed to consult their governments (documents 29 and 32).

Ghika approved Sturdza's actions and pressed the Poles to discover Litvinov's intentions (document 30). In Bucharest Mihai Arion outlined the Romanian position to Szembek (document 31). The first two sessions at Riga were carried out during Foreign Minister Ghika's official visit to Warsaw, a visit that underlined Polish-Romanian determination to defend their eastern frontiers against any Soviet aggression.[37] Ghika met with Pilsudski, Zaleski, Patek, Schaetzel, and Under Secretary of State for Foreign Affairs Josef Beck.[38] He could only reiterate his pessimism about the Riga talks, but he must have been cheered by Zaleski's public pledge that Poland would not sign her pact with the Soviets until Romania had finalized a similar treaty.[39]

The third Riga session was held on January 14. With the authorization of his government Stomonyakov agreed to discuss the rest of the pact as Sturdza had suggested.[40] At the same time he maintained that the USSR would never sign a pact that did not allude to the Bessarabian problem.[41] Equally unacceptable would be a pact that contained the words "integrity," "inviolability," or "sovereignty." The two delegates wrote a procès-verbal that mentioned areas of both agreement and disagreement (document 33).

Becoming increasingly skeptical about the possibility of Soviet concessions, Ghika shifted the Romanian negotiating priorities: Warsaw and Paris should know that the rupture, when it came, was due to Moscow's and not Bucharest's intransigence. He instructed Sturdza to replace the abstract notion of territory in article I, paragraph 2 with a concrete demarcation—the Dniester (document 34).

Meanwhile the often slow and difficult Polish-Soviet talks were showing more promise of success.[42] The Poles became apprehensive that a precipitous rupture in Riga would endanger the prospect of agreement with the Soviets. They urged the Romanians to be patient and to expect Soviet concessions (documents 35 and 36). When the fourth Riga session produced no progress (document 36), Sturdza asked Ghika to rescind his instructions to introduce the geographical definition of territory (document 37), but Ghika had already suggested the idea to Warsaw and Paris. Both Berthelot and Zaleski promised support for the Romanian position (documents 38 and 39).

The last two negotiating sessions in Riga were held on January 18 and 20, 1932. In reluctant compliance with Ghika's instructions (document 34), Sturdza proposed the Dniester demarcation *if* the Soviets agreed not to introduce extraneous questions (i.e., Bessarabia) into the text.[43] On January 20, Stomonyakov rejected the Romanian proposal.[44] Instead, he suggested the following wording for article I, paragraph 2: "Acts considered as contrary [to nonaggression] will be any attempt of a Contracting Party to resolve through violence the territorial or other existing litigations between it and the other Party." Sturdza refused to record the suggestion in a procès-verbal (document 40). The following day Stomonyakov sent Sturdza a letter reiterating the Soviet position and the last Soviet proposal; he also affirmed that the Riga stage of negotiations had ended (document 41). Although Sturdza was tempted to return the letter, he opened and copied it, an action that created controversy.[45] The Riga negotiations had ended in failure.[46]

While it is not my intention in this essay to judge either side's conduct of the Riga negotiations, the documents of both countries reveal no substantial evidence of a conciliatory spirit on either's part.[47] Neither side made serious efforts to render the Bessarabian issue less explosive. As a result of Soviet firing upon so-called kulaks fleeing across the Dniester, Romania declared a state of siege in Bessarabia.[48] After his return from Warsaw and Prague, Ghika granted the press an interview (January 15) in which he castigated the Soviets for their breach of faith.[49] In a statement to TASS Litvinov polemically restated the Soviet negotiating position but noted that agreement had been reached on many points.[50] Litvinov's statement immediately followed his and Patek's initialing of the Polish-Soviet pact, which the Polish Foreign Office had rushed through "even at the expense of abandoning some trifling point of law or some detail of wording."[51]

DEVELOPMENTS FROM FEBRUARY TO JUNE 1932

Even after Count Szembek had informed the Romanian government that the Polish-Soviet pact had been concluded, he continued to promise that Poland would not sign the treaty until the completion of a Romanian-Soviet pact (documents 43, 45, and 47).[52] At the same time, the Poles pressed the Romanians to make concessions on some "trifling points of law and details of wording" in talks that they proposed to arrange between Litvinov and Ghika in Geneva (documents 44 and 45).[53] Although disturbed by the panic in the Romanian press following the initialing of the Polish-Soviet pact (document 46), the French also assured the Romanians that they would not sign their pact with the Soviets before the achievement of a Romanian-Soviet accord (document 48). French policy in this respect did not change despite the departure of Aristide Briand from the cabinet of Pierre Laval, himself a reluctant overseer of Franco-Soviet rapprochement (document 39). In February André Tardieu replaced Laval as head of government and foreign minister, a succession that led to a slowdown in the development of closer Franco-Soviet relations.[54]

The Poles, once they had initialed their pact and seen that negotiations between the Baltic states and the USSR seemed assured of success, apparently wavered as to how far and fast they should push their Romanian allies. In Geneva Ghika patiently waited for Zaleski to arrange a meeting with Litvinov although he sensed that the proposal was no longer valid.[55] In Bucharest, Szembek and Legation Secretary Dembinski urged the Romanian government to make concessions, while in Warsaw Beck made similar appeals to Bilciurescu.[56] This confusion of policies led Ghika to accurately conclude that a dualism existed in Polish foreign policy formulation (document 50), which pitted the gentlemanly and cosmopolitan Auguste Zaleski against the singleminded and calculating Josef Beck.

Concurrently a split developed in the formulation of Romanian foreign policy. Nicolae Titulescu resented being excluded from the decisions relating to the Riga negotiations. He opposed both the initial contact with the Soviets and the continuation of the talks in Geneva; any discussion of litigations, he believed, worked to Romania's disadvantage (document 49). In order to emphasize his displeasure and in protest of the unsatisfactory development of Romanian-Soviet contacts, Titulescu submitted his resignation from his London and Geneva posts to King Carol II during a dramatic trip to Bucharest in February.[57] Titulescu won over both the King and the less tractable government to his position and his criticism of Sturdza.[58] After consulting with Romanian political leaders, Titulescu agreed to resume his posts with added powers, including the direction of all negotiations with the Soviets.[59]

Titulescu's victory in Bucharest foreshadowed an even less conciliatory Romanian attitude and a more expert and exact scrutiny of those "trifling points of law and details of wording" so disliked by Beck's faction in Warsaw. The following six months of "negotiations" bore the imprints of Titulescu's legalism and Beck's growing exasperation with Romania's stubborn independence.

Beck renewed his entreaties.[60] Ghika, however, persisted in his belief that Romania should neither change her position nor spur Zaleski to action, a policy that both he and Zaleski realized would be abetted by Tardieu's attitude (document 50).[61] Titulescu did not change Romanian policy after Ghika had returned to Bucharest. In his first meeting with Titulescu, Zaleski revealed that he had repeated to Litvinov Poland's pledge not to sign without Romania and that, despite the Soviets' threat of a press polemic, Zaleski was unmoved (document 51).[62] Titulescu told both Zaleski and the Quai d'Orsay's René Massigli that the essential prerequisite for the resumption of Romanian-Soviet negotiations was an official Soviet retraction of Stomonyakov's letter to Sturdza (documents 51 and 52).

Titulescu's meetings with Zaleski and Massigli took place against the backdrop of the debate in the League of Nations assembly on the Sino-Japanese conflict. In a speech lauded by both the Chinese and the Japanese, Titulescu emphasized the provisions of the Kellogg-Briand Pact and of article X of the League Covenant, his mind not so much on the matter at hand as on Romania's future interests and on Bessarabia.[63]

Tardieu, as anticipated, maintained a pro-Romanian policy.[64] He bluntly told Litvinov that any Soviet reservation concerning Bessarabia would prohibit Romanian-Soviet agreement (document 53). The Poles were not as supportive of their allies: a serious diplomatic incident had raised the possibility that the Soviet Union might be having second thoughts about the utility of the nonaggression pacts.[65] The Poles pressured the Estonians to resume negotiations.[66] Meanwhile the Romanians were forewarned to expect similar leverage during Pilsudski's mid-April visit to Romania (document 54). Even with the warning, Iorga and Ghika were unprepared for the vigor of the aging marshal's Francophobe declarations and his renunciation of Poland's pledge not to sign without concomitant Romanian action. Although stunned, Ghika and Iorga were not intimidated by Pilsudski's blustering (document 55).[67] In order to appease the government he had affronted and to underscore the continuing validity of the Polish-Romanian alliance, Pilsudski made a well-publicized stop in Chişinău (Kishinev) on his way back to Warsaw.[68]

Titulescu's analysis of Pilsudski's intervention motivated the formulation of a policy that, while it did not obscure the Polish government's breach of trust, was to demonstrate Romania's independence and imperturbability in the face of adversity (documents 57 and 59). Berated by Titulescu for his lack of influence, the loyal Zaleski nonetheless attempted to sway Pilsudski (document 57). Zaleski also met with Litvinov in the hope of negotiating a mutually acceptable Romanian-Soviet formula that would include retraction of the Stomonyakov letter (documents 57 and 61). The French—André Tardieu, Joseph Paul-Boncour and René Massigli—may have been sensitive to Titulescu's threat to seek loyal allies elsewhere (i.e., in Berlin).[69] In any case, they not only worked for a Soviet-Romanian accommodation along the lines of Titulescu's previously formulated conditions but urged the Romanians themselves to be amenable (documents 56, 57, 58, and 60). Throughout these Polish and French intermediary efforts in April and May, Romanian policy remained unchanged.

THE POLISH-SOVIET PACT, JUNE–JULY 1932

In the spring and summer of 1932, three changes of government made Poland's policy toward Romania shift from Zaleski's gentle persuasion to Beck's less-than-diplomatic pressure. First, the French Right of André Tardieu was defeated in the elections of May 1932. In June, a Center-Left cabinet took office with Edouard Herriot as head of government and foreign minister.[70] Second, and more importantly, the continuing political malaise in Romania was compounded as the Iorga government's serious mismanagement of the depression-spawned financial crisis became known.[71] When the government was unable to pay state employees, Iorga resigned (May 31, 1932).[72] Titulescu tried and failed to form a government of national union. Alexander Vaida-Voevod was then called upon to constitute a National-Peasant cabinet and to prepare for elections in mid-July.[73] Both Vaida, who had initiated the first Romanian-Soviet contact in 1920, and Herriot, whose government had recognized the USSR· in 1924, were perceived in Warsaw as more susceptible to Polish entreaties than their predecessors had been. Third, Poland's new aggressive diplomacy was also stimulated when the moderate Dr. Heinrich Brüning was replaced by the nationalist Franz von Papen as chancellor of Germany (document 64).

The Vaida government had hardly assumed its responsibilities when Count Szembek asked to see Grigore Gafencu, the under secretary of state for foreign affairs.[74] On June 10, Szembek informed Gafencu and Vaida that, in order to maintain Poland's solidarity with the Baltic States, Poland would shortly sign her pact of nonaggression with the Soviet Union. The Romanians, who despite their anger remained calm, pointed out that such precipitous Polish action would compromise the Polish-Romanian alliance and would invariably complicate the elections. On the same day, Titulescu complained to the French minister about the Polish démarche (document 62). The French government instructed Laroche to make a démarche to the Polish Foreign Ministry warning against placing undue pressure on the Romanian government. At the same time, the French cautioned the Romanians against using dilatory tactics (documents 65 and 66).

In separate reports the Romanian diplomatic representatives in Warsaw and Riga confirmed the authenticity of Count Szembek's information.[75] However, once the Poles had achieved the desired effect and new Romanian formulae were being elaborated, Szembek's entreaties reverted to a more diplomatic tone (document 63). In Warsaw Beck promised the new Romanian minister, Victor Cadere, that Zaleski would energetically renew his mediating efforts in Geneva (document 64). Cadere assured Beck that Romania had every intention of reaching an agreement with the Soviets.[76] He was then able to report that a delay of the Polish signing appeared to have been won.[77]

Despite fresh Romanian-Polish-Soviet contacts in Geneva, Szembek continued to tell the Romanian government that although the delay in Poland's signing would only be brief, the ratification could be postponed for a longer time (document 67). In order to clarify these conflicting reports the Romanian Foreign Ministry requested an immediate interview for Cadere with Marshal Pilsudski.[78] In the interview, which took place on July 3, Pilsudski promised Cadere a short delay in the signing. He went on to pledge that Poland would not ratify her pact without the certainty of a concomitant Romanian-Soviet pact (document 68). Since their recent experience of Polish promises had been far from pleasant, the Romanians repeatedly asked for a formal Polish pledge on nonratification (documents 69 and 71). The dualism in Polish foreign policy decision making was again manifest when Zaleski finally made the formal promise to Titulescu in Geneva (document 74). Zaleski's announcement of the pledge to Litvinov in Geneva and Patek's parallel statement to Antonov-Ovseyenko in Warsaw were apparently a bluff. Meanwhile Beck and semi-official Polish reports hedged on the promise, indicating that it was not of indefinite duration (documents 75 and 76).

The Romanians were initially unsure about the advisability of publishing Zaleski's pledge.[79] When the Polish signing became imminent, however, they prepared to publish it unilaterally. Their purpose was to mollify Romanian public opinion and reassert the validity of the Polish-Romanian alliance (document 78). When the Polish-Soviet pact was signed on July 25, the Romanian Foreign Ministry issued a communiqué to the press that included the pledge (document 80). Both Szembek (document 81) and Beck (document 82) told the Romanians that Zaleski's promise had been misunderstood. Yet Szembek's statement to the Bucharest press did not *directly* refute the Romanian Foreign Ministry's communiqué.[80] For their part, the Romanians declared to the Poles that the pledge was irrevocable (document 83).

The Polish-Romanian exchange took place concurrently with new Polish mediation efforts in Geneva. After meeting extensively with the new government and with virtually all Romanian political leaders, Titulescu had returned to Switzerland.[81] Here he immediately renewed Zaleski's mandate to act as a go-between with Litvinov.[82] The Romanians, for the sake of their French and Polish allies, were willing to reach an agreement with the Soviets as long as the Bessarabian question was not mentioned textually (document 70). The Soviets still insisted on some mention, however oblique, of the conflict (document 69).[83] Their refusal to yield on the crucial point was underscored by the draft that Litvinov gave Zaleski on July 5.[84] Since the draft was no more than the final Riga text, Titulescu became even more convinced of the wisdom of the policy he had formulated after Marshal Pilsudski's visit to Bucharest in April (document 73). On Zaleski's insistence Titulescu reluctantly agreed to meet with Litvinov, if only to witness the Polish pledge on nonratification given in front of the Soviet commissar (document 74).[85] But the Soviets refused to modify their demands. Titulescu reneged, though he agreed to maintain indirect contact.[86] Zaleski's mission had failed and he was unceremoniously replaced by Schaetzel (document 75).[87] The French were no more successful.[88] However, their efforts seem to have had a moderating effect in Warsaw (documents 70 and 74). At least they understood the legal subtleties of Titulescu's position better than the Poles (document 72).

The Romanian press had rumored the possibility of the Polish-Soviet signing for some time.[89] Even so, when the news came on July 25 it caused alarm in Bucharest and gave rise to speculation that the Polish-Romanian alliance had been weakened.[90] The Romanian government contented itself with a fruitless last-minute appeal—and the publication of Zaleski's pledge (documents 78, 79, and 80).

THE FINAL PHASE, AUGUST–OCTOBER 1932

The Romanians were delighted with France's initial reaction to the Polish-Soviet signing. The authoritative *Le Temps* declared that an eventual signing of the Franco-Soviet pact would be contingent upon the conclusion of a Romanian-Soviet pact.[91] Herriot was notably nonchalant about the Franco-Soviet pact during an interview with Dovgalevsky.[92] At Cesianu's request Herriot promised to intervene in Warsaw in order to obtain a formalization of Zaleski's nonratification pledge. He warned, however, that Romania would have to stop procrastinating and decide whether or not to reach an agreement with the USSR (document 84). The French démarche had no effect on the Poles.[93] After weathering one of Romania's periodic political crises, Vaida publicly assured all concerned that Romania stood ready to conclude a nonaggression pact with the USSR that would respect Romania's "legitimate interests" (document 86).[94]

During the last days of August and throughout September the stalled Romanian-Soviet talks were the concern of French and Polish diplomatic activity. Each country acted on its own and therefore the initiatives were uncoordinated and conflicting. When Colonel Beck visited Romania

(August 29–31) he agreed, despite the studied coolness of his hosts, to instruct Patek to present Titulescu's draft pact (document 85) to Litvinov in the guise of a Polish proposal.[95] If the Soviets accepted it, the Romanians agreed to sign it immediately. They maintained their insistence on the exclusion of any explicit or implicit mention of the Bessarabian question in the text, while Beck maintained his lack of sympathy for "trifling points of law and details of wording" (documents 87 and 88). Titulescu approved of the plan, but insisted that his draft was the only acceptable one. If the Soviets did not accept it, Titulescu believed that the talks should be terminated and Romania should proclaim the continuing validity of the Kellogg-Briand Pact.[96]

The Romanian-Polish plan was inextricably complicated by an ill-timed French diplomatic intervention in Bucharest—an intervention made with the full knowledge and approval of Dovgalevsky.[97] Herriot proposed a three-part formula for a Romanian-Soviet pact: (1) no mention of territorial or other litigations in the text; (2) specific mentions of "litigious questions" in the protocol of signature; (3) freedom for both sides to make unilateral public interpretations of the pact after it was signed. He completely reversed his policy of the month before, declaring that France would no longer delay signing the Franco-Soviet pact or countenance dilatory Romanian tactics.[98] The Romanians were appalled and immediately asked the French to support Patek's forthcoming démarche in Moscow (document 89). Realizing their mistake, the French agreed to assist the Romanian-Polish plan (document 90), but the damage had already been done. Both Beck (document 91) and the Romanians feared that if the much more favorable Herriot wording were known to Litvinov, Patek's démarche would be met by Soviet intransigence.[99]

The French intervention sent Cadere and Cesianu hurrying back to their posts. The latter and Gafencu met with Titulescu in Bad Gastein. Titulescu was equally dismayed; he considered the Herriot formula worse than anything the Soviets had proposed at Riga or Geneva. Clearly, Romania could not accept it. If Patek failed and the negotiations were terminated, Titulescu argued that Romania should ask France for just such a guarantee of nonaggression from the Soviets vis-à-vis Romania as Romania had given to them vis-à-vis the USSR when the Franco-Romanian Treaty of Friendship had been signed in 1926.[100]

Despite the realistic pessimism that the French intervention had evoked, Patek gave the Polish draft (i.e., Titulescu's) to Litvinov on September 13. Although "surprised" at being presented with a known Romanian text, Litvinov did not reject it out of hand. Since the Soviet commissar still doubted Romania's sincerity, Patek proposed that Litvinov meet Cadere, who would reassure him on that score, in Poland.[101] A second Patek-Litvinov meeting ensued.[102] It confirmed French Ambassador François Dejean's report of Litvinov's preference for the Riga text and his willingness to meet with Cadere.[103] Without Titulescu's knowledge the Romanian government decided to allow Cadere to speak with Litvinov on a train passing through Poland. For Romania, the Titulescu draft remained the only acceptable one (document 92). During the evening of September 16, Cadere met with Litvinov on a train traveling from Bialystok to Warsaw. Litvinov confirmed his predilection for the Riga text, but revealed his willingness to continue negotiations near Geneva and to exclude the words "territorial or other litigations" and "existing" from an eventual pact (document 93).

Consistent with his earlier démarches, Herriot urged the Romanians to resume negotiations in Geneva and to acquiesce in the inclusion of the words "differences" and "territorial" in the protocol of signature. Herriot also suggested that the Romanian negotiator be someone other than Titulescu.[104] Vaida and Gafencu answered that while Romania would never recognize the existence of any "litigation" or "difference" with the USSR, they would dispatch Cadere to Geneva to continue negotiations with Litvinov.[105] As they had planned at Bad Gastein, the Romanians asked for a Franco-Soviet exchange of letters guaranteeing Romanian security.[106] The French refused (document 103).

Contrary to their earlier statements, Vaida and Gafencu instructed Cadere to make major concessions to the Soviet negotiator. "Differences" was to be accepted in either article I or the protocol of signature (document 94).

Only after Cadere was on his way to Geneva was Titulescu indirectly informed that he had been replaced as negotiator and that Romania's negotiating position had been significantly altered. In a carefully calculated and typically dramatic maneuver, Titulescu refused to go to Geneva for the opening of the League assembly. Instead he proceeded directly to London and noisily resigned all his foreign posts. Sensing the inherent weakness of its position, the Romanian government vainly tried to mollify an outraged public opinion.[107] Vaida desperately implored Titulescu to change his mind, even offering to make him both prime minister and minister of foreign affairs (document 95). Titulescu bided his time in London confident of Vaida's inevitable capitulation. After the Cadere-Litvinov talks had failed, Vaida again offered Titulescu the foreign ministry. He accepted. Shortly thereafter (October 20, 1932) Vaida was replaced as prime minister by Iuliu Maniu.[108]

From the outset Litvinov effectively used not only the Herriot formula but the Romanian political crisis as points of leverage in his talks with

Cadere.[109] Nonetheless, during their second meeting Cadere and Litvinov reached agreement on every point *except* the protocol of signature. In contradiction to his earlier assurance (document 93), Litvinov insisted on wording that included "territorial litigations" or "existing differences." Cadere steadfastly refused both (document 96). Litvinov assured Cadere that these "differences" could be settled in special bilateral conferences (document 97). Despite French and Polish intervention Litvinov refused to give up "existing."[110] Both Cadere and Gafencu, however, believed a formula that would replace "existing" with analogous but more elaborate wording could lead to agreement (document 98). Vaida's hold on power was becoming more precarious each day; he was almost frantic to reach an agreement. He instructed Cadere to sign a pact that would include "differences" and circumvent "existing" (document 99).

A controversy exists about the Cadere-Litvinov meeting of October 3. If one is to believe the Romanian documents (document 100), no agreement was reached. If, however, one is to believe the Soviet documents, Litvinov wanted to accept and later was instructed to accept a circumvention of "existing" devised by Professor Iorga.[111] Cadere had unofficially suggested this formula on October 3.[112] On October 4, the French told Litvinov that the Romanians had arrived at the limit of possible concessions, and that France would delay signing the Franco-Soviet Pact until the Romanian-Soviet text was finalized. The Romanians, thus encouraged by the French, backed off from the circumventions of "existing," returning to their original formula of "differences" unmodified (document 101). In their last session Cadere and Litvinov repeated their original positions and the talks were adjourned (document 102). As he had threatened in their last meeting, Litvinov then released a polemical press account of the talks charging that Bucharest had reneged on an acceptable formula and was responsible for the negotiations' failure.[113]

Titulescu was left to pick up the pieces. On his way to Bucharest to assume the Foreign Ministry, he explained his objections to Vaida's strategy to the French: he intended to free Poland and France from their pledges not to ratify and sign; he would never condone any recognition of "litigations" or "differences" with the USSR; he would never allow a weakening of Romania's sovereignty in Bessarabia; and Romania would fall back on the guarantees of the Kellogg-Briand Pact.[114] For their part, the Soviets declared their willingness to sign the pact with the Cadere wording.[115]

Titulescu always stressed that he was first among Romanians wishing to ameliorate Romanian-Soviet relations. During his four-year tenure as foreign minister he fully proved his contention. In July 1933 Romania signed the Definition of Aggression with the USSR, an agreement in which the Soviets implicitly recognized Romanian "authority" in Bessarabia. In June 1934 Titulescu engineered the establishment of Romanian-Soviet diplomatic relations. And in July 1936 he and Litvinov initialed a pact of mutual assistance that would have recognized the Dniester frontier.[116] The last act was a direct cause of his fall from power in August 1936. It is indeed ironic that Titulescu, who had gained power by seeming to oppose closer Romanian-Soviet relations, lost power by fostering them.

Documents

Translator's Note

Documents were selected on the basis of their importance and their unavailability elsewhere. Some prohibitively long documents were not translated but their content was synopsized in the text and notes of the introductory essay. In order to avoid confusion document headings were standardized while all the important information was preserved within a uniform framework: general registry number, type of document, sender, addressee, place of origin and message number, date, nature of document, etc.

Because they were diplomatic documents, intradepartmental memoranda, and other forms of communication meant only for internal governmental consumption, many of the materials in the Titulescu Collection were poorly typed and practically unedited. Grammatical, spelling, and factual mistakes were frequent. Therefore, the translator has occasionally departed from a strict literal translation in order to lend continuity to the often semiliterate prose of the original. Brackets indicate the exercise of this license.

W.M.B.

Preliminaries to Negotiations,
May to December 1931

DOCUMENT NO. 1

Memo, ARION *to* GHIKA *and* MINISTRY OF WAR

Bucharest, 15 May 1931

I. Relative to the enclosed draft of a Polish-Soviet Treaty of Non-aggression and Peaceful Resolution of Differences, the signatory states of the Protocol of Moscow of February 9, 1929, concerning the early coming into force of the Kellogg-Briand Pact, that is Romania, Estonia, and Latvia, in addition to Finland, are invited (art. 5) to conclude similar treaties with the USSR.

Also, since it would not be possible to arrive at the conclusion of a single treaty of this kind between Romania, Poland, Latvia, Estonia, and Finland on the one hand, and the USSR on the other, the Polish draft provides (art. VI) for the retention of an organic connection between the analogous treaties that would be separately concluded between each of the aforementioned countries with the USSR [i.e., for] the simultaneous entering into force of these treaties.

In communicating the text of this draft to us, the minister of Poland,[1] in the name of his government, asked the following questions:

1. Is the Romanian government disposed to sign a bilateral pact of nonaggression with the USSR?
2. If so, is the Romanian government disposed to use the available intermediary assistance of Poland in the event of negotiations relative to the conclusion of this treaty?
3. What is the opinion of the Romanian government on the gist of the draft Polish-Soviet treaty, the subsequent Romanian-Soviet treaty to be similar to the said treaty, since by force of circumstance, it cannot be identical?[2]

Our point of view is the following:

We do not see the utility of concluding a new bilateral treaty of nonaggression of limited duration in addition to the Kellogg-Briand Pact of renunciation of war and the Litvinov Protocol for the early coming into force of the said pact, both of which are multilateral and of unlimited duration.

However, if the purpose of the new agreement is to complete the Kellogg-Briand Pact and the Litvinov Protocol, then, in our opinion, it would only be possible to attain this goal by the conclusion of a treaty of mutual assistance.

Regarding the new Polish draft of a treaty of nonaggression proposing to complete the Kellogg-Briand Pact and the Litvinov Protocol with clauses concerning arbitration and conciliation, it is to be observed:

a) that from the point of view of nonaggression, the new agreement must *neither weaken nor modify in any way the obligations of the Kellogg-Briand Pact* and of the Litvinov Protocol;

b) that from the point of view of our territorial integrity, the new agreement must carefully avoid the reopening of the question of Bessarabia;

c) and that from the point of view of the clauses of conciliation and arbitration, under the assumption that such clauses could come into play between states that do not have diplomatic relations, the new agreement must above all exclude from the questions that might be submitted to such a procedure the question of our eastern frontier.

Despite the disadvantages the new draft treaty thus presents and the difficulty of circumventing them, we nevertheless find it impossible from a political point of view to respond to the persistent interventions of Poland with a reply of nonacceptance.

II. Since for the moment it is not a question of opening direct talks between Romania and the USSR, the available intermediary assistance of Poland would be as valuable this time as her good and valuable offices were on the occasion of the conclusion of the Pact of Moscow.

III. Regarding the substance of an eventual and analogous Romanian-Soviet draft treaty, at first view it seems indispensable to us to make the following observations about the text proposed by Poland:

a) To neither weaken nor modify in any way the stipulations of the Kellogg-Briand Pact and the Litvinov Protocol, the editing of our draft must be supervised with the greatest attention by jurists.

b) In order to preserve for us the position gained on the occasion of the signing of the Pact of Moscow and at the same time in order not to give the Soviet government any pretext to claim, after the conclusion of the treaty in question, that we committed an act of aggression against the USSR by the occupation of Bessarabia, the preamble should state *"the maintenance of the existing state of peace between the two countries."*

At the same time, being unable to mention our borders with Russia in the pact, article I, paragraph 2 absolutely must protect *our existing territorial integrity* against aggression, using, for example, the formula from article I of our treaty of guarantee with Poland: "the actual territorial integrity and present political independence."

c) Concerning the Convention of Conciliation and Arbitration which, according to article IV, would be an integral part of the treaty, we cannot formulate observations because the draft of that convention has not yet been given to us. However, we consider it proper to indicate to Warsaw now that in any event we could only conclude such a Convention of Conciliation and Arbitration expressing reservations identical to those we expressed on the occasion of our accession to the optional clause of the Statute of the Permanent Court of International Justice, that is, refusing arbitration for:

1. questions arising from situations or differences prior to the ratification of the convention by the Romanian parliament;
2. basic or procedural questions causing directly or indirectly the discussion of the territorial integrity of Romania, including her ports and lines of communication;
3. all differences relative to questions that, in conformity with international law, are within the jurisdictional competence of Romania.

d) Regarding the bilateral character of the draft, it is to be stated that a single treaty of nonaggression and peaceful resolution of differences concluded between the USSR on the one hand, and Romania, Poland, Latvia, Estonia, and Finland on the other hand would demonstrate a perfect solidarity among the states that constitute the anti-Soviet chain between the Baltic and Black Seas, and from this point of view it would maintain the utility of the so-called Litvinov multilateral pact. Consequently, the bilateral form that, it is suggested, is necessary for the treaties would only be acceptable on the precondition of insuring a strict interdependence [so that] they come into force together. To this end, we feel that the text of article VI of the *Polish-Soviet* draft treaty should be more explicitly written, stipulating that "the treaty will come into force the thirtieth day after the notification *of Poland by the USSR that all the* analogous *agreements* to the present treaty *concluded separately* between the USSR on the one hand, and Estonia, Finland, Latvia, and Romania on the other, have been ratified and the *instruments of ratification* exchanged."

[*e*)] Concerning the duration of the treaty (art. VII), we consider it indispensable, in order to maintain the utility of the Kellogg-Briand Pact and of the pact concluded in Moscow on February 9, 1929, also from this point of view, that both the treaty we will conclude and the analogous treaties concluded with the USSR by Estonia, Finland, Latvia, and Poland be of unlimited duration or at least extendable by tacit agreement.

Director of Eastern Political Affairs
and Minister Plenipotentiary
M. ARION

DOCUMENT NO. 2

Draft Treaty of Nonaggression and the Peaceful Resolution of Conflicts between Poland and the USSR

The President of the Republic of Poland on the one hand, and the Central Executive Committee of the USSR on the other hand:

Animated by the desire to consolidate the political situation in Eastern Europe by means of direct agreements;

Considering that the Treaty of Peace of March 18, 1921, constitutes the basis of their relations and reciprocal engagements;

Persuaded that the peaceful resolution of international conflicts is the surest means to attain the goal desired;

Have resolved to conclude a treaty having as its end the extension and completion of the general Treaty of Renunciation of War signed in Paris on August 27, 1928, and placed into force by the Protocol signed in Moscow on February 9, 1929, and for this purpose have designated as their respective plenipotentiaries

For the President of the Republic of Poland, Mr. ———;

For the Central Executive Committee of the USSR, Mr. ———;

Who, after being communicated their full powers, found in good and due form, have agreed to the following dispositions:

ARTICLE I.

The High Contracting Parties declare that they renounce war as an instrument of national policy in their mutual relations and reciprocally pledge not to use any aggressive action or invasion against another Contracting Party.

Those acts considered contrary to the obligations in the preceding paragraph will be any act of violence or threat of violence endangering the integrity and the inviolability of the territory or the political independence of the other Contracting Party, even if they are committed without a declaration of war and avoiding all its possible consequences.

ARTICLE II.

If one of the Contracting Parties, notwithstanding its peaceful attitude, comes to be attacked by a third state, or by a group of third states, the other Contracting Party promises not to extend aid and assistance to the aggressing state or states during the entire duration of the conflict.

ARTICLE III.

The obligations stipulated in articles I and II of the present Treaty can neither modify nor endanger the rights and obligations of Poland as a member of the League of Nations, nor the obligations of Poland resulting from defensive agreements concluded by her within the framework of and in relation to the Covenant of the League of Nations.

ARTICLE IV.

The High Contracting Parties, animated by the desire to resolve exclusively by procedures of peaceful regulation all questions and litigations of whatever nature and origin that would tend to divide them and that would not be resolved by ordinary diplomatic procedures within a reasonable period of time, promise to submit them to conciliation or arbitration conforming to the dispositions of the Convention of Conciliation and Arbitration concluded and signed simultaneously with the present Treaty, of which it constitutes an integral part.

ARTICLE V.

The High Contracting Parties are agreed that the other governments, signatories of the Protocol of Moscow of February 9, 1929, be invited to conclude agreements with the USSR analogous to the present Treaty.

ARTICLE VI.

The present Treaty will be ratified and the instruments of ratification will be exchanged at. . . .

It will come into force the thirtieth day after notification by one of the High Contracting Parties to the other that agreements analogous to the

present Treaty between the USSR on the one hand and Estonia,
Finland, Latvia, and Romania on the other have been ratified.

ARTICLE VII.

The duration of the present Treaty will be three years. If it is not denounced by one of the High Contracting Parties with at least three
months' notice before the expiration of this period, it will be renewed by
tacit agreement for a new period of two years.

In witness whereof the aforementioned Plenipotentiaries have signed
the present Treaty and have affixed their seals.

Done at . . . in two copies

The. . . .

PROTOCOL OF SIGNATURE

At the moment of proceeding to the signature of the Treaty of Nonaggression and the peaceful resolution of differences dated this day, the
High Contracting Parties declare that denunciation or extension of the
Treaty, in conformity with the stipulations of article VII, will not affect
in any way the obligations of the High Contracting Parties deriving from
the Pact of Paris dated August 27, 1928.

Done at . . .

The. . . .

DOCUMENT NO. 3

Letter, ARION *to* MINISTRY OF WAR (*General Staff*)

Bucharest No. 035796, 18 June 1931

CONFIDENTIAL

Dear Mr. Minister,

In reference to my No. 35254 of June 16,[3] I have the honor to
inform you that Count Szembek, the minister of Poland in Bucharest,
presented himself at my office yesterday afternoon, June 16, in order to
inform me of the following observations of the Polish government concerning our point of view about the draft treaty of nonaggression and
peaceful resolution of differences with the USSR that I had outlined to
him during previous meetings:

   a) The Polish government raises no objection relative to our in-
       tention to mention "the desire to maintain the existing peace"
       in the preamble.

b) Regarding "the respect for the actual territorial integrity," the Polish government believes that our formulation of such a request would constitute, from the start, a serious impediment to the negotiations with Russia; that this idea should be expressed in another form; and that the text of the Polish preamble expressing the desire to consolidate the political situation in Eastern Europe would constitute a sufficient guarantee in this regard.

Naturally, we will explain this question on the occasion of the submission of our definitive response to the Polish government. [One should remember] the fact that the question of respect for actual territorial integrity in our amendments only constitutes a refinement of the Polish text of article I, paragraph 2. In the last analysis, our amendment in this regard could also be expressed in a form closer to the Polish text, if we stipulated, for example, "threatening the integrity and inviolability of actual territory or the present political independence of the other Contracting Party." The nonacceptance of this simple refinement of the Polish text would prove, without a doubt, the bad faith of the USSR.

c) Finally, regarding the organic connection that would consequently be preserved for the simultaneous entering into force of the analogous treaties to be concluded between the USSR and its western neighbors, the Polish government agrees with our suggestion.

In addition, the minister of Poland, learning that General Samsonovici, the chief of the General Staff, is about to go to Poland to meet with the allied General Staff, considers that both military bodies will have a splendid opportunity to discuss directly the basis and form of these questions.

Director [Mihai Arion]

DOCUMENT NO. 4

Memo, Szembek *(Polish Minister in Bucharest) to* Ghika

Bucharest, 31 July 1931

The proposed pact does not in any way weaken the Kellogg[-Briand] Pact, which it completes and whose theses it develops.

In its article IV [the pact] stipulates procedures of arbitration and conciliation that will be an integral part of the pact. This is necessary because, in renouncing war which until now was, in the last resort, the unique method of resolving international differences, the Contracting Parties have to replace it with an effective peaceful procedure of resolving conflict. This point of view has been adopted already in article II of the Kellogg[-Briand] Pact, of which the proposed draft is the development. These same principles also follow from a correct interpretation of the Covenant of the League of Nations, as do the procedures of disarmament which proclaim the reciprocal dependence of the principles of disarmament, security, and arbitration.

Thus, a convention of arbitration should be a part of the present pact and should be signed simultaneously [with it].

Articles V and VI affirm the regional character of the pact of nonaggression, a principle already adopted in the Litvinov Pact. They reserve for Romania, Estonia, Latvia, and Finland the possibility of acceding to it by signing analogous bilateral pacts with the USSR. The above-mentioned articles precisely state that the Polish-Soviet pact cannot enter into force until the aforementioned states have concluded analogous pacts with the USSR.

Based on the principle that the renunciation of war on the Polish-Soviet sector alone would not assure the state of peace in Eastern Europe and, on the contrary, could provoke a dangerous state of disequilibrium for the other sectors of the frontier of the USSR, the Polish government believes that only a system of pacts of nonaggression including the aforementioned states would be capable of successfully insuring the state of peace in Eastern Europe.

DOCUMENT NO. 5

Romanian draft of Treaty of Nonaggression between Romania and the USSR

Bucharest, 25 August 1931

Treaty of Nonaggression and Peaceful Resolution of Conflicts between . . . and the USSR . . . on the one hand, and the Central Executive Committee of the USSR, on the other:

Animated by the desire to maintain the existing state of peace between their countries as well as to consolidate the political situation in Eastern Europe;

Convinced that the regulation of all differences or conflicts that might arise between them ought to be effected only by peaceful procedures;

Have resolved to conclude a treaty, having as its end to extend and to complete, without modifying the basis in any way, the general Treaty of Renunciation of War signed in Paris on August 27, 1928, as well as the Protocol signed in Moscow on February 9, 1929, of the coming into force of the latter;

Have designated to this end as their Plenipoteniaries . . . the Central Executive Committee of the USSR, Mr. ———;

Who, after having been communicated their full powers, found in good and due form, have agreed on the following dispositions:

ARTICLE I.

The High Contracting Parties declare that they renounce war as an instrument of national policy in their mutual relations and reciprocally promise not to use any aggressive action or invasion *against the other Contracting Party.*

Those acts considered as contrary to the obligations of the preceding paragraph will be any act of violence endangering the *actual territorial integrity and the present political independence* of the other Contracting Party, even if they are committed without a declaration of war.

ARTICLE II.

If one of the Contracting Parties, notwithstanding its peaceful attitude, comes to be attacked by a third state, or by a group of third states, the other Contracting Party promises not to extend aid and assistance to the aggressing state or states during the entire duration of the conflict.

ARTICLE III.

The obligations stipulated in articles I and II of the present Treaty can neither modify nor endanger the rights and obligations of . . . as a member of the League of Nations, nor the obligations of . . . resulting from defensive agreements concluded by her within the framework of and in relation to the Covenant of the League of Nations.

ARTICLE IV.

The High Contracting Parties, animated by the desire to resolve exclusively by the procedures of peaceful resolution all questions and litigations of any nature or origin that would come to divide them, promise to submit them to conciliation and arbitration conforming to the dispositions of the Convention of Conciliation and Arbitration concluded and signed simultaneously with the present Treaty of which it constitutes an integral part.

Excluded from the procedure of conciliation and arbitration are:[4]

a) any question deriving from situations or facts antecedent to the ratification by the Romanian parliament of the Convention of Conciliation and Arbitration to be concluded;

b) any question of basis or procedure possibly leading, directly or indirectly, to the discussion of the actual territorial integrity and the sovereign rights of Romania, including those pertaining to her ports and lines of communication;

c) differences relative to questions that according to international law, fall within the jurisdiction of Romania.

ARTICLE V.

The High Contracting Parties agree that the other signatory governments of the Protocol of Moscow of February 9, 1929, as well as *those that subsequently adhered to it and Finland* be invited to conclude agreements with the USSR analogous to the present Treaty.

ARTICLE VI.

The present Treaty will be ratified and the instruments of ratification exchanged at. . . .

It will come into force the thirtieth day after the notification of Poland (Romania) by the USSR that all of the agreements analogous to the present Treaty *concluded separately between the USSR on the one hand, and Estonia, Finland, Latvia, Lithuania,*[5] *Persia, Romania (Poland), and Turkey* on the other hand, have been ratified *and the instruments of ratification exchanged.*

ARTICLE VII.

The duration of the present Treaty will be the same as that of the General Treaty of Renunciation of War signed in Paris on August 27, 1928, and of the Protocol signed in Moscow on February 9, 1929, that is to say, unlimited.

Or else:

The duration of the present Treaty is five years from the date of its coming into force. If it is not denounced by any of the High Contracting Parties with a notice of at least one year before the expiration of that period, it will be considered as renewed by tacit agreement for a new period of five years and so on subsequently.[6]

In faith of which, the aforementioned Plenipotentiaries have signed the present Treaty and have affixed their seals upon it.

Done at . . .

In two copies, the. . . .

DOCUMENT NO. 6

Intradepartmental memo by CRETZIANU

Bucharest, 27 August 1931

On the occasion of the interview that he had with Count Szembek on Tuesday, August 25, at 6:00 P.M., Minister Ghika gave the former the text of the Romanian draft treaty of nonaggression and arbitration with the USSR (text annexed to the report of Minister Arion of July 14, 1931).[7]

The next day Count Szembek wrote Minister Ghika a personal letter in which he said that he had found some "quite important" differences between the Romanian and Polish texts and that, delaying for this motive [his] departure for Warsaw, he desired to be received by Minister Ghika in the morning.[8]

The audience was fixed for 12:30 and the undersigned attended as temporary director of Eastern Political Affairs.

The Polish minister told the minister of foreign affairs that he did not wish to send our draft to Warsaw because the said draft departed too much from the text of the Polish draft. It contained exactly those precise mentions of territorial questions that the Polish government believed should be avoided at all costs since they would cause, from the start, a categorical refusal on the part of the USSR.

[*However, even the Polish draft talks* (arts. I & II) *about territorial integrity and inviolability. Aug. 28, 1931. AC* (Alexander Cretzianu). Manuscript note to the above.]

Minister Ghika replied that the text given to Count Szembek did not represent in our conception a rigid "take-it-or-leave-it" text and that we were ready to discuss whatever passage in our text the Polish government deemed unsuitable.

Count Szembek then elaborated that the article in the Romanian text that bothered him and that provoked his new request was article IV to which we had added a paragraph that said we [would] not allow arbitration or conciliation for questions that could lead, directly or indirectly, to a discussion of the actual *territorial* integrity of Romania.

Minister Ghika told the minister of Poland that in this article we mentioned reservations identical with those made on the occasion of our accession to article 36 of the Statute of the Permanent Court in the Hague, reservations of vital interest to us because we could never allow the USSR, directly or indirectly, to raise the Bessarabian question before an arbitration tribunal. The minister of foreign affairs called the attention of Count Szembek to the fact that Poland also made some reservations on the occasion of her accession to article 36 of the Statute of the Permanent Court of International Justice, and that it was not improbable that she is making similar reservations in the pact of arbitration with the USSR.

The minister of Poland replied that he, too, appreciated the interests of a higher order that compelled Romania to avoid any possibility of arriving at an arbitration in the Bessarabian question. However, he believed that a means of obtaining this end could be achieved without textually inserting our reservations in an article of the draft treaty. For example, a new wording of the preamble could be sought that would give us full satisfaction in this order of ideas.

We then brought up . . . the text of article IV of the Polish draft in which occurs the phrase, "all questions and litigations of any nature or origin that exist." In any case, this wording would be made to conform with the formula that would be introduced in the preamble. We added that the text of the additional paragraph proposed by us in article IV could be modified in the following manner: "However, those questions expressly reserved at the time of accession of Romania to the voluntary dispositions contained in the Statute of the Permanent Court of International Justice will be excluded from the procedure of conciliation and arbitration." Thus, none of those direct mentions of territorial questions that might have tended to provoke a "non possumus" on the part of the Soviets would figure in the text of the treaty and, at the same time, our right to refuse any arbitration in the question of Bessarabia would be safeguarded.

Count Szembek also called Minister Ghika's attention to the differences that exist between the Polish and Romanian texts in articles V and VI. He did not know if Finland would take part in the system of proposed treaties. In any case, he does not believe that the eventuality of including Persia and Turkey among the signatory states must be examined because he claims that these states also have concluded similar treaties with the USSR. The minister of Poland did not insist on the question of extending the treaties to include Lithuania, but he did not appear to be disposed to allow such a possibility.

Both the minister of foreign affairs and Count Szembek agreed that the latter differences were not of capital importance and that they could easily be adjusted. However, insofar as article IV is concerned, Count Szembek declared that he would inform Warsaw that Romania absolutely demands that it is made unequivocably clear in the text that will be proposed to the USSR that the question of Bessarabia will never be subject, directly or indirectly, to arbitration.

[*On August 30, Mr. Dembinski, Poland's chargé d'affaires, informed me that he had received a letter in which Count Szembek told him that speaking on the*

*telephone from Lvov, the Polish Ministry of Foreign Affairs had told him that the
reservations we invoked on article IV would not constitute an insurmountable
difficulty and that the question could be resolved in a way satisfactory for us.
Sept. 1, 1931. A.C.* Manuscript note on the above.]

It was agreed that the negotiations will be resumed by Minister Ghika
and Mr. Zaleski in September in Geneva.[9]

The minister of Poland said that he did not know the text of the treaty
of arbitration that the Polish government would propose to the Soviets
as [an] annex to the pact of nonaggression. In his opinion this is the crux
of the question and he does not believe that this time [as in the past] they
will be able to overcome the difficulties presented by a neutral arbi-
trating tribunal acceptable to the USSR. From 1926 until this time it has
not been possible to reach an agreement between the USSR and Poland
in the negotiations that have taken place concerning the conclusion of a
treaty of arbitration.

ALEXANDER CRETZIANU

DOCUMENT NO. 7
(Reg. No. 68352 of 26 November 1931)

Letter (copy), BILCIURESCU *to* GHIKA

Warsaw No. 3864, 21 November 1931
MR. LITVINOV ON THE CONCLUSION OF A PACT
OF NONAGGRESSION WITH ROMANIA—<u>CONFIDENTIAL</u>

Dear Mr. Minister,

Confirming my telegram No. 3863[10] of today, I have the honor to
report to Your Excellency that today at the Foreign Ministry, I was read
passages from a recent report by Mr. Patek, the Polish minister in
Moscow, about his interview with Litvinov immediately after the former's
return to his post.[11]

The commissar of foreign affairs told Mr. Patek that Russia could not
accept the draft pact of nonaggression proposed by Poland because of
the clause that makes its coming into force dependent on the ratification
of similar pacts with all the bordering states.[12] This [rejection] is motivated by two [considerations]: first, the Soviets do not wish to negotiate
such pacts through the mediation of Poland, but directly with each state;
and second, among these states is Romania, which does not have

diplomatic relations with the Soviets and with which, on the contrary, they have a territorial litigation.

And coming thus to speak about Romania, Litvinov added that the Soviets were not thinking of resolving this litigation by force of arms. The proof is that they consented to sign the act of February 9, 1929, placing into force the Kellogg[-Briand] Pact ahead of time with Romania too. But, Russia has no interest in proposing the negotiation of a pact of nonaggression to Romania. However, if Romania so desires, she only has to propose such direct negotiations to the Soviets—she has enough avenues for this—*and the Soviets are disposed favorably to consider Romania's proposal.*

Finally, Mr. Litvinov proposed that they take the text accepted by France for a pact of nonaggression as the basis for the discussions between Russia and Poland.[13]

In asking Mr. Schaetzel, the chief of the Eastern Political Section, who had given me all this information, to tell me how the Polish government viewed this proposal, he answered that the question was still being studied, but that he believed the Polish government would not accept the French draft as a basis of the negotiations because it contained things unsuited to relations between Poland and Russia: questions of colonies, commercial relations, etc., that cannot be accepted by Poland, which has a common frontier with Russia.

To give the conversation a more interesting turn (more interesting to me, at any rate), I said, "And then, the French draft does not have clauses relative to other states as has the Polish draft," adding, "If the Soviets refuse a pact with Poland containing such clauses, how would you consider the further development of the negotiations?"

Mr. Schaetzel then told me, just about verbatim, that he believed that "a way must be found because, assured of the conclusion of pacts of nonaggression between the Soviets and the bordering states, Poland could make the concession of removing from her draft the article under discussion because the negotiations could be continued on the basis of the Polish draft."

Since my visit to Mr. Schaetzel today was the result of the fact that yesterday, at lunch at my residence, he told me that he had important things to tell me, I could deduce that his communication—which, more-over, he was obliged to make to me—was intended to encourage the Romanian government to take an initiative that, leading to posi-tive results, would facilitate the Polish-Soviet negotiations for a pact of nonaggression.

According to Mr. Schaetzel, this very day Mr. Patek will have another interview with Litvinov in order to discuss the same questions. He

promised to communicate to me anything that might interest us from
the new report of the Polish representative in Moscow.

In the newspaper *Kurjer Warszawski* of November 13, there appeared
an article entitled "It Is Necessary to Start with the Neighbors" in which,
citing a German newspaper on the latest declarations of Molotov, president of the People's Commissars, it was said: "In another speech
Molotov reproached Litvinov for not having worked [hard] enough
toward the conclusion of pacts of nonaggression with France and
Poland, despite the fact that by a better exploitation of existing possibilities, one could undoubtedly arrive at such a result."

"It was nevertheless necessary to persist, among other [things], in
taking a benevolent attitude in the Bessarabian question in order to
improve the relations of the Soviets with Romania," because then, after
the elimination of this obstacle, one might energetically work for an
amicable orientation toward the Soviets.

Having only now seen this article, I have not been able to discover
what German newspaper published the above [information], nor do I
have at hand the text of the Molotov speech in question. The words
reproduced do not appear to be from the speech of the president of the
Commissars delivered on November 6, already published "in extenso"
by *Izvestiia* of November 12 (or 13?), so that they are (probably) from
another of the three "archpacifist" speeches, as *Kurjer Warszawski* called
them.

Tomorrow being Sunday, and since I am leaving Warsaw in the
evening, Dr. Davidescu will remain to search for the source that was
used by the aforementioned Polish newspaper.[14]

It seems evident to me that, if the words attributed to Molotov are
authentic, they throw sufficient light on the explanations made by Mr.
Litvinov to Mr. Patek as, in such a case, they acquire the significance
of an invitation to the Romanian government to talk with Moscow
directly.

Gr. Bilciurescu

DOCUMENT NO. 8

Aide-mémoire (copy) by Arion

Bucharest, 23 November 1931

CONFIDENTIAL—FOR MEMORY

In face of the pressure that is being exerted upon us to negotiate a
bilateral treaty of nonaggression directly with the Soviets analagous to

the ones it is proposed they conclude with Finland, Estonia, Latvia, and Poland, it must not be lost from view that whatever the interest might be in maintaining the solidarity among the states that constitute the anti-Soviet chain from the Baltic to the Black Sea, our principal guide permanently remains the one articulated by Ion I. C. Brătianu on the occasion of the verbal instructions given to our delegation to the Romanian-Soviet Conference in Vienna, to wit: "There is no room for any discussion about the union of Bessarabia, which is and must be ours."

"Romania must not on any account depart from her present situation in the question of Bessarabia," said Titulescu in his telegram of last May from Geneva, enregistered as No. 30773/931. If Romania were to commit the error of considering the question of Bessarabia as open, she could only play into the hands of the Soviets because "a plebiscite would fatally follow as the unique solution of resolving the conflict without war." "Only the mediation of a friendly power can reconcile Romania's necessity not to depart from her present international position in the question of Bessarabia with the necessity to obtain Russia's recognition of the frontiers. In truth, the mediator speaks in his own name and has no need of full Romanian powers which in case of failure (would be) looked upon as a written proof that Romania considers the question of Bessarabia as 'open' and as 'unresolved from the international point of view.' "[15]

Finally, in our quality as "beati posidentes" [sic] we must avoid anything that might compromise our possession of Bessarabia. We must not forget that time works in our favor.

Consequently, independently of the question if and under what conditions one could superimpose a new treaty of nonaggression on the Kellogg-Briand Pact and Litvinov Protocol, in any event we must never (on the occasion of eventual negotiations with the Soviets) admit any discussion about Bessarabia. [We must] maintain the debate *within the strict framework of a treaty of nonaggression.*

Moreover, only under these preceding conditions do Minister Ghika and I agree to state: (1) that we would be able to yield to the insistences of our allies to negotiate directly with the Soviets for a pact of nonaggression; (2) that there exists any possibility that these negotiations would succeed.

M. ARION

DOCUMENT NO. 9

Cabinet letter (copy), GHIKA *to* WARSAW LEGATION

Bucharest, 28 November 1931

STRICTLY CONFIDENTIAL

Dear Mr. Minister,

In answer to your report No. 3864[16] of November 21 and [No.] 3866 (Polish-Soviet pact) of November 22, I have the honor to inform you that, after requesting the advice of the French government about the opportunity of making direct contact with the USSR, our minister in Paris has informed me that the French government has no objections to a direct contact between Romania and the Soviets and that in case of failure the obligations of France toward Romania will remain unchanged.[17]

Consequently, you will begin an action in the following manner: using the pretext chosen by you, you will seek to have a meeting with the representative of the Soviets (of course, neither at our Legation nor at the Soviet Legation), in order to be able, once contact is established, to make proper soundings regarding the possibilities and methods for negotiations with Moscow for the pact of nonaggression. The Romanian government will not allow the Soviets to take us to Vienna or to another Western city, there to promote another noisy breach over the question of Bessarabia coupled with the usual offensive communications in the press, a delicate and humiliating situation for Romania [which would be] placed in a position of a defendant. Your colleague in Riga will also have a meeting with the representative of the Soviets.

Although Poland's impression is that the Soviets are alarmed by the situation in Manchuria and desire a relaxation in the West and so the moment is favorable for Romania to arrive at a better state of affairs with Moscow [through the pact of nonaggression], I admit that I am not as convinced of the more favorable intentions of the Soviets and I wonder if Russia's new attitude does not correspond with the desire to separate Poland and Romania and to discover how far Polish solidarity with us goes in the question of Bessarabia.

Please accept, Mr. Minister, the assurance of my high consideration.

GHIKA

DOCUMENT NO. 10
(Reg. No. 70035 of 5 December 1931)

Decoded telegram, BILCIURESCU *to* MINISTRY OF FOREIGN AFFAIRS

Warsaw No. 4026, 4 December 1931

In reference to my report No. 4015.[18]

During a long interview with the Soviets' minister, who was surely prepared by his conversations with Zaleski and with the director of Eastern
Policy,[19] he confirmed Litvinov's statement relative to the Moscow government's desire to negotiate directly with Romania while indicating the
difficulty of the question of Bessarabia. For an entire hour we opposed
our arguments, discussing as two colleagues without governmental
instructions. Of course, he mentioned the need for a plebiscite, con-
testing our rights and invoking, among other things, the famous letter of
General Averescu.[20] I said that undoubtedly the Romanian government
[would] allow neither a plebiscite nor any reservations on the question of
Bessarabia.

Then the Soviet representative said: "Hence, you are of the opinion
that this question must not be touched [upon] in [the] pact."

These words left me with the impression that the Soviets are inclined
to negotiate on this basis.

He will ask, by this evening's courier, for instructions from Moscow
and will inform me of the response as soon as possible.

Please telegraph me if you believe it would be proper for me to inform
the French ambassador.

BILCIURESCU

DOCUMENT NO. 11

Decoded telegram, GHIKA *to* WARSAW LEGATION

Bucharest No. 70035, 5 December 1931

[In reference] to [your No.] 4026:[21] please inform the ambassador
of France[22] about the result of your private conversation with (your)
Russian colleague. You will take the opportunity of this contact to
manifest your personal fears, shared by many Romanians with good
sense, lest the current action of the Soviets for pacts of nonaggression be
foredoomed to produce, even to have as a sure result, a weakening of

the Polish-Romanian front and thus of the political system that today is supported by French policy. In truth, today we live vis-à-vis the Soviets with the Litvinov Protocol and the Kellogg-Briand Pact, Poland and Romania being united. Why arrive at a situation (tomorrow) in which Poland signs for herself alone and Romania the same? Does not the French ambassador agree that we lose instead of gain a better position? And definitely, will not France indirectly suffer a diminution of her own position by changing a regime that assures Poland is tightly united with Romania?

GHIKA

DOCUMENT NO. 12
(Reg. No. 70305 of 7 December 1931)

Decoded telegram, CARP *to* ARION

Ankara No. 2053, 6 December 1931
STRICTLY CONFIDENTIAL

Today the minister of foreign affairs again called me to inform me that the Soviet ambassador had received a response from Moscow and to put me in direct contact with him at Mr. Surits's home.[23] The Soviet ambassador confirmed that his government is disposed to enter into negotiations with Romania for "normalization of relations between both countries; that he considers the question of Bessarabia as not being of an urgent nature; and that as a result it does not constitute an obstacle to such a normalization, being able to remain open. He, Surits, is thus disposed to transmit to Moscow a formal proposal of the Romanian government. The place of the negotiations will then be fixed by common accord between both governments."

[While there] was no talk of alliances, it does not mean the information of Tewfik Rusdi Bey was unfounded.

CARP

DOCUMENT NO. 13

Telegram, GHIKA *to* ANKARA LEGATION

Bucharest No. 70690, 11 December 1931

Referring to your 2075.[24] For motives that, given our alliance [with] Poland, are readily understood, the Romanian government considers that the place where the negotiations will take place must be Warsaw, between our minister there and the representative of the Soviets.

GHIKA

DOCUMENT NO. 14
(Reg. No. 72749)

Decoded telegram (copy), CESIANU *to* MINISTRY OF FOREIGN AFFAIRS

Paris No. 892, 9 December 1931

Saw Berthelot regarding your telegram [*sic*] Nos. 68453 and 70298.[25] Berthelot read me a telegram by which the Polish foreign minister complained that Romania had also made démarches through our representatives in Riga and Ankara, not just via Warsaw [concerning an eventual Romanian-Soviet treaty of nonaggression].[26] Berthelot was somewhat surprised that it was explored and discussed in three places.

Just as I entered Berthelot's office, the Soviet ambassador was leaving it. Berthelot told me that among other things he also spoke with him about Romania. Dovgalevski told him that Litvinov had said that he was ready to negotiate directly with Romania accepting with equanimity either the text of the treaty with France or that with Poland; that the Soviets did not harbor aggressive intentions against Romania but that the question of Bessarabia cannot be brought into discussion, remaining "reserved."

Regarding the affirmations of Tewfik Rusdi Bey, Berthelot did not attach importance to it, considering it a "simple personal opinion."[27]

Regarding the Baltic countries, up until now there have not been any sort of negotiations between their governments and the Soviets.

Berthelot asserted [that] it would be good to negotiate as soon as possible and he believes, without insisting however, that the place suitable for [the] meeting would be Warsaw, affirming that we must work hand in hand with the Poles.

CESIANU

DOCUMENT NO. 15
(Reg. No. 72180)

Letter (copy), BILCIURESCU *to* GHIKA

Warsaw No. 4109, 10 December 1931
ABOUT THE NEGOTIATIONS OF A PACT OF
ROMANIAN-SOVIET NONAGGRESSION

Dear Mr. Minister,

Confirming my telegrams of yesterday under No. 4099 and of today No. 4108,[28] I have the honor to report to Your Excellency that at noon yesterday Mr. Antonov-Ovseyenko, the minister of the Soviets, was at my office and informed me that the answer of Moscow was affirmative— the said government agrees to negotiate a pact of nonaggression with Romania in which the question of Bessarabia would not be mentioned in any way—and that it proposed Ankara as [the] place for conducting the negotiations.

I informed Mr. Laroche, the ambassador of France, of the response this very evening. However, he had already been informed by Paris.[29]

Today I saw the chief of Eastern Policy, Minister Schaetzel, who, in the absence of Messrs. Zaleski and Beck, directs the Foreign Ministry. He already knew from Riga and Ankara that we had also made soundings there and that the Soviet representatives in those two capitals gave the representatives of Romania the same answer given to me.

Minister Schaetzel was of the opinion that the Soviets had evidently chosen Ankara deliberately, on the one hand so that we would not be in daily contact with Poland during the negotiations, and on the other hand so that they would be held in a place where the atmosphere was entirely favorable to Russia, conducted, on the Soviet side, by Mr. Surits, their ambassador in Turkey.

The present Soviet ambassador in Ankara seems to be a man with great influence both in Moscow and with the Turkish government. He is a great enemy of ours and of Poland and, moreover, energetic and intransigent—capable of demanding from us much more than what Litvinov himself would demand. The Polish government claims that Surits declared, on I don't know what occasion, that, in the case that Russia concludes a pact of nonaggression with Romania, the Romanian-Polish alliance, if it had no offensive character, would no longer have a rationale for existing.

Given that, Mr. Schaetzel, who would prefer that our negotiations take place in Warsaw, believes that we could try to request a different place for [the] negotiations, invoking technical difficulties resulting from the excessive distance of the Turkish capital from both Moscow and Bucharest.

I wonder if it would not be preferable for us—if we cannot negotiate where we wish—to negotiate at Istanbul instead of Ankara.

Regarding Poland, she will continue negotiations in Moscow where she has the advantage of treating directly with Litvinov, a relatively understanding man and one who decides rapidly, and of having Mr. Patek, who started the negotiations and who is an excellent negotiator.

BILCIURESCU

DOCUMENT NO. 16
(Reg. No. 71861 of 13 December 1931)

Decoded telegram, TITULESCU *to* MINISTRY OF FOREIGN AFFAIRS

London No. 3127, 12 December 1931
STRICTLY CONFIDENTIAL

Yesterday I saw Zaleski. . . .

Then, Zaleski told me about his negotiations with the Soviets for the pact of nonaggression. "Things are going well for Romania," he said, "because the Soviets seem to be disposed to conclude an identical pact with Romania without raising the question of Bessarabia. However, the fact that Turkey is also mixed up in the question, either as a result of her own initiative or as a result of a Romanian initiative, makes the situation difficult. The Soviets have told Turkey that in order to conclude a pact of nonaggression with Romania, a third disinterested power would have to intervene in Moscow and that it would also be necessary that Romania 'unmake' her alliance with Poland. Of course the Soviets would not dare to speak about such conditions in Warsaw. Poland has informed Moscow that she would not sign the pact without Romania. In fact Poland could sign without Romania, on condition never to ratify the pact if Romania did not also sign one of the same kind."

Since I do not know anything about Romania's actual negotiations in this question, I contented myself with asking Zaleski, strictly personally and for information, what a pact of nonaggression would add to the obligations of the Kellogg Pact. Zaleski answered that the pact of nonaggression would be accompanied by a treaty of conciliation, which constituted a step forward. Then I asked, "But if in virtue of this treaty of conciliation the Soviets wish to discuss the question of Bessarabia?"

Zaleski answered that on the occasion of the editing of the treaty all we have to do is to exclude the question of Bessarabia from the differences that can be made the object of conciliation. "And if the Soviets refuse?" I asked. Zaleski answered that Litvinov had told Patek that he would sign a pact of nonaggression with Romania without mentioning Bessarabia and if the Soviets break their word we have only not to sign the treaty.

You will permit me to share [with you] an anxiety as far as I am concerned. A treaty of conciliation without the formal exclusion of Bessarabia does offer a legal opening for the Soviets to raise the question of Bessarabia in the future with our consent. On the other hand, a request for formal exclusion of Bessarabia, refused by the Soviets, especially if the agreement with Poland had been signed and only lacked ratification, is a new occasion for public contestation of our eastern frontier, which could only do us harm. Perhaps my anxiety is derived from my ignorance of the negotiations taking place.[30] Still, I considered it my duty to share it with you..

TITULESCU

DOCUMENT NO. 17

Minutes (copy), conversation of GHIKA *with* PUAUX *(French Minister in Bucharest)*

Bucharest, 18 December 1931

CONVERSATION OF MINISTER GHIKA WITH THE MINISTER OF FRANCE, DECEMBER 16, 1931, CONCERNING THE PACTS OF NONAGGRESSION WITH THE USSR

The minister of France, having asked for an audience, was received by Minister Ghika on the morning of December 16, 1931. On the basis of instructions received from Paris, Mr. Puaux told the minister of foreign affairs that the French government was interested in speeding up our official establishment of contact with the Soviets with a view to concluding a pact of nonaggression. (France would like the Franco-Soviet pact to be concluded as soon as possible in order to place herself in a more favorable situation vis-à-vis Germany.)

Minister Ghika answered that the Romanian government was not to blame for the delay that had occurred. In truth although on the one hand, the minister of Poland in Bucharest persistently intervenes with us on the question of the pact, Poland, on the other hand, was not yet prepared to communicate to us the text on the basis of which Polish-Soviet negotiations are taking place in Moscow. (On December 15) with [much] difficulty and following the insistent requests of Minister Ghika, Count Szembek informed him that he had received the text in question, still in Polish, and that he would forward it after having it translated.[31]

The minister of foreign affairs added that he had regretfully discovered, as Count Szembek himself had stated, that telegrams sent to Warsaw by the Polish Legation in Bucharest were poorly understood and were criticized by Mr. Zaleski and the respective policy section in a mistaken manner, to our disadvantage. Such erroneous interpretations had their echo in Paris (see telegram No. . . . . of . . . December signed by Mr. Cesianu). For example, Minister Ghika recently informed Count Szembek that the Soviet minister in Warsaw had asked Mr. Bilciurescu if we were eventually disposed to reestablish diplomatic relations.[32] Minister Ghika added that the Romanian government would only accept such a reestablishment of diplomatic relations after a formal written recognition of our rights in Bessarabia. The telegram through which the minister of Poland reported this to his government was so poorly written that it had resulted in the Polish minister of foreign affairs complaining that Romania had tied the pact of nonaggression to reestablishment of diplomatic relations on the basis of recognition of Bessarabia.

In general terms, the minister of foreign affairs told Mr: Puaux that he finds that Poland does not display enough susceptibility in face of the efforts made by the Soviet government—on the surface at least—to separate Romania from Poland. For example: (1) Why hasn't the Polish government asked Moscow for explanations regarding the Soviet government's refusal to agree to the Romanian-Soviet nonaggression pact being discussed through Poland? (2) Why didn't the Polish government protest when the Soviet government rejected Warsaw [as the location for] the Romanian-Soviet negotiations?

Minister Ghika added that if the Moscow government did not accept negotiations in Warsaw, we would probably select Riga. We did not want to send a Romanian delegate to Moscow because he would find himself isolated, disarmed, spied upon by microphones, and exposed to having [his] code stolen.

Again Minister Ghika explained to Mr. Puaux that the Romanian government never began negotiations with the Soviets in Ankara. Mr. Carp received instruction to speak with the Turkish government about the pact with the Soviets—so much and no more. For the moment, in Warsaw and Riga, we have made only unofficial inquiries. When we know the location in which we agree with the Soviet government to start negotiations, we will authorize our respective representative to begin official contact with the Soviet representative. Minister Ghika wondered if, after all, the location in question wouldn't be Paris.

DOCUMENT NO. 18
(Reg. No. 73237 of 21 December 1931)

Decoded telegram, BILCIURESCU *to* GHIKA

Warsaw No. 4225, 20 December 1931

Your Excellency's telegram No. 67648 intersecting with mine, No. 4214, please be so kind as to telegraph me if I should comply.[33]

I wish to add that Zaleski, whom I saw accidentally in the evening and who knows that the Soviets have refused Warsaw, urged me to insist to Your Excellency to agree to Moscow where Romania would go for the second time.[34] This is also where Poland and Estonia negotiate, and probably where Latvia's negotiations will start.[35]

In this way the negotiators will be able to be in daily contact with and profit by the experience of Patek, whereas in any other capital we would be isolated, which would hinder reaching an agreement. He insisted on our interest in concluding a pact with the Soviets, an act, moreover [that would] imply the tacit renunciation by the Soviets of [their] claim to Bessarabia.

BILCIURESCU

DOCUMENT NO. 19
(Reg. No. 74779 of 30 December 1931)

Decoded telegram, ZANESCU *to* GHIKA

Rome No. 2741, 29 December 1931

The political director informed me of the following personal answer from the ambassador of Italy in Moscow regarding conversations he had with Litvinov about the pact of nonaggression with us.[36] Litvinov allowed that he would treat directly with Romania on the following conditions:

1. [If] the question of Bessarabia were not raised;
2. [If] no mention were made in the text of the pact of either the League of Nations or of recourse to any form of arbitration (it seems that these last two conditions were made to both Poland and France).

Litvinov added that conclusion of a pact of nonaggression with us does not necessarily imply reestablishment of diplomatic relations. As Mr. Attolico must arrive momentarily in Rome, I will not miss [the opportunity] to see him immediately after his arrival and will telegraph Your Excellency all the supplementary details.[37]

ZANESCU

DOCUMENT NO. 20
(Reg. No. 74934 of 30 December 1931)

Decoded telegram, CARP *to* MINISTRY OF FOREIGN AFFAIRS

Constantinople No. 2212, 30 December 1931
STRICTLY CONFIDENTIAL

Referring to my telegram No. 220 [*sic*].

The Soviet ambassador communicated to me the following answer of the people's commissar of foreign affairs on the proposal [of] Riga transmitted by me: he asks that in order to facilitate the negotiations the location be Moscow. However, if the Romanian government insists on Riga, the Soviet government will not refuse. [At the same time], he asks that the Romanian government definitely fix the date for the start of the negotiations.[38] I await your answer in Constantinople, where the Soviet ambassador is to be found.

CARP

DOCUMENT NO. 21

Telegram, GHIKA *to* CARP

Bucharest No. 74934, 31 December 1931

Answer to 2212.[39]

Please tell the Soviet ambassador, the Romanian government noting that the Soviet government does not reject Riga, that the negotiations for the pact of nonaggression will begin there. Chargé d'affaires Sturdza [is] receiving the mission to conduct them.

The starting date [is] January 5.

GHIKA[40]

The Riga Negotiations, January 1932

DOCUMENT NO. 22

Letter, GHIKA *to* STURDZA

Bucharest No. 119, 31 December 1931

Dear Mr. Chargé d'Affaires,

Although the Soviet government desired our direct negotiations for the conclusion of the pact of nonaggression to take place in Moscow, it nevertheless consented to negotiate with us in Riga. Consequently, you are charged with conducting these negotiations "ad referendum," remaining in daily telegraphic contact with the Romanian government.

I have the honor to send you general instructions (through these strictly confidential lines).

As a point of departure, it remains understood that the question of Bessarabia be left out and unmentioned. (In the last interview that took place between Litvinov and the Italian ambassador, the Soviet commissar declared again that the question of Bessarabia would remain outside any discussions.)[41] I do not dwell on the abnormal character of this situation, which can only be conceived within the framework of the mentality of the Soviet leaders. I will not judge the value and the logic of the pact of nonaggression that will result from this direct contact with the Soviets. In face of pressures [on Poland and Romania] by the French government to speed up the conclusion of concomitant pacts of nonaggression, the Romanian government is resigned and determined to begin direct negotiations (reluctantly and very conscious that the new pact represents neither a strengthening of our positions, nor a better guarantee that the actual state created by the Litvinov Protocol). The rhythm of these negotiations seems to be accelerated on the part of the Soviets and [this] haste is shared by our allies in Warsaw and Paris.

From our information it appears that the USSR is waiting for our proposals; thus, the initiative belongs to us.

I am enclosing our draft.[42] When you present it to the Soviet representative, you will call it clearly "the Romanian draft" although, in reality, it is the text of the Polish draft with modifications.

You will observe that in the preamble our draft is based on the Protocol of Moscow of February 9, 1929 (the Litvinov Protocol) for the coming into force of the Treaty of Renunciation of War signed in Paris on August 27, 1928 (the Kellogg-Briand Pact) reconfirming that a state of peace exists between the two countries. We consider such an affirmation essential, keeping in mind the reservations formulated by the USSR on the occasion of its accession to the Kellogg-Briand Pact (in his note of August 31, 1928, to France's ambassador in Moscow, Litvinov said that the Soviets consider that "[an] armed occupation of foreign territory" has the character of an act of war contrary to the Treaty of Renunciation of War).

Concerning article I, paragraph 2, I draw your attention to the importance we attach to the words "every act of violence impairing the integrity and the inviolability of territory *that presently is found under the sovereignty of the other Contracting Party.*"

It is of central importance to us that this wording be accepted without change by the USSR. Given that this point could produce some resistance on the part of the Soviets, you will keep in mind, in order to respond to the eventual objections, that according to stipulations of international law, the definition of territory is "the space over which a state exercises its sovereignty." The above phrasing is imposed since, in compliance to the Soviets' desire, we have consented to put aside the question of Bessarabia.

Article II was already accepted by Moscow in the negotiations with Poland. As our text does not introduce any important modification, I do not believe it will cause any Soviet opposition.

Article III is of evident value, comprising the affirmation of the legitimacy and permanence of our alliances with Poland and with other states as well as of our obligations deriving from the Covenant of the League of Nations. Thus, while there is still no doubt that the Soviets would be very eager to disrupt our military alliance with Poland, we do not believe that the Soviets will oppose the text of this article because, according to our information, Moscow has already accepted a similar article in the Polish draft.

Article IV contains an addition to the Polish text, specifying that controversies deriving from facts antecedent to the Convention (thus including the question of Bessarabia) will not be liable to [the] procedure of conciliation.

Articles V and VI, similar to the Polish text, establish the interdependence and simultaneity of the coming into force of the bilateral pacts of nonaggression concluded by the USSR with all the states on her western border, clauses of a capital importance for maintaining the established solidarity between the states that comprise the anti-Soviet chain from the Baltic to the Black Sea and that, from this point of view, maintain the utility of the said Litvinov unilateral [*sic*] Protocol.

Finally, a protocol of signature specifies that, independent of the fate of the pact of nonaggression, the Treaty of Paris of 1928, as well as the Protocol of Moscow of February 9, 1929, remain in force in their entirety.

Aside from this summary analysis, I believe it necessary to insist upon our tactics, with which you will be inspired in making contact with the representative of the Soviets—always keeping in mind, for greater adaptability, his personal and all other psychological elements, which you have under your control.

It is clear that the Soviets are in a hurry and are desirous of rapidly arriving at the signature. They hope that in Geneva their position will be better in the attack they will launch against "the Russian Clause" that we are currently invoking. We are proceeding only in order not to remain isolated, and in order to respond to the desire of the French government (and secondarily of the Polish government). Consequently, you will conduct the negotiations, on your part, with [an] interest devoid of any sign of emotion; you will not appear impatient to learn the response from Moscow after the presentation of our text, and you will not hotly debate the Soviet representative. But, as you have told us, as your interlocutor finds in you one who is interested, with a certain admiration for the Soviets' progress on economic grounds—agricultural and industrial—you will estimate to what extent this personal expression of interest vis-à-vis the internal policy of the Soviets could produce a friendly atmosphere that, through telegraphic transmissions to Moscow, would definitely have a happy result in the sense of approval there of the text we present.

I am sending along to you, for your strictly personal use, the text of the Polish draft. I intend to send to you later our project for the Convention of Conciliation foreseen in article IV.

Please accept, Mr. Chargé d'Affaires, my personal assurance of consideration.

GHIKA

DOCUMENT NO. 23

Romanian draft of Treaty of Nonaggression between Romania and the USSR

His Majesty, the King of Romania on the one hand, [and] the Central Executive Committee of the USSR on the other hand:

Animated by the desire to reaffirm the political situation in Eastern Europe by means of direct accords as well as to maintain and to consolidate the existing state of peace between the two countries, consecrated by the Protocol of Moscow of February 9, 1929, for the early coming into force of the Treaty of the Renunciation of War signed in Paris on August 27, 1928;

Convinced that the peaceful resolution of all international conflicts is the surest method to attain the goal aimed at, and persuaded that no international engagements concluded previously constitute an impediment to the peaceful development of their mutual relations nor are they contrary to the present treaty, having as [their] end to extend and complete the above-mentioned Protocol and Treaty of Moscow and Paris, have designated to this end their Plenipotentiaries, to know. . . .

Who, after having been communicated their full powers, found in good and due form, are agreed on the following dispositions:

ARTICLE I.

The High Contracting Parties, verifying that they have renounced war as an instrument of national policy in their mutual relations, reciprocally pledge not to indulge in any invasion or aggressive action by way of land, sea, or air against the other Contracting Party.

Acts considered contrary to the engagements foreseen in the preceding paragraph will be every act of violence impairing the integrity and the inviolability of the territory that is presently found under the sovereignty of the other Contracting Party, as well as its political independence, even if such an act were committed without declaration of war or without having the character of an act of war.

ARTICLE II.

If one of the High Contracting Parties, notwithstanding its peaceful attitude, comes to be attacked by a third State or a group of third States, the other Contracting Party pledges not to give aid and assistance to the aggressor State or group of States during the entire duration of the conflict.

In case one of the High Contracting Parties resorts to an act of violence against a third State, the other Contracting Party will be free to denounce the present Treaty without prior warning.

ARTICLE III.

The international rights and obligations resulting for each of the two High Contracting Parties from accords, pacts, treaties, or all other arrangements concluded before the coming into force of the present Treaty remain intact: the engagements stipulated by the present Treaty will neither modify them nor impair them.

ARTICLE IV.

The two High Contracting Parties, animated by the desire to resolve and to solve only by peaceful means all litigations and conflicts that might spring up between them whatever their nature, pledge to submit all the litigious questions they have not been able to resolve within a reasonable period to a procedure of conciliation conforming to the dispositions of the Convention of Conciliation concluded simultaneously with the present Treaty, of which it constitutes an integral part.

This stipulation does not apply to disputes having their origin in facts antecedent to the present convention and that belong to the past.

ARTICLE V.

The High Contracting Parties are agreed that the other signatory governments of the Protocol of Moscow dated February 9, 1929, as well as Finland be invited to conclude (with the USSR) accords analogous to the present Treaty.

ARTICLE VI.

The present Treaty will be ratified and the instruments of ratification exchanged at. . . .

It will enter into force the thirtieth day after the notification to Romania, by the government of the USSR, that analogous accords between the USSR on the one hand, and Estonia, Finland, Latvia, and Poland, on the other hand, have been ratified and the instruments of ratification exchanged.

ARTICLE VII.

The duration of the present Treaty is three years. If it is not denounced by either of the High Contracting Parties with a warning of at least six months before the expiration of this period, it will be considered as renewed by tacit agreement for a new period of two years and henceforth, until denunciation in the time period foreseen above.

PROTOCOL OF SIGNATURE

The High Contracting Parties declare that article VII cannot be interpreted in the sense that the extinction of the Treaty after [its] term or after denunciation, may in any measure impair the obligations resulting from the Treaty signed in Paris on August 27, 1928, as well as the Protocol signed in Moscow on February 9, 1929, nor impair in any way the said obligation.

DOCUMENT NO. 24

Presentation, GHIKA *to* COUNCIL OF MINISTERS

Bucharest, 5 January 1932

There already exist reciprocal promises of nonaggression between Romania and the Soviet Union through the fact that both states are signatories of the multilateral Treaty for the Renunciation of War concluded in Paris on August 27, 1928 (the Kellogg-Briand Pact), and of the Protocol of Moscow of February 9, 1929 (the Litvinov Protocol), on the basis of which the said treaty entered into force early between the USSR and its neighbors to the west. The Protocol of Moscow presents, therefore, an unusual importance as far as Romanian-Soviet relations are concerned because, in the preamble, "the maintenance of the existing peace" is mentioned. The Soviet Union, recognizing that she was in a state of peace with Romania, thus forever renounced her pretensions that Romania committed an act of war through the fact of the occupation of Bessarabia.

So, the necessity of negotiating a new Romanian-Russian pact of nonaggression was not imposed inexorably. The new facts that pushed us in this direction are the following:

At the beginning of last May, the minister of Poland informed us that negotiations had begun between the Soviet and Polish governments for the conclusion of a pact of nonaggression by which [it was proposed] to specify and to enlarge the obligations undertaken in the Kellogg-Briand Pact [at the same time] completing it with a treaty of arbitration and conciliation. The minister of Poland was authorized to tell us that Poland made the conclusion of such a pact conditional on the conclusion of a similar pact between Romania and the USSR, and to offer us the useful intermediary assistance of his government in this regard. I did not fail to tell the minister of Poland that there were eventual conditions for the conclusion of such a pact on our part:

1. The new draft was not to weaken or modify in any way the utility of the Kellogg-Briand Pact and the Litvinov Protocol;
2. That, in accordance with the text of the pact, any damage to actual territorial integrity would be considered aggression;
3. That excluded from the questions that could be submitted to the procedure of arbitration and conciliation [was] the question of our eastern frontier;
4. That there existed an absolute interdependence between the coming into force of our pact with the USSR and the coming into force of the pact between Poland and the USSR, so as not to lead to the dislocation of our alliance.

On the other hand, we were informed on May 31 by our Legation in Paris, on the basis of a communication of the French minister of foreign affairs, that on June 5 negotiations would begin in Paris between the French and Soviet governments for the conclusion of a pact of commerce and a pact of nonaggression and of arbitration. Both our Legation in Paris and the Legation of France in Bucharest kept us informed about the progress of these negotiations, which have now led to the elaboration and initialing of the text of a pact of nonaggression and of conciliation, which was approved by the French government. In the text of the pact of nonaggression, which was early communicated to us, it is formally provided that "if one of the Contracting Parties attacks a third State, the other Contracting Party may denounce the pact without warning." As a result France remains at liberty to give us her military aid in case we should be attacked by the USSR.

Concerning the Polish-Soviet negotiations, they were interrupted during the summer and were only restarted last November. On the occasion of the restarting of the negotiations in Moscow, the Soviet government declared that it was not willing to treat with Romania through Poland, and that they desired direct negotiations, leaving it to Romania to take the initiative for those negotiations. In face of the persistent interventions of the French government and the similar insistence of the Polish government, and in order not to remain isolated, we were obliged to give in to these requests, giving instructions to our representatives in Warsaw, Riga, and Ankara to make contact with their Soviet colleagues in order to make some preliminary soundings. The question of the site where the negotiations would take place was raised on this occasion, and in this realm of ideas we proposed Warsaw and then Riga whereas the Soviet government proposed Ankara and then Moscow. Finally, we agreed on Riga, where I gave instructions to our chargé d'affaires to carry out these negotiations "ad referendum," keeping in daily telegraphic contact with the Romanian government. At the same time, I sent him the draft pact of nonaggression we had settled on.[43] This was on the basis of the Polish draft modified to suit our special situation vis-à-vis the USSR. The question of Bessarabia continuing unmentioned—without dwelling on the abnormal character of this situation, which can only be conceived within the framework of the mentality of the Soviet leaders—we considered [it] indispensable to ground ourselves, even in the preamble of our draft, on the Litvinov Protocol, again affirming that a state of peace exists between the two countries. At the same time, article I paragraph 2 provides in so many words that "acts considered contrary to the pledges foreseen in the preceding paragraph, will be every act of violence threatening *the integrity and inviolability of territory currently found under the sovereignty of the other Contracting Party,* as well as its political independence even if such an act were committed without declaration of war or without having the character of an act of war."

This wording is, moreover, in conformity with the definition given by international law to the notion of territory, which is "the space over which a state exercises sovereignty." And it is evident that Romania's sovereignty is exercised over Bessarabia. Thus any confusion is excluded regarding the line of demarcation there against which no aggression can be committed.

Article II of our draft is reproduced after the French and Polish text, to wit: "In case one of the High Contracting Parties resorts to an act of violence against a third State, the other Contracting Party will be free to denounce the present Treaty without warning."

In this way our alliance with Poland will maintain all its efficacy in case one of us is attacked by the USSR. Moreover, article III, similar to the Polish text, specifies that "the international rights and obligations deriving for each of the two High Contracting Parties from accords, pacts, treaties, or all other arrangements concluded before the coming into force of the present Treaty remain intact: the obligations stipulated by the present Treaty will neither modify them nor impair them."

This strengthens, along with the respect of our defensive alliances previously concluded, the rights and duties that result for us from the Covenant of the League of Nations.

[As for] article IV, foreseeing the conclusion of a convention of conciliation, we want to make it clear that the procedure of conciliation will apply only to disputes having their origin in facts subsequent to the conclusion of the pact of nonaggression—thus excluding from such a procedure the question of Bessarabia.

Articles III and VI, similar to the Polish text, establish the interdependence and simultaneity of the coming into force of the bilateral pacts of nonaggression concluded by the USSR with all the states on her western border, clauses of primary importance in view of maintaining the developed solidarity between the states that constitute the anti-Soviet chain between the Baltic and Black Seas, and that maintain from this point of view the utility of the so-called Litvinov multilateral Protocol.

This interdependence of the simultaneous entering into force of the bilateral pacts of nonaggression that will be concluded by the USSR was suggested by the Polish government from the start. This new verification of solidarity and loyalty on the part of our ally constitutes a gratifying ray on the eve of direct negotiations with Russia—negotiations that we did not desire and to which we are resigned.

DOCUMENT NO. 25

Telegram, GHIKA *to* PARIS LEGATION

Bucharest No. 597, 6 January 1932

For your knowledge, my instructions given to Chargé d'Affaires Sturdza on December 31 and approved by the king and Council of Ministers yesterday do not conceal [the fact] that the Romanian government begins direct contact with the Soviets for the pact of nonaggression without illusions, without an appetite [for them] and only with resignation and in a spirit of solidarity with [our] allies: Poland and France.

Our public opinion receives the negotiations and the realization of the pact with timidity and disbelief, the majority of the newspapers being hostile to the developments. In the most favorable hypothesis—that is, if the Soviets accept the text of our draft, where we did all we could to guarantee our positions, without mentioning Bessarabia—we will have a confirmation of the situation established in 1929 after the Litvinov Protocol, with a more powerful specification relative to "the inviolability and integrity of the territory under our sovereignty." On the other hand, if we are constrained to accept a vaguer formula, our situation will not be strengthened in comparison to what it has been so far, and the Soviets alone would profit in their presentation and their action at the Disarmament Conference.

In your conversations with Berthelot and, more important, with

Laval, putting into relief our spirit of solidarity and the care we have taken in regard to our allies, please find out if somehow the French government would not be inclined, before the signing of the eventual Romanian-Soviet pact, to exchange with the Romanian government a secret letter complementary to our treaty of friendship by which the French government declares that it considers the Treaty of Paris of 1920 concerning Bessarabia as in force as far as France is concerned, despite [the fact] that its entering into force is conditional on the ratification of the five signatory powers, of which one, Japan, has not ratified.

GHIKA

DOCUMENT NO. 26

Letter, STURDZA *to* GHIKA

Riga No. 40, Annex 1, 6 January 1932

Dear Mr. Minister,

I have the honor to transmit to Your Excellency herein the text of the Soviet draft for [a] pact of nonaggression with Romania.[44]

The characteristics of this draft are:

1. From the first, a placing on the agenda of the Bessarabian litigation, which we were promised would be overlooked, and the adaptation of the entire text, vis-à-vis the French and Polish texts, with contestations of our sovereignty over a part of our territory.
2. Suppression of the possibility of denouncing the pact in case Russia first attacks another power ([the] possibility foreseen in the initialed French and Polish texts).
3. The introduction (art. 3) of a general obligation not to take part in any accord hostile to the other party, thus an obligation still larger than that of economic nonaggression, which was refused by Poland and the Baltic powers.

Judging from this text it would seem that Russia, pure and simple, wants to take us to Vienna again. It is evident how well our government acted in refusing Moscow or Ankara as [the] location for the negotiations and in electing the procedure that it is following.

I do not doubt that the USSR is determined to find the means to noisily reopen the question of Bessarabia during the course of negotiations. I believe, however, that the definitive gesture in this regard is reserved in Moscow's thinking for the end of the negotiations, and that this first attempt could be, up to a point, more of a bluff. Perhaps, then, I could get the text under discussion suppressed from the preamble and continue the negotiations with regard to the other points of contention. I am nevertheless convinced that the question of Bessarabia will be reopened by the Soviets at another time during the negotiations, or very probably even after the negotiations, between the eventual initialing and signing or ratification.

It remains to be seen if it would not be to our advantage for the interruption to take place earlier, before the Soviets are given the advantage of a text, even if only initialed, that would serve them in Geneva.

Mr. Stomonyakov will pay his first visit to me tomorrow and I propose to use the following language:

"The Romanian government only entered into these negotiations with the indirect but precise promise that the question of Bessarabia would not be raised. I notice with surprise that the Soviet government begins exactly with the opening of this question. My government will never accept any version of the principal part of your preamble—only its pure and simple elimination. In case this elimination is not obtained, I will immediately withdraw from the ongoing negotiations. It is, therefore, up to you to judge whether, in order to gain time, it is useful for us now to examine the other points, about which the disagreements do not appear so great.

Please accept, M. Minister, the assurance of my highest consideration.

MIHAIL R. STURDZA

P.S. I add that I have denied to the press today that Romanian-Russian negotiations have really begun, and I will do so until after the solution of this previous question.

Naturally, I kept my French and Polish colleagues informed of the course of events, and, to the extent that it is useful, the Latvian and Estonian governments.[45]

DOCUMENT NO. 27

Russian draft of Treaty of Nonaggression between the USSR and Romania

The Central Executive Committee of the Union of Soviet Socialist Republics, and

His Majesty, the King of Romania:

Animated by the will to consolidate the peace;

Having the firm conviction that the establishment of peaceful relations between the two Contracting Parties corresponds to their interests;

Recording that the establishment of such relations brings no prejudice to the existing territorial litigation between the two Contracting Parties about Bessarabia which is not regulated by the present Treaty;

Considering that the situation of which mention is made in the preceding paragraph also found its expression in the signature by the two Contracting Parties of the general Treaty on the Renunciation of War of August 27, 1928, and of the Protocol of Moscow of February 9, 1929;

Have resolved to conclude the present Treaty and have named for this purpose their Plenipotentiaries, to wit:

The Executive Committee of the Union of Soviet Socialist Republics . . .

His Majesty, the King of Romania . . .

Who, after having communicated to one another their full powers found in good and due form, have agreed to the following dispositions:

ARTICLE I.

Each of the Contracting Parties pledges never to undertake against the other, either separately or in conjunction with other Powers, any aggression on land, at sea, or in the air, and in no case to resort to war against the other.

ARTICLE II.

In case one of the Contracting Parties should become the object of an aggression on the part of a third State or group of third States, the other Party pledges to observe neutrality during the entire duration of the conflict.

ARTICLE III.

Each of the Contracting Parties pledges not to take part in any agreement hostile toward the other Party or found to be contrary in law or in fact to the present Treaty.

ARTICLE IV.

Each of the Contracting Parties pledges never to allow on its territory the sojourn or the activity of organizations having as [their] end armed struggle against the other Party, or of organizations or persons claiming the role of government or of representing all or part of its territory.

ARTICLE V.

The present Treaty will be ratified. The acts of ratification will be exchanged at. . . . It will come into force on the day of this exchange.

ARTICLE VI.

The present Treaty is concluded for the duration of three years. If one of the Contracting Parties does not denounce it six months before the end of the three-year period, the validity of the Treaty will be automatically prolonged for a new duration of two years.

Done in two copies in . . . on. . . .

DOCUMENT NO. 28

Intradepartmental memo, STURDZA *to* MINISTRY OF FOREIGN AFFAIRS

Riga, [?] January 1932

CONVERSATION OF THE ROMANIAN REPRESENTATIVE AND
THE SOVIET DELEGATE, 7 JANUARY 1932[46]

Returning the visit that the Soviet minister in Riga had paid him by chance five weeks before, the representative of Romania met with the Soviet delegate. On this occasion, texts of the respective drafts of [the] pact of nonaggression were exchanged. The present meeting took place at the Romanian Legation, where the Soviet delegate paid an official visit.

NOTE: This is not a procès-verbal; the notes were taken and the editing made unilaterally.

ROMANIAN REPRESENTATIVE: I had hoped to carry on this business with the good Mr. Svidersky.[47] It was an unpleasant surprise to learn that they were sending us the terrible Mr. Stomonyakov.

SOVIET DELEGATE: Terrible? But no! Why?

RR: They assured me only Mr. Litvinov himself was to be feared more. Exchange of diverse courtesies. Exchange of opinions on the procedure. The SD would like the conclusions arrived at during the sessions, once consigned in a procès-verbal, to constitute definite obligations. On this [point] the RR produced the following formula [that he had] previously written: "It was decided by both the one and the other party that all proposals made, all provisional agreements at which one might arrive, every partial text exchange, would constitute an obligation for the one or the other party only within the general framework of the total agreement, an agreement that would be only taken 'ad referendum.' "

SD: "Ad referendum?" Why "ad referendum?" I have full powers. It is I, Stomonyakov, who represent the Soviet government. You have full powers too, so we can negotiate.

RR: I negotiate "ad referendum." It is an old procedure still much appreciated. In your negotiations with Poland, for example, I believe that it was utilized.

SD: But not at all. We signed a protocol on December 21 with Mr. Patek. The engagements are definite.

RR: But until then how did you conduct the talks? When we reach our December 21 we too will sign definitive texts, perhaps. It is only the beginning of the year.

SD: But no, I tell you, whenever Mr. Patek signed it was always definitive. Really, I am quite perplexed. I do not know what to do.

RR: Let's do the same as Messrs. Berthelot and Dovgalevsky. Their text, at least, was initialed A.R.

SD: Well, all right, we'll see.

RR: That's it, we will see.

SD: Besides, we are not there [yet]. Today we ought to discuss a question of principle.

RR: You're right, today we will simply enter into preliminary contact to see if the negotiations are possible.

SD: What? Surely, the negotiations began yesterday with the exchange of texts, and if that's not called "beginning".....

RR: Of course they'll be started, as soon as the texts are considered. Besides, I think that we will do well to proceed methodically. [Since] it is the Romanian text that was submitted first, you'll probably want to be the first to give your opinion. I will listen to you without interruption.

SD: Yes, by all means. That's what I'm going to do. You know, do you not, that there is a serious litigation between your government and mine, a territorial litigation—Bessarabia. You know of course that the Soviet government has never renounced its rights to that province, and we will do no such thing on this occasion, any more than we did on the occasion of the Kellogg Pact and of the Protocol of Moscow. The main question is, are we negotiating a treaty of nonaggression or something else? We wish, in the interest of general peace, to altruistically make a "beau geste." But we leave the question of Bessarabia open. You are being egotistical: you want to profit from the situation in order to expand your country. You wish on this occasion to extort from us the recognition of your sovereignty over a territory that you have occupied by force of arms (*here he opened the Romanian draft and pointed to paragraph 2 of article I*). We will not allow it, we will not recognize it. The present situation is not an obstacle to an accord being concluded between us, but we do not want you to profit from this pact to take something else from us. You also have claims against us. You have some, haven't you? So, we do not ask that you renounce them by this pact. We are not acting for an egotistical end, it is for the general peace; but we ought to formally declare from the preamble of our pact that the question of Bessarabia remains open.

RR: May I, in my turn . . . ?

SD: Please do. (*Offers cigarettes and refreshments.*)

RR: The Romanian government only decided to consider negotiations with the Soviet government on the indirect but precise assurance that the question of the eastern frontiers, of eastern Moldavia, would not be mentioned. I am, therefore, extremely surprised that it is precisely that question with which your government tries to open the said negotiations. Romania is determined not to allow its sovereignty over such and such other parts of its territory to be called into question in any text whatever; [she will not allow] what you call the question of Bessarabia to be evoked in any way whatever in the pact that we are trying to establish. It would, therefore, be impossible for me to even begin these negotiations before you purely and simply remove paragraphs 5 and 6 from the preamble.

SD: The Soviet government consulted its legal counselors and they decided that a pact of nonaggression with Romania could not be signed without making mention of the Bessarabian litigation, from the beginning of the pact. If we do not so declare it, our rights would be limited.

RR: You did it anyway in Moscow in 1929.

SD: In Moscow Mr. Litvinov made the formal reservation.

RR: In the protocol?

SD: No, but solemnly, after the signing, in front of all the delegates.

RR: Are you going to do something similar this time, too?

SD: Yes, we could not let this pass. It is the Council of People's Commissars that wrote the preamble. We cannot pass over it. It is an official document that I present to you.

RR: I am obliged to repeat it is in flagrant contradiction of the promises on the basis of which we agreed to make the first contact.

SD: Who told you about these promises?

RR: Your government is certainly as well informed as I am about this report.

SD: But tell me, who?

RR: Mr. Stomonyakov, it is quite simple, to dispel all doubt on this subject I ask you this precise question. Should I formally record at this time that the Soviet government refuses to negotiate and conclude a pact of nonaggression without touching upon the question of Bessarabia?

SD: It is you that want at all cost to touch upon the question of Bessarabia. Look. (*The SD read paragraph 2 of article I of the Romanian draft, emphasizing the word "presently"*).

RR: (*smiling*) Look, I thought that this expression would sit nicely with you . . . that you could think that "presently" does not mean forever.

SD: (*also smiling*) You are optimistic.

RR: Do you imagine that we will write a pact of nonaggression without stipulating the inviolability of our respective frontiers and the integrity of our territory?

SD: In principle, you are right; in fact, we cannot recognize your sovereignty over Bessarabia.

RR: It is impossible for us to force you, but if you cannot guarantee us that you will not attack us at some point on our present frontier, that you will invade none of the provinces presently under our sovereignty, I do not see what we are doing here!

SD: Do you want a formal pledge that we will attack you neither on your territory nor on what you call your territory? I give it to you immediately.

RR: In making this distinction? It's not worth it. Mr. Stomonyakov, realize that you will never obtain from us even the simple taking into consideration of a text that declares or implies the existence of a legal dispute over our eastern frontier.

SD: But the dispute exists, you said so yourself.

RR: Yes, but I will never write it, you may be sure.

SD: This territory that you have taken from us. . . .

RR: Retaken.

SD: We have offered you a plebiscite.

RR: Let us leave this question. We are negotiating a pact of non-aggression.

SD: And you want to extort from us a tacit consent. All your press says so.

RR: Which newspapers do you read?

SD: We will not give you our consent.

RR: We cannot take it from you. All we want is not to touch upon this question.

SD: It is what we want too, to start off by saying that it remains open.

RR: To emphatically declare that a question remains open—that is touching upon it quite a bit. No, you must pledge faithfully not to touch upon it, and keep your pledge; otherwise I [will] not budge a step. You will not take us for a second time to Vienna. You can be sure about that.

SD: That is not our intention.

RR: I cannot overlook it. For the great, the immense Russia, little Bessarabia is an interesting political possibility that will always exist. For us it is a question of our independence, of our existence. We will accept no ambiguity, no reticence. We do not play with this type of question. It is useless to try. On any other question you will find in me the most patient and most conciliatory interlocutor. I see something we can agree to right off. I am sure of it.

SD: What?

RR: For example, article II of your draft: if we leave it as it is, they will say we are negotiating a treaty of alliance.

SD: We're not there yet (*examination of the text*). Ah, yes, I see what you mean. Naturally, we can fix that. It is not of importance.

RR: You see!

SD: But it is not me, it is you who are terrible. You make a mountain out of everything.

RR: One mountain, just one. After that it's the valley, and then the plain.

SD: I don't know: in face of the unexpected turn the discussion is taking, I must consult my government. I will ask you two questions to summarize our conversation. May I report to Moscow that the Romanian government refuses to sign any pact in which the question of Bessarabia is mentioned in any way; [and] that the Romanian government does not intend to use these negotiations to extort a consent from us relative to Bessarabia?

RR: You may report that to Moscow with confidence. My government accepts that this question is in no way to be touched upon during the course of the negotiations that are about to open.

SD: But they are open.

RR: Yes, of course, in a certain way. Tell me, Mr. Stomonyakov, I would like to consult you on a small question of protocol. I ought to repay your visit tomorrow, [but] perhaps you would prefer it to be in several days.

SD: Yes, yes, that's it. I will telephone you when you should come. It is not worth [the trouble] before I receive an answer from Moscow.

The conversation developed on an extremely cordial and courteous tone and even . . . here and there.

Pro forma

STURDZA

DOCUMENT NO. 29
(Reg. No. 1265 of 12 January 1932)

Decoded telegram, STURDZA *to* MINISTRY OF FOREIGN AFFAIRS

Riga No. 54, 11 January 1932

Today I had my third meeting with Mr. Stomonyakov.[48] Conforming to the instructions [he had] received in the meantime from Moscow, he formally declared that the Soviet government refuses to sign a pact of nonaggression with us without adoption of its text or of an instrument somehow annexed mentioning that the question of Bessarabia remains open.[49] The Soviet government is of the opinion that without this precaution it would sanction our sovereignty over Bessarabia, which Russia will never recognize. In my turn I reiterated to Mr. Stomonyakov that it was the desire of the Romanian government to entirely exclude, explicitly and implicitly, the question of Bessarabia from the discussions, that in its opinion to sign a pact of nonaggression, conceived in the essential terms of such a diplomatic instrument, cannot prejudice the position that the Soviets intend to maintain in the question of Bessarabia [and] that, on the other hand, refusing [would] give us some expression of this position.

Mr. Stomonyakov told me that neither can his government allow that it could be deduced from its silence on such an occasion that it had renounced its rights. I told Mr. Stomonyakov that, in these circumstances, I did not see on what grounds we could reach an understanding. He then proposed the signing of a separate procès-verbal in which I could officially take note of the Soviet reservation, stating [his] opinion that this procès-verbal could be written without containing the word Bessarabia. I replied that it would be impossible for me to sign such a procès-verbal. He then proposed, without guaranteeing that it would sufficiently satisfy Moscow, that he send me a note in which he would inform me about the formal reservation of the Soviets, that I take note of that note, and that we proceed to the discussion of the articles. I also declined this offer. Regarding my last declaration, he expressed the opinion that the negotiations had been broken off. Only in order to avoid our being accused by someone of intransigence, I sought a formula that would impede this "break" at the second meeting, proposing to Mr. Stomonyakov that we agree to leave the examination of the preamble for the end of the negotiations and that we now proceed to the discussion of the other points. He said he could only accept this formula [if] the words "examination of the preamble" were replaced with "examination of the existing litigation."

In what followed, we agreed not to consider the conversations as broken off before we had informed [our] governments of the foregoing and had received instructions. I believe that the Soviet government, realizing the impossibility of drawing us further down [their] prepared course, will break off the conversations at the next meeting, or perhaps even before.

The sooner the rupture takes place, the more probable we will be followed by the Baltic States.

I will give every attention to this possibility.

STURDZA

DOCUMENT NO. 30

Telegram, GHIKA *to* STURDZA

Bucharest, 12 January 1932

On [your] No. 54.[50] I approve your attitude. We will wait for the Soviets' next move. If we can believe the observations of the Polish minister in Moscow, the Soviet procedure was to be expected, and after their violent debut concerning Bessarabia a new, more acceptable phase of negotiation will now follow. But I fear that the Polish sources, in their desire to achieve a result, delude themselves. Today I will inform Count Szembek of the content of your telegram, with the request that he inform us of the suggestions of the Polish government and that it discover the exact intentions of Litvinov on the spot in Moscow. At the same time you should know that the French government is taking steps that it is believed correspond to its desire to reach the conclusion of a pact of nonaggression.

GHIKA

DOCUMENT NO. 31

Intradepartmental memo, ARION *to* GHIKA

Bucharest, 12 January 1932

Mr. Minister:

I informed the minister of Poland of the content of telegram No. 54[51] from Riga and told him the following:

1. That Romania cannot allow the question of her sovereignty over Bessarabia to be placed in discussion at Riga;
2. That if we agree, due to the insistence of our allies and only to keep in step with them, to negotiate the conclusion of a treaty of nonaggression with the USSR, nevertheless our allies cannot expect that Romania will surrender for this even the least bit of her present position vis-à-vis the USSR, either by the text of the treaty or by any other act;
3. That if the USSR does not change [its] attitude to conform with the previous assurances, according to which the question of Bessarabia would not be mentioned on the occasion of our negotiations, then these negotiations will certainly be broken off;
4. That consequently we ask him to bring the above to the attention of the Polish government in order to make démarches in Moscow corresponding to ·its desire to arrive at the conclusion of analogous and concomitant treaties of nonaggression between the USSR and all its neighbors between the Baltic and the Black Sea, and to inform us of the suggestion of the Polish government as well as asking Mr. Patek to find out the exact intentions that Mr. Litvinov might have relative to the conclusion of such a treaty with Romania.

> M. ARION, Minister Plenipotentiary
> Director of Eastern Political Affairs

DOCUMENT NO. 32
(Reg. No. 1610 of 13 January 1932)

Decoded telegram, STURDZA *to* MINISTRY OF FOREIGN AFFAIRS

Riga No. 55, 13 January 1932

Referring to [my] No. 54.

I extract the following dialogue from the discussions of yesterday [as] being of special interest to the Polish government.

ME: You promised that you would leave out the question of Bessarabia; we would not have consented to these conversations otherwise.

STOMONYAKOV: We never promised that. I said, perhaps, that we leave it open. . . .

ME: I am compelled to remember the incident of that procès-verbal, the one that gave you the occasion to liquidate this subtlety—[a] procès-verbal that is, it would seem, the origin of our negotiations.

STOMONYAKOV: It is not true: I know what you are talking about [and] there is no connection between that incident and today's negotiations.

STURDZA

DOCUMENT NO. 33
(Reg. No. 2198 of 14 January 1932)

Decoded telegram, STURDZA *to* MINISTRY OF FOREIGN AFFAIRS

Riga No. 56, 14 January 1932
VERY URGENT, STRICTLY CONFIDENTIAL

Today I had my third conversation with the Soviet delegate. Mr. Stomonyakov told me in the name of his government, in the most express and definitive manner, that it is impossible for the Soviet government to submit to our desire to conduct negotiations and to conclude a pact in which its principal position in the question of Bessarabia is not recorded, and that Soviet Russia will never sign a pact of nonaggression with Romania that contains the following three words: (1) integrity, (2) inviolability, and (3) sovereignty.[52] Nevertheless, he added that in order to demonstrate its conciliatory spirit, his government had authorized him to accept the proposal I had made during the last session to bypass the discussion of the preamble for the examination of the pact. Just as categorically, I reminded Mr. Stomonyakov of my government's opinion, leaving it to him to judge if in such circumstances this examination was of any utility. He answered affirmatively. We decided to begin the negotiations, fully conscious of the tactical mistake we might be making by postponing a rupture, but taking into account our situation vis-à-vis Paris and Warsaw and desiring to leave the theory of the Soviet bluff, dear to Mr. Patek, every chance of being proven true.

After a long session we arrived at the conclusion of a procès-verbal without any preamble, stating, by simple annexation of texts without any commentary, the existing differences and recording two or three possibilities of agreement on secondary points. At the next session, that is, tomorrow January 15 at 6 o'clock [P.M.], we will begin the discussions in earnest about each article in turn. If we begin, as is logical, with article I, I am sure that [we will] have the same excellent motives for a rupture as today, to judge from the declarations of the Soviet delegate today, which I naturally did not record, declarations that he will repeat to me. For one in my position, all considerations seem to call for a rupture, with the possibility of leaving the door ajar for a Soviet return.

STURDZA

DOCUMENT NO. 34

Telegram (copy), GHIKA *to* STURDZA

Bucharest No. 2482, 15 January 1932

Answer to [your] 56.[53]

From what you tell us about the state of negotiations, I see that their success seems to be, at the very best, dubious. Given the advantage we would gain at the Disarmament Conference from the nonconclusion of the pact in question, please be so kind as to not lose sight of our interest in seeing that the rupture comes eventually from the Soviet side.

I have full confidence in your tact to obtain this result. However, I should inform you that, as a result of my interventions with France and Poland to make démarches in Moscow corresponding to their desire to arrive at the conclusion of the projected treaties of nonaggression, it should not be ruled out that the Soviets [might] adopt a more conciliatory attitude, although I am very skeptical in this regard.

In this respect, today the minister of Poland informed me that Poland maintains the principle of interdependence of the coming into force of the pacts of nonaggression, and that whereas the USSR was in such a hurry to conclude these pacts, Litvinov [now] asks Patek to postpone the negotiations for a few days on the pretext of the visit of the minister of the Permanent Court to Moscow. The Polish government, on the other hand, believes that it is better that the eventual negotiations between us and the Soviets go gradually, coming to a head during the time of the Disarmament Conference. I see in this an early result of that démarche I informed you about in my telegram No. 1603.[54]

However much we might remonstrate in Paris and Warsaw that a pact of nonaggression that would not provide in some form or other a precise demarcation of where aggression could not be committed would be meaningless, we have no objection to replacing it with a concrete notion like that of a geographic line if the USSR shows a categoric aversion to the abstract notions of integrity, inviolability, and sovereignty.

Of course, this line could only be the Dniester—a line already mentioned in the Romanian-Soviet agreement of Tiraspol for the settlement of disputes, *without the word* "Dniester" being considered either provocative or inadmissible by the Soviets.

GHIKA

DOCUMENT NO. 35
(Reg. No. 2687 of 16 January 1932)

Decoded telegram, BILCIURESCU *to* MINISTRY OF FOREIGN AFFAIRS

Warsaw No. 141, 15 January 1932

Answer to your No. 1846.[55]

Today I spoke with Zaleski, who told me that once he had received the telegram from Count Szembek he had given telegraphic instructions to the Polish minister in Moscow to insist to the Soviet government in the desired sense, and that today he would telegraph [him] again. He added that he viewed the question calmly, that he did not believe that we were in a hurry, because only if we obtain the text that suits us will we sign the pact before the Disarmament Conference, otherwise [we will] not, our situation at the conference being very good thanks to the negotiations. Litvinov, being occupied with the visit of a high Persian official, the negotiations of Poland's minister in Moscow have been interrupted for two to three days. So Zaleski informed the bordering states not to display an air of haste as does the Soviet negotiator, but to postpone the negotiations until Patek resumes his. Once they have something new from him, they will let us know.

Without intending to put the slightest pressure on us, the foreign minister further told me he believes that we could accept a pact in which the Soviets renounce [their] reservation concerning Bessarabia in exchange for our renunciation of the words "territory where we exercise sovereignty."

I answered that our position was a minimum, whereas the Soviet reservations would be the equivalent of our demanding to record formal recognition of the union of Bessarabia.

I have the impression that the ambassador of France is of Zaleski's opinion.

BILCIURESCU

DOCUMENT NO. 36
(Reg. No. 2752 of 16 January 1932)

Decoded telegram, STURDZA *to* MINISTRY OF FOREIGN AFFAIRS

Riga No. 60, 16 January 1932

I am transmitting the procès-verbal of today's session, probably the last of the negotiations.

The delegates decided to pass to a more careful examination of the points on which agreement was not achieved in the preceding session.

Addressing article I, the delegate of Romania asks that the definition of acts contrary to the obligation of nonaggression, a definition that is essential to this pact, be expressly recorded in it, and that this definition include "expressis verbis" the terms "territorial integrity," "inviolability," and "national sovereignty."

The Soviet delegate, repeating his declarations of the preceding session, declared that his government is prepared to undertake the obligation not to resort to action against Romania, but that he was not in the position, for the reasons he had expressed, to accept the proposed terms. The Soviet delegate proposes to seek through common efforts another wording that, [while] giving Romania material satisfaction in the question of nonaggression, would [still] be acceptable to the Soviet government.

In the opinion of the Romanian delegate, an explicit guarantee of territorial inviolability and integrity is an essential clause of any pact of nonaggression. He considers the search for a text that would not comprise the desired terms as superfluous, and he declares that he cannot renounce them, any pact of nonaggression not recording them being unacceptable to this government.

In the situation created both delegates decided "to report to their governments."

We decided to enter into the negotiations because we had the impression from our allied colleagues, especially Polish ones, that if we persisted in the fiction of a simple previous contact, we could be accused of not making even the slightest effort toward the commonly desired end, and so conveniently escaping our responsibility.

A quarter of an hour before today's session my Polish colleague came to beg me, following an urgent telephone call from Warsaw, in the name of his government and Mr. Patek, not to break off conversations formally, in any case before Monday the eighteenth.

Also in the name of Mr. Patek, he again reaffirmed the conviction that the Soviets would yield and that they would carry their bluff to the extreme limit.

By today's procès-verbal this limit is reached, and I believe that no friendly and allied government could ask us to go further. On the other hand, this procès-verbal permits us to consider and declare the negotiations as broken off at any moment we wish. Such a declaration, [made] as soon as possible, seems opportune vis-à-vis Warsaw, which we presume asks breathing space until Monday only with the aim of permitting Mr. Patek to sign before the Polish government is faced with its responsibilities and obligations of solidarity.

Concerning our position vis-à-vis our adversaries only, a more rapid procedure would surely have been better. Caught, however, between them and our allies, I believe that what resulted was the only thing possible for us.

STURDZA

DOCUMENT NO. 37
(Reg. No. 2757 of 17 January 1932)

Decoded telegram, STURDZA *to* MINISTRY OF FOREIGN AFFAIRS

Riga No. 61, 16 January 1932

In answer to your telegram No. 2482.[56]

If we are obliged to renounce the guarantee of integrity and inviolability of territory subject to national sovereignty, and if we will satisfy ourselves with the promise not to pass the line of demarcation—a promise corresponding to that of the Statute of Tiraspol—I believe nothing would be easier to obtain (of course without prejudice to the "de jure" reservation of the Soviets on Bessarabia that forms the chief point of the negotiations). However, I ask not to yield, and to prevent this change from somehow being made known to the Soviet delegate through Paris or Warsaw until we are convinced that we will not obtain the formal recording of at least those two notions of integrity and inviolability (the term "sovereignty" being the only one I am absolutely sure we will never obtain), or before we seek to get in exchange for this concession the expunging from the preamble and the entire pact of any mention of the litigation over Bessarabia. From what has been revealed by the Soviet delegate himself, I know that the Soviet government intends, in case its position on the question of Bessarabia is not declared in the pact itself, to make a noisy reiteration of its position on the occasion of the conclusion of our pact. The only way to frustrate Mr. Litvinov's intentions is, I believe, to be satisfied only with the most solemn declarations. Count Szembek's information regarding the maintenance of the principle of interdependence perplexes me. My Polish colleague, who up until now told me "that this clause if not dead yet is already buried (it is Patek who dropped everything)," informed me yesterday that even as of that date it had died, and that the Polish government had definitely renounced it. This information was given by the ministers of Poland to the respective Baltic governments, which, I am told by the most competent sources, have not yet followed Poland's example; they are leaving the renunciation to which they are committed for another moment in the talks, entirely for motives of procedure in the negotiations. In face of the situation, I suggest that I make a proposal to the Soviets that in exchange for a formula of the type you indicated in today's telegram they renounce any reservation on the question of Bessarabia within the framework of the pact, and that I bring the negotiations to their conclusion because of their probable refusal.

STURDZA

DOCUMENT NO. 38
(Reg. No. 2758 of 17 January 1932)

Decoded telegram, BILCIURESCU *to* GHIKA

Warsaw No. 174, 16 January 1932

In making the communication to Zaleski in confirmation with Your Excellency's telegram No. 2483,[57] a little while ago he told me that he understood our point of view [only] too well because we could only conclude a pact of nonaggression that means a step forward, and not backward. In his opinion, it would be well, for the time being, to leave out the preamble and article I and to seek an agreement to edit the rest of the pact with the Soviet delegate in the hope of finding an acceptable formula by common accord in the meantime. If not, then at the moment when all the pacts are ready, he will be able to put pressure on the Soviets, threatening not to sign if they do not reach an understanding with Romania too. So as not to compromise the whole question because of the article in the Romanian pact, the Soviet government will be obliged to yield. On this occasion he assured me that Poland [would] not sign without Romania. Then he read me part of a recent telegram from Patek, who had been able to see Litvinov again. The latter recognized that he had said that he consented not to talk about Bessarabia in the negotiations with Romania, but this was not a formal promise! And, he said that the reservation concerning the question of Bessarabia could be made the object of a separate act or an exchange of notes.

I told Mr. Zaleski that the Romanian government (would) surely never accept this. He answered that perhaps the People's Commissar for Foreign Affairs, regretting the signing of the act of 1929 without the reservation of Bessarabia, imagines that he will now succeed in introducing [it] in [the] pact, but that in the long run he will probably be satisfied on this occasion too to make only a verbal statement after the signing of the pact.

BILCIURESCU

DOCUMENT NO. 39
(Reg. No. 3184 of 19 January 1932)

Decoded telegram, CESIANU *to* MINISTRY OF FOREIGN AFFAIRS

Paris No. 983, 18 January 1932
STRICTLY CONFIDENTIAL. ANSWER TO NO. 2479

(*Will answer that he can communicate our proposal and Soviet counterproposal[.] Political director tells us that he has given requested authorization by courier[.] Useless to telegraph more.* Manuscript note on what follows.)

This morning I saw Berthelot, who told me: "In such conditions surely and incontestably you cannot conclude the pact. The attitude of the Soviets surprises me, since before you began the discussions they said and repeated that they had peaceful and benevolent intentions toward Romania and desired the conclusion of the pact. I would like to see the last Romanian text and the counterproposal of the Soviets."

To my question concerning what the Poles would do, he told me: "Our ambassador in Moscow says that the Polish ambassador, Patek, told him that the Poles would be inclined to accept the Soviet request to initial before Litvinov's departure for Geneva. This, Berthelot added, did not correspond either to other news that he has, or to the opinion of Marshal Pilsudski, who—perhaps by way of a joke—expressed himself very strongly about your handling of the Soviets." To a question of mine, he answered: ["]France is not inclined to sign. She will keep an eye on the interests of her allies and agreed to discuss the pact of nonaggression because she believed that it would make the discussion of a real Franco-Soviet commercial policy easier."

Please quickly respond if I can give the Quai d'Orsay the copy of the Romanian proposal and the Soviet counterproposal. At lunch at the Legation I spoke with Prime Minister Laval, to whom I briefly exposed the difficulties encountered in the Romanian-Soviet conversations. He answered: "What purpose do such conversations serve? They are not very important given that it is the Soviets."

Speaking with Berthelot and referring to the massive Soviet [military] preparations, [a] question that was also the object of yesterday's discussions of the joint commission [session] of the army and of the foreign [affairs] commissions of the Senate, he replied, "I believe it is exaggerated and really quite inconsistent with other information that is less alarming. As a matter of fact, I believe the Soviets do not have, nor can they have, aggressive intentions because it is feared that the general in command would overthrow the present government or would be placed in a position to do so. Currently, the danger is greater for them than for others."

Berthelot leaves on January 23 for Geneva. Referring to Lausanne, he had the impression [that] it will miscarry.

CESIANU

DOCUMENT NO. 40
(Reg. No. 4494)

Report (copy), STURDZA *to* GHIKA

Riga No. 66, 21 January 1932

Dear Mr. Minister,

In the January 18[58] session of my negotiations with Mr. Stomonyakov I had the very strong impression that from then on the Soviets, sure of the inevitable rupture, would hasten to bring up the question of our intransigence concerning the acts of aggression (paragraph 2 of article I of our protocol) in order to avoid a return to the original [source of] conflict: the Soviet pretension[59] that their reservation on the territorial question be recorded in the preamble or in the rest of the pact.

In order to avoid this maneuver I decided to take the responsibility for the following proposal, recorded in the procès-verbal of that day: (1)

we consent to change the text of paragraph 2 of article I thus: "Considered as acts contrary to the obligations stipulated in the preceding paragraph will be any act of violence impairing the inviolability of the territory defined by the Dniester and the other land, sea, and air frontiers of the two states, even if these acts. . . ." etc.; (2) this on the express condition that neither [a] reduction of the general value of the pact be produced nor a subject foreign to the primary purpose of this pact be introduced in any part of its entire and definitive editing.

The situation resulting from this proposal was the same as at the beginning of the negotiations—Moscow reneging on its obligation made to our allies to leave the question of Bessarabia out—but these allies' desire to take full account of the possible Soviet bluff was satisfied. In truth, we agreed to ignore the essential difficulty presented by the preamble of the Soviet draft and to seek to agree on all the other points, so that a commonly agreed text was even drawn up between Mr. Stomonyakov and me for all the articles of the pact except the one relative to the procedure of conciliation, which the Soviets refused to arrange between us, and except paragraph 2 of article I.

Yesterday Mr. Stomonyakov gave me Mr. Litvinov's answer to the accommodating proposal that we made. This answer was the following ("taken in dictation from the Soviet delegate"):

1. The Soviet government cannot conclude a pact of nonaggression with Romania without formally recording its reservations on the question of Bessarabia;
2. Neither can the Soviet government agree to our last definition of the acts contrary to the pact of nonaggression because it cannot recognize our present borders.

In exchange, it proposes the following formula: "Considered acts contrary to the obligations stipulated in the preceding paragraph will be any attempt of a contracting party to resolve through violence the territorial or other existing litigations between it and the other party."[60]

Mr. Stomonyakov requested that we record the response of Mr. Litvinov in a procès-verbal of the session. I note in passing that the negotiations of Riga were only a prolonged attempt on the part of the Soviets to obtain the signature of the Romanian delegate on any piece of paper where the Bessarabian litigation was mentioned.

Not being able to write the procès-verbal that he desired, Mr. Stomonyakov today sent me the enclosed letter.[61]

Naturally, my first idea was to return it to him. However, I did not do so because my Polish colleague, after being informed by me and following telephone conversations with Warsaw, asked me to leave the door open between Stomonyakov and me until after the former's departure, observing that the return of the letter would make it very difficult for the Soviet delegate to return to the interrupted conversations. I believed it necessary to satisfy the request of the minister of Poland (1) because Mr. Stomonyakov himself stated that we did not take note of the response of his government, (2) because I maintain the option of returning the letter in question even after an interval of some time, explaining "that after searching we were not able to find a place for classification either in the Legation registry or in the archives of the Romanian Department of Foreign Affairs."

I add that before taking my leave of Mr. Stomonyakov I told him that I remained at his disposition in case he believed he could pledge at that time that a subject foreign to the pact would not be introduced one way or another into our negotiations.

I have the honor to ask Your Excellency to be so kind as to accept the assurances of my highest considerations and of my devotion.

MIHAI R. STURDZA

DOCUMENT NO. 41

Letter, STOMONYAKOV *to* STURDZA

Riga No. 4, 20 January 1932

Mr. Delegate,

In a session of this day I informed you that my government cannot accept your proposal of the eighteenth of this month, [just] as it was not able to accept the first version you proposed for the second paragraph of article I of the pact of nonaggression, for the reason that it cannot sign any formula containing explicitly or implicitly its recognition of the illegal occupation of Bessarabia.[62] At the same time, today I again confirmed to you that the government of the Union of Soviet Socialist Republics is ready to give [a] formal pledge not to resort to armed force to settle this territorial litigation as well as any other litigation between the two states, and, consequently, I proposed to you to give the following wording to the second paragraph of article I:

Considered as acts contrary to the obligations stipulated in the preceding paragraph will be any attempt(s) by one Contracting Party to resolve by violence the territorial or other litigations between her and the other Contracting Party.

Whereas you have refused the introduction of my above-mentioned declaration in the protocol of the session, I am constrained, in order to avoid any possible misunderstanding and given the importance of the question, to resort to this method to record the declaration that I made to you today by authority of my government.

At the same time, I state that you believed it necessary to refuse the proposal of the government of the Union and to declare that, until the acceptance of a firm pledge not to have the question of Bessarabia intervene in this pact in any manner, you no longer found that it was useful to continue the negotiations [that had] begun, and that you would be ready to resume them when this condition is accepted.

I take this occasion to present to you, Mr. Delegate, the assurance of my high consideration.

B. STOMONYAKOV

Developments from February to June 1932

DOCUMENT NO. 42

Letter (copy), BILCIURESCU *to* GHIKA

Warsaw No. 1478, 26 April 1932

THE LITTLE INTRIGUE OF MR. STOMONYAKOV—<u>CONFIDENTIAL</u>

Mr. Minister,

Referring to the ministerial note No. 6119 of last February 3,[63] I have the honor to report to Your Excellency that today I talked for a long time with Mr. Patek, the Polish minister in Moscow, for the moment in Warsaw, and I took the occasion to seek information about the question of the alleged "incident" between him and Litvinov and the alleged "establishment of responsibility" that Mr. Stomonyakov mentioned to Mr. Sturdza in their interview of January 20 in Riga.

Mr. Patek told me that in his discussion with Litvinov in November 1931, regarding the negotiation of a pact of nonaggression with Romania concomitant with the other bordering states, when the latter raised the question of Bessarabia, he said one day that such a pact with Romania could only be concluded if the question of Bessarabia were left "aside."[64]

Later Litvinov, again meeting with Mr. Patek, read him his notes that he had made (it seems that the people's commissar makes such notes after each conversation of more than average importance), in which he had written that the question of Bessarabia must be left "open."

Mr. Patek interrupted him, observing that he had not used this word, but had said "left aside." At this Litvinov, without any sort of retort, took out [a] pencil and corrected the notes, writing "left aside" in place of "left open."[65] (He used the French words, as in the note of Your Excellency's department, but Litvinov's notes were written entirely in Russian, a language that Patek knows at least as well as Litvinov.) It was not a question of protocol or any such thing.

It doesn't mean a thing that Mr. Litvinov defended himself by saying that, since these were Mr. Patek's words, he was not obliged [by them].

But, as the Polish minister to Moscow told me, Mr. Litvinov's notes, corrected or uncorrected, have no significance because much later, that is the day after the initialing of the pact with Poland, on January 26, Litvinov freely, compelled by no one, and addressing himself to Russian journalists, gave an interview to TASS in which he twice used the formula that in the negotiations with Romania the question of Bessarabia is left "aside."[66] Mr. Patek let me see his dossier to show me the very text published by *Izvestiia,* as well as the article [that] appeared in the same newspaper on January 28, where the same thing is repeated.

As a result, Mr. Patek concluded, we should not take Stomonyakov's insinuations seriously, especially when, two months later, Litvinov himself confirmed in an interview, featured in the official newspaper of Moscow, that it was still an accepted principle to "leave aside" the question of Bessarabia in the Romanian-Soviet negotiations. The recognition in this way of the Soviets' promise [not to raise the Bessarabian issue] excludes any "establishment of responsibility" [for the breakdown of the Riga negotiations], as Stomonyakov claimed with the aid of alleged letters from Litvinov during the discussion[s].

GR. BILCIURESCU

DOCUMENT NO. 43

Intradepartmental memo by ARION

Bucharest, 21 January 1932

On January 21 the minister of Poland telephoned me that the negotiations about a Polish-Soviet pact of nonaggression had been concluded and that Mr. Zaleski had given instructions that the pact not be signed until we too had completed our negotiations with the Soviets with the aim of concluding an analogous pact.

Asking me what news we had from Riga, I answered by telephone that both we and the Soviets are firmly maintaining our positions and that the last news received from Sturdza did not evidence any convergence of our points of view.

Count Szembek told me that he will come to see me tomorrow. I immediately informed Mr. Filality about the above.

M. ARION

DOCUMENT NO. 44

Intradepartmental memo by ARION

Bucharest, 22 January 1932

On January 22 the minister of Poland came to see me in order to make the following two communications:

1. The Polish government proposes that the question concerning the litigation relative to Bessarabia be regulated in a manner consistent with the declarations that Mr. Ghika just made in Prague, that is, by direct conversations that he would have with Mr. Litvinov in Geneva.[67]
2. Mr. Zaleski understands that the Soviet formula article I, paragraph 2, is unacceptable to Romania. Still, a way out could be found if the Romanian government authorized Mr. Sturdza to respond to Mr. Stomonyakov's letter along the lines that, for the Romanian government, there do not exist litigious territorial questions with the Soviets and that, in undertaking the negotiations, his only goal was to establish that neither of the contracting parties considers resorting to an act of aggression against the other. In the negotiations on the pact, this would tend to suppress paragraph 2 of article I.

I replied to Mr. Szembek:

1. That we had no knowledge that Mr. Sturdza had received any letter or note from Mr. Stomonyakov.
2. That it seemed even more strange that Mr. Stomonyakov would address any note to Mr. Sturdza as the latter informed him during the negotiations that "if I had not known that a note can be rejected, Mr. Litvinov would have taught us that this can be done" (allusion to the rejection of our note of protest addressed to the Soviets via France on the occasion of aggression carried out by the Red Army in Manchuria contrary to the Kellogg Pact);
3. That in any case we will not allow, either in the text of the pact or in any other annexed act (exchange of letters, notes, procès-

verbals [*sic*], etc.), any mention that there exists any territorial
litigation between us and the Soviets;

4. That according to the latest news received on January 21 from
   Riga, contrary to the promise of the Soviets not to invoke the
   question of Bessarabia on the occasion of negotiation of the pact
   of nonaggression, Mr. Stomonyakov persists, by order of Mr.
   Litvinov, in the pretension of formally recording the Soviet
   reservations about Bessarabia, moreover making mention of "the
   existing territorial litigations" even in the formula proposed for
   the editing of article I, paragraph 2.

5. According to the same news from Riga, Mr. Sturdza refused to
   formally take note in the procès-verbal of these Soviet proposals—declaring himself ready, however, to resume negotiations whenever Mr. Stomonyakov should be in a position to give
   him the assurance that the question of Bessarabia would no
   longer be introduced in the negotiations by any means.

   Consequently, I observed that the negotiations have been
   stalemated. They could be considered suspended until the
   Soviets give us the above assurances.

6. Finally, despite Mr. Szembek's explanations that the suppression of article I, paragraph 2, of which Mr. Zaleski's telegram
   spoke, did not refer to our draft, but to the last Soviet formula,
   I felt obliged to make it clear to him that article I, paragraph 2
   of our draft is not suppressible; it is similar to the corresponding
   paragraph in the Polish draft, with the single difference that it
   contains the formula of sovereignty that is imposed both because of our different situation, and in order to define with pre-
   cision the line of demarcation where aggression cannot be committed and without which demarcation the pact of nonaggression would be meaningless.

                                *   *   *   *

   Mr. Szembek told me he would telegraph to Warsaw the clarifications
that I made and that he hoped the negotiations would be resumed in
Geneva between Messrs. Ghika and Litvinov personally, according to the
declarations made to the press by Mr. Ghika in Prague.

   He added that he noted a difference between the information gar-
nered from Mr. Patek in Moscow about Litvinov's intentions concerning

the conclusion of our pact and the intransigent attitude adopted in the name of the same Litvinov by his delegate in Riga.

M. ARION

DOCUMENT NO. 45

Intradepartmental memo by ARION

Bucharest, [?] January 1932

Coming to see me on January 26, the minister of Poland told me that, judging from a telegram sent two days ago from Mr. Patek in Moscow, the intransigence of Mr. Stomonyakov is not shared by Mr. Litvinov, who continues to believe that we will reach an agreement about the text of the pact of nonaggression, the conclusion of which it seems he really desires.

Consequently, Count Szembek insisted "that we do not close the door" in Riga, and that we continue to negotiate, seeking a new formula, perhaps in the geographic domain, although his opinion [is that] the last Soviet formula could constitute a new basis for negotiation because although this formula mentions territorial litigation, it nevertheless does not specify that it is a question of those [*sic*] existing, thus of Bessarabia.

I answered that for us the last Soviet formula is unacceptable because, contrary to their promise . . . not to open the question of Bessarabia, through this formula the Soviets only intend to mention . . . in the text of the treaty the same territorial litigation that we would not allow to be mentioned either in the preamble—which we are determined not to accept under any form—or in an act.

Coming to the Franco-Soviet negotiations, Count Szembek told me that the minister of France does not believe that the changes recently experienced at the Quai d'Orsay modify the course of the negotiations with Russia.[68] In any case, added Count Szembek, Poland will conclude the pact of nonaggression with the USSR even if France now would refuse to conclude a similar pact. On this occasion he renewed 'the assurance that, according to the instructions of Mr. Zaleski, the Polish-Soviet pact will not be signed until we reach an agreement with Moscow. However, he asked me to continue to negotiate, and told me he also intended to see Mr. Iorga to inform him of the desire of his government.[69]

M.A.

DOCUMENT NO. 46

Intradepartmental memo by ARION

Bucharest, [?] January 1932

On January 28 I received a visit from Mr. Puaux who, after I had informed him about the stage reached in our negotiations with the Soviets, pointed out to me the difference between the text telegraphed to us by Mr. Sturdza and the one apparently made known to him by the Quai d'Orsay regarding the last Soviet formulation of article I, paragraph 2.

Inspecting the texts we noted that in fact the formula telegraphed to us by Mr. Sturdza as the proposal of Mr. Stomonyakov on the occasion of their last interview sounds like this:

Acts considered contrary to the obligations stipulated in the preceding paragraph will be every attempt by one Contracting Party to resolve by violence the territorial or other litigations existing *between her and the other Contracting Party.*

And in the letter Mr. Stomonyakov sent after the interview but also on January 20 to Mr. Sturdza, the word "existing" is no longer present in the Soviet wording of the formula. Thus, this last attenuated wording is the one communicated to France by the Soviets themselves.

However, I pointed out to Mr. Puaux that even thus attenuated— through elimination of the word that, [in] characterizing territorial litigation, really mentions the Bessarabia litigation—the Soviet formula continues to be unacceptable because it does not specify the indispensable demarcation [line] where aggression cannot be committed. The only means, in our opinion, for the pact to be operable would be the definition, still to be discussed, of the notion of aggression and of aggressor.

I also told him on this occasion that if our so-called initial formula of sovereignty and our use, in the interests of clarity, of that indispensable demarcation did not please the Soviets, [then] we had no objection to an eventual replacement of that abstract formula with a concrete notion of a geographic line—[a] line that, moreover, we had already designated with the Soviets in 1923 for the settling of conflicts on the Dniester without that designation having been considered then by the delegates of the USSR as either provocatory or inadmissible.

Before we parted, the minister of France especially dwelled upon the inexplicable attitude adopted by the Romanian press on the question of

our negotiations in Riga generally and that of the initialing of the
Polish-Soviet pact in particular. Concerning these last questions, he told
me that, thanks to the manner in which the Romanian newspapers have
interpreted it, a real panic has been launched in all Bucharest circles and
probably throughout the country in the face of "an alleged abandoning
of Romania by Poland"!? According to information received by Mr.
Puaux from Paris, nothing indicates that Poland will sign before the
Romanian-Soviet negotiations are concluded. Consequently, he does not
see our interest, independent even of the assurances given to us by
Poland in this regard, in the Romanian press alleging that until now
"we have been defeated?"

Reasoning along the same lines, I believe it useful to add that today
the minister of England, who is ill, also sent me Mr. Greiffenhagen, the
secretary of the Legation, to interest himself in the repercussions on us
of the fact that Poland initialed the pact with the Soviets during the
present phase of our negotiations in Riga.

M. ARION

DOCUMENT NO. 47

Intradepartmenal memo by ARION

Bucharest, [?] January 1932

Count Szembek told me Friday evening January 29, 1932, that, according to instructions received from Warsaw, he shortly before made
the following communication to Prime Minister Iorga:

*The Polish government refused, despite Litvinov's insistence, to sign the pact of
nonaggression with the USSR, given the difficulties [that have] intervened in
the Romanian-Soviet negotiations and it does not intend to do so if Romania were
not to arrive at an agreement.*

Count Szembek added that this communication, which he was authorized by his government to make to the Romanian government, naturally was not intended to be broadcast to one and all.

M. ARION

DOCUMENT NO. 48
(Reg. No. 5569 of 31 January 1932)

Decoded telegram, GHIKA *and* CESIANU *to* MINISTRY OF FOREIGN AFFAIRS

Paris No. 1014, 31 January 1932

Berthelot again told me that, regarding the pact with the Soviets, the attitude of the Romanian government could not be different in face of the path taken by the Soviet government—a path that contradicts its previous affirmations. He repeated that neither France nor Poland and the other interested states would sign anything without us.

The impression at the Quai d'Orsay is that the Soviets, who have swallowed all the blows and provocations of the Japanese without any reaction, are disoriented for the moment, and that in Geneva Litvinov will try to pick up the thread of the conversations with Romania.

Communicated to H. M. the King   Signed GHIKA
                                                   CESIANU

DOCUMENT NO. 49

Aide-mémoire by ARION

Bucharest, [?] February 1932

FOR MEMORY

By a private letter received from Geneva on February 10, I am informed that Mr. Titulescu is of the opinion that it would have been necessary to refuse all discussion with the Soviets, or at least to delay it in order to outline it quietly in Geneva.

He takes his stand, in effect, on the following point of view:

When one is in the situation of "beati possidentes" one must avoid anything that can be considered as disturbing possession. For uncontested possession finishes at the end of a certain lapse of time as being equivalent to a juridical title. Instead of that, eight years ago we were in a large capital [Vienna] loudly proclaiming that which we [already] knew. Three years ago we were in another great capital [Moscow] to hear the same short sentence ["Bessarabia belongs to the USSR"], and now we have given rise to the same result.[70]

And to implicitly or explicitly admit that there is a litigation equals being led to accept a judge someday.

M. A.

DOCUMENT NO. 50
(Reg. No. 9996 of 23 February 1932)

Decoded telegram, GHIKA *to* MINISTRY OF FOREIGN AFFAIRS

Geneva No. 143, 22 February 1932

ANSWER TO NO. 9369

Zaleski has left for Zurich for a Polish commemoration, but I believe it would be a tactical mistake to reiterate a position he spontaneously reached with such clear considerations and conclusions which correspond to our present position and with our interest[s]. I believe that [in response] to the insistence of the minister of Poland it would be well to answer in a decided manner both to him and through Bilciurescu in Warsaw in this way:

> The Romanian government long ago realized that the intention of the Soviets was not only to come to Geneva with a pacifist mask supported by the pacts of nonaggression, in order to support there the German thesis of complete disarmament, but also to attempt to split Romania from Poland and to break the solid front presented by Russia's neighbors. This tactic was mistaken because their solidarity was maintained and strengthened by the fact that even the states [that] signed the pacts would not place them into force on account of the Soviets' attitude vis-à-vis Romania, [namely,] bringing up from the start a question that should not have been either discussed or mentioned. For Romania the episode is closed and the question could not be reopened except by a new [and] acceptable attitude on the part of the Soviets."

It is certain that at the head of the Polish Ministry of Foreign Affairs there are two men and, as a result, a possible duality of policy, but I established when I was in Warsaw that Marshal Pilsudski considers the question of the pact of nonaggression as without meaning; at the same time, in Paris, Berthelot appears more interested than Laval and the fact that today Tardieu is minister of foreign affairs permits us to affirm on the basis of the declarations that he made to me here that France meanwhile does not look upon the pact of nonaggression favorably.

GHIKA

DOCUMENT NO. 51
(Reg. No. 11915 of 3 March 1932)

Decoded telegram, TITULESCU *to* MINISTRY OF FOREIGN AFFAIRS

Geneva No. 104, 2 March 1932
STRICTLY CONFIDENTIAL—FOR HIS MAJESTY, THE KING

I saw Zaleski today, who told me about a recent conversation with Litvinov.[71] The latter asked him when Poland would sign the pact of nonaggression. Zaleski answered that she will do so when Romania and Estonia are also ready to sign. Litvinov replied, "This means that Poland's hands are tied." Zaleski answered: "You can present things as you wish, that is, [as] Poland 'cannot' sign. I am telling you she does not want to sign without her allies." Litvinov replied, "Must I interpret your declaration as a refusal to sign and publish a communication to this effect in Moscow?" Zaleski answered, "You are free to do as you wish, but such a presentation being inaccurate I would also publish a communication placing things in focus." Litvinov then replied that he had never accepted the interdependence of the signings Poland spoke about. Zaleski replied that he did not ask Litvinov to accept the Polish point of view because he had no need for it—but, that this was the Polish point of view.

Then Litvinov said that he could not sign the pact with Romania because she asked for the recognition of Bessarabia. Zaleski replied that his information was exactly the opposite: that is, that the Soviets ask that Romania recognize the question of Bessarabia as open. It is a question of intervening both in Moscow and in Bucharest so that an acceptable formula might be found.

I answered Zaleski that in today's situation it was no longer a question of formula but of fundamentals. I showed him that if Bessarabia were not talked about at all, perhaps a formula could be found. But today, when Romania is in possession of the letter of the Soviet delegate to Sturdza by which the illegality of our possession of Bessarabia is affirmed, any formula one might find leaves the question of Bessarabia open. Thus Romania is in a worse situation today than yesterday.

Zaleski said I was right, but that perhaps the Soviets would withdraw the letter so that work might be resumed all over again.

Then Zaleski asked me if I knew officially that Marshal Pilsudski had arrived in Romania.[72] Very embarrassed, I answered that I knew from the newspapers that he was coming but officially I did not know since Romanian diplomats were not informed as Polish ones [were] of everything that was going on at home. Zaleski told me that, according to his information, Marshal Pilsudski arrived yesterday in Romania and he would immediately telegraph him [about] the question of the letter so that in the conversation he was to have with His Majesty the King he would be informed and could, if need be, make suggestions.

I then asked Zaleski what was the reasoning behind Poland's desire for the signing of a pact in the efficacy of which she did not believe. Zaleski answered that, quite apart from the political argument that can be made vis-à-vis Germany, this pact is desired by Latvia because it is imposed [on her] by the Soviets as a condition for more active commercial relations. And Poland cannot split away from the Baltic States.

I answered: "But don't you believe that such a pact would hinder our defense in the question of disarmament? Because, it will be said that vis-à-vis the Soviets we have assured security." Zaleski answered that he did not believe so, since everybody knew that the Soviets lie.

In continuation I concluded, "It would be so if disarmament were only the work of the chancelleries. It is, however, the work of public opinion, and publicly you cannot say that the Soviets lie, and that, therefore, their promises do not constitute security. Then, Romania is not in Poland's situation, having neither [a] recognized border nor a large military budget. So we must not forget that under such conditions it is much more difficult for us, at the time of the Disarmament Conference, to pass over the argument of geographical situation in exchange for deceptive appearances."

TITULESCU[73]

DOCUMENT NO. 52
(Reg. No. 13401 of 10 March 1932)

Decoded telegram, TITULESCU *to* MINISTRY OF FOREIGN AFFAIRS

Geneva No. 107, 9 March 1932
STRICTLY CONFIDENTIAL—WITH THE REQUEST THAT IT BE
SENT TO H.M. THE KING

. . . . [74]

Massigli told me that the Soviet ambassador in Paris asked the Quai d'Orsay to intervene with France's allies to hasten the signings of the pacts of nonaggression and asked me what our position was. I answered that Romania began these negotiations on the basis of the assurance that the question of Bessarabia would be left out. But the Soviets found a way to send us a written protest against the illegality of Romania's possession of Bessarabia. Therefore, as long as the Soviets do not annul their written protest by another letter, any pact of nonaggression makes Romania's situation worse than it is today because it will always be interpreted in the light of the Soviet protest. Today we have a delicate situation because our eastern frontier is contested. But if pacts have [any] value, the Kellogg Pact impedes the Soviets from making war over Bessarabia. If we signed a pact of nonaggression without the retraction of the recent Soviet protest, we [would] have a still worse situation than today because not only [would] we have the contested frontier of the East, but also we [would] have agreed that this border is contested. This would mean that we [would] open the door to peaceful procedures like arbitration, plebiscite, etc., to regulate litigation that we alone [would] have recognized as existing. This is inadmissible.

Massigli told me that I was right and that he will communicate these points of view to the Quai d'Orsay.

TITULESCU

DOCUMENT NO. 53
(Reg. No. 16671 of 27 March 1932)

Decoded telegram, CESIANU *to* MINISTRY OF FOREIGN AFFAIRS

Paris No. 1102, 27 March 1932
STRICTLY CONFIDENTIAL

In Geneva Tardieu had conversations with Litvinov that among other things, touched upon the question of the Romanian-Soviet pact of non-aggression. Litvinov declared that the Soviets do not intend to resolve the question of Bessarabia by force, but ask that it be reserved; Tardieu answered that a formula must be found that removes any cause of armed conflict with Romania from an eventual pact of nonaggression, and to this end it is better that the Soviets no longer make any reservation.

Tardieu asked me if Romania really intended to conclude that pact of nonaggression. I answered that in any case Romania would only work in agreement with France. In my turn I asked if France really intended to sign the Franco-Soviet nonaggression pact. Tardieu answered, "It would have been preferable if France had never begun discussions for a

Franco-Soviet pact, but once begun and the question being irritating, a method will have to be found to escape the present impasse."

CESIANU

DOCUMENT NO. 54

Telegram (copy), GHIKA *to* PARIS LEGATION

Bucharest No. 19283, 7 April 1932

Returning from Warsaw, the minister of Poland resumed his usual proddings concerning the pact of nonaggression with Russia, claiming that when Marshal Pilsudski passes through Bucharest soon he, too, will be steadfastly insistent. In order to convince me of the necessity of a resumption of negotiations he alleges that Estonia is on the eve of signing, having actually agreed with the Soviets today. Since in Geneva the Estonian delegate appeared very desirous that Romania do nothing with the Soviets and very pleased that the negotiations between Estonia and Russia had reached a dead end, please make contact with your Estonian colleague in order to find out the stage of the question. I needn't tell you that Romania does not at all desire a resumption of the negotiations and that at least as long as France omits the question, that is until June according to Mr. Puaux,[75] we do not wish to reopen this distasteful affair.

GHIKA

DOCUMENT NO. 55

Memo by GHIKA

Bucharest, n.d.

RECORD OF THE MEETING THAT TOOK PLACE BETWEEN
MARSHAL PILSUDSKI, MESSRS IORGA, GHIKA, AND COUNT SZEMBEK
AT THE PRIME MINISTER'S OFFICE ON APRIL 14, 1932, 12:20 P.M.

After the usual banalities, the marshal opened the announced question of the pact of nonaggression. In a violent tone and using strange expressions, as for example that of "hysterical policy," he began with a very violent attack against France, "whose leaders, from reciprocal hatred, change the political line from one day to the next, Tardieu throwing into the garbage pail what Briand did, for example the pact of nonaggression; and God knows that not Poland but France was the one who pushed in this direction and forced Warsaw to put into motion this Polish-Soviet train. So, what does the way in which France today abandons everything mean?" (It appears that Marshal Pilsudski made this foray against France in order to clear Poland of any suspicion that she would play the Soviet game for any price.)[76] In continuation, the marshal declared that Poland followed a policy ordained by her alliance concerning Romania and by her sphere of influence (Pilsudski let the word "protectorate" escape regarding the Baltic States). And, the Baltic States would sign. The Russians, who have very powerful means of economic pressure over Finland [and] Latvia as well as over Estonia, compelled all of them to take this step. So when Tallinn signs, then Poland will sign in her turn, without further solidarism with Romania if she remains in her present negative position.

I took note [of this]. Mr. Iorga allowing me to speak first, I asked the marshal some questions, which left him rather puzzled, about the manner in which it [i.e., Poland's determination to sign the Polish-Soviet pact] concerned the alliance and also its effects on Polish policy vis-à-vis the Baltic States. I observed that after Riga we had nothing more to do. If there existed any desire to resume the negotiations, the Soviets are the ones who must manifest it, on the basis of an initiative from Warsaw or Paris and under the express conditions that the question of Bessarabia is no longer brought up for discussion and that Moscow annul in the most explicit manner all that was said (privately, as far as we are concerned) at Riga and, in particular, annul the written document about the existence of the litigation.

I added that the Soviet game is, among other things, to make use of the Kellogg Pact to raise the question of Bessarabia and to oblige us on the basis of article II [to agree to] an arbitration or a plebiscite.

Mr. Iorga stressed the point that we had nothing more to change.

In staccato sentences, the marshal repeated: "I am not French! If I make policy with twenty people who change tomorrow what they did yesterday, you'd like that a lot, wouldn't you!" Annoyed, I concluded by telling him: "Everybody knows, Mr. Marshal, that you are Polish. Your imprisonments both in Germany and in Russia are eloquent in this regard. Please believe that even here, with all the very old appreciation and sympathy for France, which we are not the only ones to feel so deeply, we know how to remain Romanians when the interests of the country demand it."

Marshal Pilsudski repeated in every possible way the point of view he had already expressed, insisting on the value of the Kellogg Pact, followed by the Litvinov Protocol, and of a simultaneous ratification (we made it clear to the marshal that in Romania, such ratifications were the prerogative of the King and were not by vote of Parliament).

On the occasion of a conversation between Messrs. Iorga and Argetoianu with His Majesty the King, which followed this meeting at the Prime Ministry, the same subject was taken up again.[77] We arrived at the conclusion that in the year in which the Disarmament Conference was held, despite the Dniester massacres and despite the repulsion of our public opinion and of the Romanian government, we could not refuse a pact with the Soviets.[78] However, it was decided that it devolved upon the interested parties to again take up the thread of the negotiations with us, and to give us guarantees concerning the removal of the question of Bessarabia.

GHIKA

DOCUMENT NO. 56
(Reg. No. 21798 of 19 April 1932)

Decoded telegram, CESIANU *to* MINISTRY OF FOREIGN AFFAIRS

Paris No. 1448, 18 April 1932
STRICTLY CONFIDENTIAL—ANSWER TO NO. 20807

I had a meeting at the Quai d'Orsay, which had received nearly similar news from Puaux referring to the marshal. The Quai d'Orsay recognizes the delicate situation of Romania, but it believes that a Romanian-Soviet pact of nonaggression, although it would no more mean a full guarantee for Romania than for anyone else, would have, however, some moral value. Thus it believes that concluding such a pact would be somewhat advantageous for Romania, not disadvantageous. Thus negotiations must be begun to escape . . . [the] present impasse.

I asked: "But in order to do this after France and Poland have talked with the Romanian government, who will do what is necessary to resume the conversations, since neither Romania nor—probably—the Soviets will take the first step? Would it be either France or Poland? Does the Quai d'Orsay believe that the Soviets will give up all further talk of Bessarabia when the talks resume?" To both questions no answer was given to me [the Quai d'Orsay having] to discuss [them] with the Prime Minister. I asked, "Does the Quai d'Orsay believe either that Poland would sign without Romania or, admitting that Poland is determined to do it, does she believe they will do so without informing France and, if France is informed, what would France say?" And following on that, "But if Poland with or without the knowledge of France would sign, what would France do? Would she sign too?" The Quai d'Orsay reserved its response. It will prepare a note for Tardieu and will give him the entire dossier on the question of the pacts of nonaggression. Tardieu arrives tomorrow afternoon and on Wednesday, will probably be obliged to be in Geneva where all the prime ministers and foreign ministers of the Great Powers are arriving to discuss disarmament. Tomorrow I will be in Lille to inaugurate the Romanian section of the northern region's commercial fair. Wednesday I will make contact with the Quai d'Orsay, then will have an audience with Tardieu.

CESIANU

DOCUMENT NO. 57

Telegram, TITULESCU *to* MINISTRY OF FOREIGN AFFAIRS

Geneva No. 137, 22 April 1932

STRICTLY CONFIDENTIAL—WITH THE REQUEST TO TRANSMIT
TO HIS MAJESTY THE KING

I.

With all the multiple duties imposed upon me [as] delegate to the Disarmament Conference, I am continually busy with the grave problem of Romania's relations with the Soviets.

I will begin by telling you my opinion of Marshal Pilsudski's declarations, which you kindly sent to me by your telegram No. 20807.[79]

If the marshal wanted to put pressure on Romania, I answer, one does not speak like that to allies.

If the marshal wanted to show his true intentions, I answer, one does not behave like this toward allies.

A threat and a fait accompli are equivalent in relations between two allies because the one, like the other, destroys the essential basis of an alliance: mutual trust.

Poland, by the voice of the marshal, told us categorically that between the Baltic bloc and Romania she opts for the former. And she did it without judging whether the negative attitude of Romania is justified or not.

For Marshal Pilsudski, Poland's signing of the pact with the Soviets does not depend on an element in our domain of action, but purely and simply on an external condition, completely independent of our will; the signing of Estonia.

And Poland proposes to carry out this action, which has neither logical basis nor justice, concerning the very question that is the object of our alliance: the defense of Bessarabia.

When it is a question of Bessarabia, if Poland refuses us her aid even in the easy form of a refusal to sign with the Soviets, it is difficult to believe that she will give us aid in the form of the great sacrifice of human lives, material, and money that even a defensive war implies.

The signing of Poland without Romania amounts to a denunciation of our treaty of alliance. What must Romania do? [She must] look upon these things calmly. And for nothing in the world [must she] ask Poland not to sign without us.

Romania must [first] show Poland that she sacrifices her own interests if she signs without us, and then say to her, Do what you want.

If Poland believes that she had [a] rationale so strong as to [make her] sign without us, she will do so whatever may be our requests. But if Poland will realize that [in] sacrificing Romania for the Baltic bloc [she] basically sacrifices herself and [that] we did not hinder in any way the liberty of action that she believes she had, then she will come back to Romania like the prodigal son.

Thus if we intervene with her and Poland does not sign, she will claim that she has made a sacrifice to defend our interests and will demand the price of the sacrifice.

Not only do we owe nothing to Poland for doing her duty because Poland did her duty, but also we avoid transforming Poland into Romania's savior just when she was at the point of abandoning her.

II.

This is the line I have been taking in my work here. And the results up to now prove that we are not mistaken.

Immediately upon receiving your telegram I spoke to Paul-Boncour (Tardieu was absent from Geneva).[80] I informed him of what had happened; I showed him that Marshal Pilsudski's action endangered the alliance; and I told him very clearly that Romania would not raise even her little finger to divert Poland from the road she had taken.

Very correctly, Boncour telephoned the Quai d'Orsay and the result of this intervention was very favorable.[81] Boncour probably also talked to Zaleski, since after my conversation with Boncour, Zaleski came to see me twice and today I had a third conversation with him at the League of Nations.

In the first conversation, Zaleski asked me to believe that he personally was not responsible at all for the marshal's declarations. I know Zaleski [is] a loyal man and I said I believe[d] him, but of what use [is he] if Colonel Beck has more influence over the marshal?

I frankly told Zaleski the consequences of signing without us, but I added that Romania would not at all hinder Poland from taking the road desired by the marshal.

In the second conversation Zaleski told me, asking that I keep it absolutely confidential, that he had written the marshal that if the Baltic States sign without Poland the thing is not serious, but if Poland signs without Romania then the Soviets will have succeeded in the stratagem they have been following for years, namely, to split Romania from Poland, and Poland will be the first to feel the consequences.

In the third conversation this morning at the League, Zaleski told me that he had spoken to Litvinov about the retraction of the letter to Sturdza and had the impression that this would be possible.[82] Zaleski believes that the impression he gained that the Soviets wish to reach an agreement with us is connected to the Soviets' fear of Japan. The information received by Zaleski is that Japan is urging the White Russians to massacre the Red Russians and this makes Litvinov desire to conclude nonaggression pacts in Europe more rapidly.

Zaleski added that he will go to Warsaw for four days with the sole aim of dissuading Marshal Pilsudski from being influenced by those who advise him to sign at one time with the Balts and without Romania.

I thanked Zaleski for the information he had given me and for his personal sentiments—repeating again however, that Poland alone knows where her own interests [lie].

I have just seen Tardieu. I spoke to him in the manner indicated and also pointed out the political consequences of Poland's signing without Romania, and why I consider that under today's circumstances the best method to save Poland from error is not to request anything ourselves; she [must see] the correct path alone. I then talked about the conditions under which we would resume discussions with the Soviets: among others, retraction of the letter to Sturdza, and avoidance of any mention of the existing litigation on Bessarabia.

Tardieu answered: "You are right—both in method and in reason. Romania must not show herself fearful of Poland's attitude or request anything of her. But it is our [i.e., France's] duty to explain to the Poles and to impede them from doing what is not permitted. So I am pleased to tell you that once I found out about Marshal Pilsudski's declarations, and before Cesianu made the démarche that he was instructed to make, I telegraphed Warsaw that we do not agree to Poland's signing with the Baltic States without Romania. Moreover, I told Litvinov not to think about the signing of the pact with France so long as he wished to extort a recognition of the existence of the Bessarabian litigation from Romania. I ask you, however, if Litvinov carries out the necessary conditions of which you speak, will you accept that we French work on a draft pact of nonaggression and that through our mediation you reach an agreement with the Soviets?"

I answered, "Yes, but on the condition that I take part in the editing committee, that is that you show it to me before and you agree with the Romanian government before sending it to the Soviets as French suggestions."

Tardieu answered, "That's how I understood things."

After I had seen Tardieu, as I was writing this telegram Massigli also came to see me on Berthelot's part to talk about the Russian question. I spoke to him in the same way as to the others. Massigli said that if his information were correct, *things were not received with the same calm in Bucharest, that the declarations of Marshal Pilsudski had produced emotion and that Romania in her turn would have asked* France to intervene for a resumption of the negotiations with the Soviets. I answered that I was pleased he was mistaken. On this issue Romania had nothing to ask of France as she had nothing to ask of Poland. Here, it is not a question of a threat of war, of a financial crisis, or other imminent dangers. Here, it is only a question of political relations dependent on the will of each. In such cases we inform France—and that's all. When Romania is struck to the heart by the Soviets' exorbitant pretension that we get smaller while they decide what territory to recognize, Romania should not call upon the assistance of her allies; [on the contrary,] they themselves should [hasten] with aid.

And I added: As a matter of fact, your information does not correspond with the telegram I received from Minister Ghika. You may tell Berthelot that I have the approval of my government when I declare:

1. Poland's attitude pains us but we will not resort to begging. Romania will shape her attitude toward Poland by her attitude toward us, established of her own free will.
2. We will only resume negotiations with Russia under the communicated conditions; it is up to Poland and France to obtain them; we will only enter [onto] the scene afterwards.
3. Once these conditions [are] met, we will be ready to resume negotiations with the Soviets. [At that stage] French assistance

in reaching an agreement will be not only useful but necessary. We will be disposed to negotiate in good faith and rapidly, but I must forewarn you that [a] definition of aggression and the clarification of the territory on which it will not take place are indispensable conditions for us.

If with such language we do not obtain what we need from France and Poland, who know too well that a Romania *thus abandoned* will immediately find herself mounting actions in other capitals, Berlin and even Moscow for example, *which we do not wish to see and which they have no interest in seeing,* then with other language we [would] obtain even less.

All that I have gained for Romania in my political career was [on] the front of struggle and of resistance, not of prayers and of pleadings. In the same spirit, I also intend to defend the country's interests in this question.

TITULESCU

DOCUMENT NO. 58
(Reg. No. 22753 of 26 April 1962)

Decoded telegram, CESIANU *to* MINISTRY OF FOREIGN AFFAIRS

Paris No. 1163, 25 April 1932
STRICTLY CONFIDENTIAL

I had a long conversation with the Quai d'Orsay, as a result of my telegram No. 1148.[83]

The Quai d'Orsay told me that Zaleski, on his own initiative (or may I say, at the suggestion of the Polish government), had talks in Geneva with Litvinov for the resumption of Soviet-Romanian talks.[84] The Quai d'Orsay believes that the desired modality for the resumption of Romanian-Soviet relations would be that those conversations be restarted from the top, that is, like *new talks, considering the ones that took place in Riga as null and void. This way of proceeding would have the advantage of avoiding the withdrawal of Stomonyakov's written request, to which withdrawal* it would not seem probable that the Soviets would consent if we asked for it, as it would mean that they themselves repudiated it.[85] The Quai d'Orsay also told me that if Romania asked France for its good offices for the preparation of the terrain in view of the resumption of talks with the Soviets, they would gladly do it, in this eventuality also making contact with Poland. The French government, says the Quai d'Orsay, would like to know, in advance of making any probe, what the exact intentions of the Romanian government are concerning the pact of nonaggression and the chances for resuming conversations with the Soviets. The opinion of the French government, says the Quai d'Orsay, is that it would be delicate if Romania alone, today when the road to negotiating pacts of nonaggression has been taken by all the neighboring states, does not do the same. However, France will not put any pressure on Romania to decide to do as the other countries. And, France believes that, although the pact of nonaggression only represents a very relative guarantee, the position of Romania would be nonetheless much more advantageous in arriving at a pact of nonaggression than in avoiding the pact. It is certain that if all the neighboring states sign and ratify such pacts, and Romania does not, it will give rise to criticism. And if the Poles sign and we do not it will be interpreted by the Soviets to mean that Polish-Romanian friendship is shaken. The Quai d'Orsay told me that according to the latest information they had from the chargé d'affaires in Warsaw, Poland will ratify if the Baltic countries ratify. However, the Quai d'Orsay assured me that although Poland is decided, even if Romania were to remain in the same situation as today, she will do nothing to hurry these matters concerning her and the Soviets. I told the Quai d'Orsay that in case our government were to make an appeal to the good offices of France to probe the terrain for an eventual resumption of conversations with the Soviets, it would have to be assured in the first place that the Soviets will no longer bring up in the discussion the question of Bessarabia or, under any form, the intangibility of the present frontiers with the Soviets, since it would mean a new impasse and a second failure—a failure due to the Soviets of course—and it would be much more displeasing than today's situation, for which we are not at fault. [They] answered that of course the Soviets must understand that the question of Bessarabia or anything relative to frontiers is particularly out of order, so that—eventually—new talks may have a chance to produce a nonaggression pact.

CESIANU

DOCUMENT NO. 59

Letter, GHIKA *to* CESIANU

Bucharest, 27 April 1932

Mr. Minister,

I have the honor to inform you, for your personal information, that in the question of the most recent declarations made in Bucharest by

Marshal Pilsudski concerning Poland's decision to sign and ratify [her] pact of nonaggression with the Soviets after the Baltic States arrive at agreement with the USSR [that] on this terrain, the Romanian government maintains the following policy.

Romania will not do anything vis-à-vis the Soviets and remains in the same attitude, which is dictated by obvious motives of dignity and political interest. If the Polish government considers that its policy vis-à-vis the Baltic States demands that the pact of nonaggression with the Soviets be signed and ratified without a similar concomitant [one] on the part of Romania, Romania can only take note and record this negative manner of understanding the value of the alliance between both nations, with all the consequences that will be produced both in Romanian public opinion and in other states. France will evaluate, in her turn, if such a situation does or does not injure her general situation and will or will not make démarches in Warsaw as she believes useful.

[It is] evident that Romania, especially during the year of the Disarmament Conference, could not refuse a new proposal to conclude a pact of nonaggression with the USSR if one came tomorrow. The Romanian government, however, will only accept a resumption of contact on the express condition that everything that transpired at Riga be nullified and considered as nonexistent and that Poland and France, the states interested in the conclusion of the Romanian-Soviet pact of nonaggression, promise that we will not again find ourselves confronted by a Russia that proclaims [as] existing and open the litigation concerning Bessarabia.

As a result of an active exchange of views by telephone with Mr. Titulescu in Geneva, he explained this situation both to Mr. Zaleski and to the French delegation.

I have the honor of transmitting to you herein enclosed, confidentially and only for your personal knowledge, Mr. Titulescu's telegram 137[86] as well as my last telegram No. 22964.[87]

Concerning these last telegrams, I believe it is necessary to explain to you that when I informed Mr. Puaux of Marshal Pilsudski's declarations I did not show "any great emotion" and that, on the contrary, I was very categoric in stating that Romania, although saddened with good reason, looked upon the consequences of this eventual course of her ally with cold blood and full knowledge of the future repercussions. [It is] likely that the minister of France, alarmed by such a situation, has desired to stimulate, by any means possible, the interest of the Quai d'Orsay in the prospect of an energetic intervention in Warsaw and, consequently, believed [it] necessary to relate that great emotion prevails here in this regard.

For a better balanced coordination, please keep in contact with Mr. Titulescu to find out in time the result of his conversation in Geneva with the Polish minister of foreign affairs and with Mr. Tardieu and the French delegation.

DOCUMENT NO. 60
(Reg. No. 24009 of 9 May 1932)

Decoded telegram, TITULESCU *to* FOREIGN MINISTRY

Geneva No. 141, 5 May 1932
STRICTLY CONFIDENTIAL—WITH THE REQUEST THAT IT BE
TRANSMITTED TO HIS MAJESTY, THE KING

Massigli has come in recently to talk to me about the Russian question. He said that he had received from Berthelot a draft pact of non-aggression between us and the Soviets in order to ask my opinion of it. Massigli told me he answered Berthelot that, given the conversations he had had with me, he could not present this draft pact of nonaggression as he was sure that it would not give me satisfaction. Massigli added he told Berthelot that even if he presented it to me, he would advise me not to accept it, and that he asked to write another draft that took account of the essential demand which I have made, to wit, precise definition of the territory over which aggression cannot take place. He suggested [to Berthelot] utilizing the formula "the territories over which Romania today exercises authority."

I thanked Massigli and told him that until I saw the text, I could not express any opinion. As a result, I could not make contact concerning this question with the Romanian government, which has the material power of decision.

I asked Massigli what was being done with the previous question. He answered that material withdrawal of the letter by the Russians would be possible, but that nullification in writing of the letter given to Sturdza, as we have asked, is difficult to obtain.

I replied [that] I clearly refused a pure and simple delivery of the letter. With their characteristic bad faith, the Soviets will say tomorrow that they did not receive it back and that we do not wish to produce it or that we destroyed it.

Massigli answered that I was right and that perhaps the formula to be sought would be that Romania and the Soviets write reciprocally that the negotiations of Riga, including the correspondence exchanged, are null and void. Since only the Soviets wrote us and we not them, the letter addressed to Sturdza would be nullified. I answered that at first sight I see inconveniences in this reciprocal formula, but until I see it in writing I reserve any opinion. I added, in so many words, the following: "Permit me to tell you sincerely that France made a great mistake when she undertook her action [to further] signing of nonaggression pacts with the Soviets on the part of all their neighbors. In truth, before undertaking this action, France alone should have determined the answer to the following question: Do the Soviets have an interest in signing the pact of nonaggression with France and Poland? If not, it is absurd that France and Poland consent to sign, playing the game of the Soviets who could say tomorrow, 'Now that you have signed pacts of nonaggression, your security is assured, so disarm!' If, however, the Soviets have a serious interest in signing pacts of nonaggression with France and Poland, then the duty of France is to profit by this interest, by this unique occasion, to obtain from the Soviets the definitive recognition of Bessarabia. By their diplomatic action of today, France and Poland protect their own interests in the future, avoiding the sacrifice of military assistance in case of aggression that is provided by the treaty of alliance. What opportunity will be presented again—an opportunity for Romania to deal with the Bessarabian question once and for all—like the present one, in which the Soviets need our allies France and Poland? Difficult to answer. Once the pacts of nonaggression are signed by France, Poland, Romania, and the Soviets, the latter would no longer have the [same] interest in recognizing Bessarabia. Romania was extremely generous, agreeing to enter into such negotiations only on condition that the question of Bessarabia remain open, that is, that her situation tomorrow not be worse than that of today.[88]

Once the question was placed on a lower level, so much lower that I ask why you negotiate, I, who today for the first time enter into this question, permit myself, given the situation, to frankly say to France: 'On this ground we do not intend to budge. And as a result, the demands that I formulated are necessary, 'sine qua non,' and their complete satisfaction will never erase my regret that France permitted this precious occasion for definite settlement of our conflict with the Soviets to be lost.' " Massigli answered that I was absolutely correct, that he had spoken to Berthelot to this effect, and that France wishes to help us along the lines expressed by me.

TITULESCU

DOCUMENT NO. 61
(Reg. No. 27753 of 27 May 1932)

Decoded telegram, TITULESCU *to* FOREIGN MINISTRY

Geneva No. 153, 26 May 1932

STRICTLY CONFIDENTIAL—WITH THE REQUEST TO BE TRANSMITTED
TO H. M. THE KING

The Polish delegation informs me that Zaleski saw Litvinov in Berlin on May 24[89] and that Zaleski communicated the following: "Litvinov would be inclined to consider as null and void all the correspondence of Riga if both parties would come to an agreement on a suitable basic text." Zaleski made his reservation concerning Romania's way of viewing it. Then, in his own name, Zaleski suggested to Litvinov that in article I the word "authority" be substituted for the word "sovereignty," and that in the preamble Patek's formula, communicated to Bucharest but about which no response had been received, be utilized.[90] Not knowing Patek's formula, I asked the Polish delegation of what it consisted. They told me that it was a question of declaration in which both parties left out litigious questions. The Polish delegation added that, in the conversation with Zaleski, Litvinov asked that the litigious questions be "left out."

My personal opinion is that Zaleski should make no suggestion in his own name. To talk about the litigations that exist between us and the Soviets means talking about Bessarabia, since everybody knows that this is the litigation between us. I consider the formula inadmissible and Zaleski's procedure as imprudent.

TITULESCU

The Polish-Soviet Pact, June to July 1932

DOCUMENT NO. 62

Intradepartmental memo by GAFENCU

Bucharest, 11 June 1932

Count Szembek informed me yesterday morning that he wished to see me. I went [to the Polish Legation] at 3:30 so it was I who made the initial visit. On this occasion, Count Szembek informed me that the Polish government planned to sign the pact of nonaggression with Russia in the second half of June, that is, between June 15 and 25.

Poland justified this decision in this way: her policy vis-à-vis Russia was always supported by two factors, collaboration with Romania and collaboration with the Baltic States.

Collaboration with Romania is assured by the Polish-Romanian treaty of alliance, whose substance was even strengthened by article III of the Polish-Russian pact of nonaggression [since it] recognizes that the treaties of alliance of the two contracting states remain in full vigor. Poland has no treaties of alliance with the Baltic States. So, she desires to express her solidarity with the Baltic States by a common action vis-à-vis Russia.

The Baltic States have completed the negotiations with Russia concerning their pacts of nonaggression and are determined to sign these pacts. The time of the signings of these pacts is the end of June, when the Baltic parliaments will meet to give a definitive legal form to the pacts with Russia.[91] At that time Poland wants to sign too.

Count Szembek insists that this signing does not at all slight Poland's obligations to Romania.

The visit that Marshal Pilsudski made to Chisinău two months ago clearly showed not only that Poland intends to give full value to the treaty of alliance that ties us, but also that she has every intention of

making common cause with our policy, which is based on our rights in Bessarabia.

I answered Count Szembek that the information that had been given me was so serious that I asked him to communicate it directly to the prime and foreign minister. As for me, especially in my capacity as his former collaborator in the negotiations that led to the conclusion of the Litvinov Protocol, I could not hide from him [my belief] that Poland's decision ends a policy of close Polish-Romanian collaboration in the eastern question, [a] policy that until today has produced the best results, and that it is an obvious weakening of the Polish-Romanian alliance. In this regard, political arguments and the impression produced in public opinion take precedence over legal arguments.

It is obvious that our entire public opinion will see Poland's decision as a weakening of the Polish-Romanian alliance.

Count Szembek then came to the Foreign Ministry, where he repeated before Prime Minister Vaida the declarations he had made to me both concerning Poland's decision to sign the pact of nonaggression toward the end of the month and concerning the Polish government's point of view that this démarche did not in the least weaken all the political, juridical, and military obligations that Poland has toward Romania.

Minister Vaida answered that he was very surprised at the Polish minister's démarche and that he was perplexed as to why Poland places a higher value on her solidarity with the Baltic States than on her full solidarity with Romania in a problem so delicate.

The prime minister asked Count Szembek to communicate only this state of perplexity to the Polish government and to state that while the Romanian government has every desire to successfully complete the negotiations for a Russo-Romanian pact of nonaggression, it cannot negotiate under the pressure of a deadline that can only make her situation vis-à-vis Russia worse.

At the same time, the prime minister drew the Polish minister's attention [to the fact] that the Polish government's decision to sign without Romania and before Romania has reached an agreement with Russia [on a] pact of nonaggression, was unusually inopportune today when Romania finds herself in the middle of an electoral campaign. It is a period of anxiety in which naturally all ideas and all currents abound. It is not good to weaken belief in allies and our alliances in precisely such a period. Only those hostile to our alliance and our common policy could profit from this

The prime minister continued [discussing] the inopportunity of the Polish decision given the fact that Mr. Titulescu, who has been exploring the possibility of reaching an understanding with Russia, has been

immobilized for a month by the political crisis in Bucharest and the new government has only been at the helm of state for twenty-four hours.

Such are the motives for which the prime minister is convinced that Poland will renounce the deadline about which the Polish Minister informed us.

Count Szembek said that he would communicate all this to the Polish government. [He will push the matter] in order to be able to give a good answer to the prime minister in the first days of next week.

*   *   *   *

On June 10 Mr. Minister Titulescu saw Mr. Puaux and talked in the same vein about the inopportunity of the Polish government's decision to sign the pact of nonaggression with Russia before Romania reaches an understanding with Russia. On this occasion Minister Titulescu particularly insisted on the argument that, because Romania finds herself in the middle of the electoral campaign, it is not right to weaken belief in our allies in precisely such a period and that this could only profit our adversaries.

Coming to see me at the ministry on the morning of June 11, the minister of France told me that he had learned of the Polish government's decision from Mr. Titulescu; that even yesterday he had telegraphed the Quai d'Orsay [about] the conversation he had had with Mr. Titulescu; and that on this occasion he had insisted that Paris intervene in Warsaw to get the Polish government to withdraw its deadline for signing.

I brought Mr. Puaux up to date on the meeting the prime minister and I had had the day before with Count Szembek. The minister of France told me that he would send a second telegram to his government to inform them about what we communicated.

GR. GAFENCU

DOCUMENT NO. 63

Intradepartmental memo by GAFENCU

Bucharest, 16 June 1932

On the occasion of the conversation I had with Count Szembek during the evening of June 14, 1932, at the dinner given in honor of the representatives of the Polish-Romanian press, he expressed the hope that

the Polish General Gasiorowski, once [he had] returned to Warsaw, would persuade the Polish government to reconsider the deadline fixed for the signing of the pact of nonaggression with the USSR.[92] The minister of Poland added, however, that in this case he hoped that the Romanian government would use this delay to resume negotiations with Mr. Litvinov in Geneva through Mr. Titulescu.

In this last regard, I replied to Count Szembek that Mr. Titulescu, in accordance with our already established point of view, believes that as long as we have not reached a formula acceptable to both parties through the mediation of our allies, making contact with Mr. Litvinov would be not only useless but injurious because, in place of a relaxation, we risk arriving—in case of failure—at a more accentuated tension of our relations with Moscow.

At the same time I made it clear to Count Szembek that it would be desirable for Poland to continue the mediating action of Messrs. Zaleski and Patek with a view to finding, according to our suggestions, the acceptable formula that would allow us to resume negotiations with Russia in Geneva under the best conditions.

The minister of Poland replied that Mr. Patek was not currently in Moscow and that it would be difficult for the Polish government to treat a question of this importance through a chargé d'affaires. I observed that Mr. Zaleski, who is a close personal friend of Mr. Titulescu, is in the best position to carry out this role of mediator when Mr. Litvinov is again . . . in Geneva.

At the same time I again told Count Szembek that new formulae are in the process of being elaborated by us and that presently I hoped to bring them to his knowledge to be used by Poland—as suggestions on her part, of course—in the discussions she will have when carrying out her role as mediator with the USSR.

*   *   *   *

Informing Mr. Titulescu of the preceding, he approved yesterday, June 15, the answer I had given to Count Szembek the day before.

At the same time Mr. Titulescu approved the texts of the preamble and article I, which I herein enclose, specifying that he was not opposed to completing the preamble with Patek's suggestion, to wit, "would not be able to either impair or profit in any way from the present situation of the two countries," but that he only accepts the introduction of such a formula in the preamble if the Soviets accept, concerning article I, paragraph 2, at least the formula "over the Dniester and the shore of the Black Sea."

Consequently, Mr. Titulescu accepts the introduction of Patek's suggestion in the preamble only if the Soviets accept the Zaleski formula for article I, paragraph 2 (see telegram 27753/932),[93] according to which the word "sovereignty" in our initial draft is replaced by "authority."

G. GAFENCU

PREAMBLE

His Majesty the King of Romania on the one hand, the Central Executive Committee of the USSR on the other hand:

Animated by the desire to reaffirm the political situation in Eastern Europe by means of direct agreements, to maintain and consolidate the state of peace existing between the two states, *as well as to clarify the reciprocal obligations arising from the Protocol of* Moscow of February 9, 1929, for the early coming into force of the Treaty of Renunciation of War signed in Paris on August 27, 1928;

Convinced that the peaceful resolution of all international conflicts is the surest means for attaining the desired end;

And persuaded that no international obligations previously concluded constitute a hindrance to the peaceful development of mutual relations nor are contrary to the present treaty;

Have resolved to conclude a treaty that, having as [its] end the extension and completion of the aforementioned Protocol and Treaty of Moscow and Paris, would not be able to either impair or profit in any way the present situation of [either of] the two countries;

Have designated to this end as their Plenipotentiaries, to wit. . . .

ARTICLE I.

The High Contracting Parties confirm that they have renounced war as an instrument of national policy in their mutual relations and reciprocally promise not to carry out any aggressive action against the other Contracting Party.

Acts considered as contrary to the obligations stipulated in the preceding paragraph will be any armed attack, invasion, or other acts of violence directed on the ground, on the sea, or in the air against the other Contracting Party over the Dniester and the shore of the Black Sea (*against the territories comprised between the Dniester, the shore of the Black Sea, and the frontiers of each of the High Contracting Parties with their other neighbors*), even if such acts are committed without declaration of war or without having the character of an act of war.

DOCUMENT NO. 64

Letter, CADERE *to* VAIDA-VOEVOD

Warsaw No. 2108, 14 June 1932
STRICTLY CONFIDENTIAL

Mr. Prime Minister,

I have the honor to inform Your Excellency that, after the courtesy visit [of arrival] that I made to Count Romer, the director of protocol at the Ministry of Foreign Affairs, today I saw Mr. Beck, undersecretary of state in this department. The conversation lasted about an hour and a half and I had the opportunity to learn [his] opinion about many current problems.

However, the principal object of our conversation was, naturally, the question, so important for us, of the imminent signing of the Polish-Soviet nonaggression pact. Because my letters of accreditation can be presented to the president of the republic only at the beginning of next month, our meeting did not have the character of an official intervention on the question of the pact on my part, [and] our conversation, as it developed, took on a more casual tone. I did not use this first occasion to show Mr. Beck the absolute necessity of not causing any weakening of the intimate collaboration between the two allied countries and of not rushing this question at an inopportune moment for us. [Rather I explained to him] the influence that Poland's decision to sign now could have on our public opinion, keeping in mind that we find ourselves in the middle of an electoral campaign, and I also drew his attention to the unfavorable impression that such an act on the part of Poland could produce on foreign public opinion, which I had the occasion to ascertain personally at the time of my trip through France.

As I telegraphed Your Excellency, Mr. Beck enumerated the known arguments that place the Polish government in the situation of no longer being able to postpone for very long the signing of the pact initialed five months ago. He also repeated the objections of Marshal Pilsudski on the occasion of his visit to Bucharest and reminded me of the advanced stage in which the problem is found in the Baltic countries.

Under the impression that the most recent events in connection with Danzig and with the new state of affairs in Germany are influencing the Polish government's decision,[94] I was able to confirm [the existence of] a visible effort not to betray any irritation at Germany's recent provocations. Mr. Beck spoke to me with easy irony about the way in which the president of the Reich dismissed Dr. Brüning at the moment when the

latter had entered into conflict with the Reichswehr—[the] organization
that is still the apple of the old field marshal's eye—as well as the way in
which the present government has been set up—a government in which
only Prussian Junkers figure. Otherwise, my interlocutor believed that
this change of regime created an unambiguous situation. Mr. Beck
added, however, that while the laws of a country could be easily
changed—by a squadron of cavalry—her customs are much more difficult to change. The leaders must realize this difficulty, and in the laws
that they draft they [must] not go beyond the customs of the country
except in limited measure. It is obvious that the habits of Germany will
not change in the near future and thus her anti-Polish behavior will
continue.

This sally of Mr. Beck's poorly concealed his anxiety concerning the
possibility of a radical change of affairs in Germay (constitution, mon-
archy, etc.) because in an expansive moment he added, "[It is] evident
that for a change of frontier something more than a few squadrons of
cavalry is necessary."

Mr. Beck's last words on the issue of the pact were that Mr. Zaleski will
make new efforts in Geneva to obtain from Litvinov an assurance that
negotiations with us would give proof, on the part of the Soviets, of a
spirit of conciliation larger than [they have shown] up to now. Mr. Beck
believes that the positive or negative intentions of the Soviet government will be immediately discernible from the first contact. He left me to
deduce that the decision of the Polish government depends upon the
result of Mr. Zaleski's conversations with Litvinov, who is still in Geneva.
If Mr. Zaleski gains the impression that the Romanian-Russian negotiations could be successfully resumed this time, the Polish government
will seek a new way of giving us the necessary time for negotiations. In
the contrary case, however, the Polish government would no longer be
able to delay the signing. It appears that a telegram from Mr. Zaleski
giving the result of his meetings with Litvinov is awaited in Warsaw this
very day.

*   *   *   *

On another subject, Mr. Beck expressed his great satisfaction concerning the personalities who compose the new French government and
Franco-Polish collaboration. He has friendly relations with Mr. Paul-
Boncour who was in Poland in April 1926, a month before Marshal
Pilsudski's coup d'état, to study the organization of the corps of border
guards in Poland. Through the eastern regions of Poland, Mr. Beck
accompanied Mr. Paul-Boncour and the relations between them are
also cordial at the present. However, the Polish government also has

other friends in the present French government, for example Mr. Painlevé, and thus the collaboration with Mr. Herriot's government will surely be close.[95] The eventual departure of Mr. Philippe Berthelot from the Quai d'Orsay has not tended to impress Mr. Beck unduly.

*   *   *   *

I must add that during the course of our conversations, Mr. Beck expressed repeatedly and in categorical and inspired terms his deep conviction concerning the fundamental and inflexible character of the Polish-Romanian alliance. I am sure that Mr. Beck expressed a profound personal conviction, being at the same time the faithful interpreter of the equally categoric convictions of Marshal Pilsudski and Polish governing circles.

Please accept, Mr. Prime Minister, the assurances of my very high consideration.

VICTOR CADERE

DOCUMENT NO. 65

Intradepartmental memo by GAFENCU

Bucharest, 17 June 1932

The Minister of France came to see me yesterday, June 16, at 3:00 and brought me up to date with what he had shown to the prime minister and Minister Titulescu during the morning. He read me Mr. Laroche's telegram, which reports to the French foreign minister his démarche to Colonel Beck in the question of the Polish-Russian nonaggression treaty.[96] The French démarche had the aim of persuading the Polish government not to sign before the Romanian government, and not to impose a deadline upon Romania in order not to weaken [the latter's] position vis-à-vis Russia. Mr. Beck answered that the Polish general who was in Bucharest [General Janusz Gasiorowski] had no communication to make concerning Poland's signing and that, moreover, Poland had not decided on a deadline for signing her nonaggression pact with Russia. On the other hand, however, Count Szembek had not gained the impression, from the conversations he had had with the Romanian prime minister, that the Romanian government is desirous of hastening the conclusion of nonaggression pact with Russia. Colonel Beck continued on the difficulties that Romania's failure to settle on a policy concerning this problem had caused Poland. Nonetheless, he promised Mr. Laroche "not to bully the new government and to give it time to arrive at an understanding with Russia concerning the pact of nonaggression."

Mr. Puaux showed me that he too realized that Beck's statements did not at all correspond with the declarations that the Prime Minister had made to Count Szembek, as was related to Mr. Puaux not only by me but also by Count Szembek himself.

On the other hand, Count Szembek has told the minister of France that the new Romanian government and Mr. Titulescu are determined to bring the negotiations with Russia through Polish mediation to a good end, and that he insistently intervened with the Polish government not to set an irrevocable deadline, in order to make the Romanian government's burden lighter.

I also remarked on the curious nature of Mr. Beck's declarations, telling Mr. Puaux that I was informed of the decision of the Polish government to sign her pact of nonaggression without waiting for Romania not only directly, by the Polish government and Count Szembek, but also indirectly—even by the Latvian government.[97] I also showed France's minister the method by which we intended to arrive at an understanding with Russia concerning the conclusion of a pact of nonaggression. Finally, I told him that Mr. Titulescu would not begin negotiations with Litvinov until he was presented with an acceptable formula by the representatives of France and Poland.

I showed these formulae to Mr. Puaux, who took note of them in order to communicate them to Paris as his own suggestions.

*   *   *   *

Mr. Kirchholtes, Germany's chargé d'affaires, came to see me yesterday, June 16, at 5:00 and told me that he had learned that Poland had the intention of signing her pact of nonaggression without waiting for Romania any longer. He added that the German government was very surprised at Poland's attitude and he asked me what significance it had, as it would totally change the situation in the East.

GAFENCU

DOCUMENT NO. 66

Intradepartmental memo by FILALITY

Bucharest, 18 June 1932

The secretary of the French Legation came to see me today to read me the following telegram received from his government as [a] response to one of Mr. Puaux.

> The French government has intervened with the Polish government in making it understand that it should abstain from putting unwonted pressure on the Romanian government; however, the French government believes that the Romanian government should realize the inconveniences that would result from leaving the negotiations at a dead end.
>
> This state of affairs places Poland in a false situation. Mr. Patek cannot delay [his] return to Moscow, and it would be quite difficult for him to steal off when Litvinov returns.
>
> Also, the French government hopes that the Romanian government will show a desire to succeed.
>
> The French government remains ready with the Polish government to seek a formula of agreement.

The secretary added that Mr. Puaux telegraphed to Paris the subsequent conversation with Mr. Vaida and Titulescu, so that the French government knows exactly what the Romanian position is.

FILALITY

DOCUMENT NO. 67

Telegram, GAFENCU *to* TITULESCU

Bucharest No. 34340, 28 June 1932

Count Szembek came to see me this morning to talk with me again about the question of the nonaggression pact. I connected this démarche of the Polish minister with the return to his post of Mr. Kobilanski [*sic*], counselor of the Polish Legation, in Bucharest, who spent about two weeks in Warsaw. Mr. Kobilanski is considered Marshal Pilsudski's crony and an intimate friend of Colonel Beck.[98]

The Polish minister said that the result of the negotiations in Geneva between Zaleski and Litvinov is awaited impatiently in Warsaw because the future decisions of the Polish government depend on it. To my question about what the Polish government will do in case Litvinov thwarts an understanding between Russia and us, Count Szembek categorically replied: "We will no longer be able to postpone the signing of our draft. We are obliged to sign."

I pointed out to the Polish minister that if this were so, an action on which hinged the security of the eastern frontier and the value of the Polish-Romanian alliance depended on the good or bad faith of Mr. Litvinov. If the Russian foreign minister consents to reach an understanding with us, the value of the Polish-Romanian alliance remains intact; if not, the Romanian-Polish front is broken, Poland signs separately, and Romania remains [up] in the air.

Under such conditions, and given that Mr. Litvinov surely knows the intentions of the Polish government, as the German government and the Latvian government know them, the Russian foreign minister would consequently be an imbecile if he made the conclusion of the Romanian-Russian Pact easier. And I also told Count Szembek [that] if this equivocal attitude of Poland toward us was meant to be a pressure to push us to an understanding with Russia, it is useless; we have proved that we are determined to arrive at an understanding that, naturally, does not weaken our situation vis-à-vis the Soviets. However, if Poland's attitude truly signifies an intention to sign the pact of nonaggression separately, I must again draw [his] attention [to the fact] that such an action deprives the Polish-Romanian alliance of any real political value in our eyes and in the eyes of our friends and adversaries.

During the entire discussion the Polish minister maintained the attitude of a man who knew that the decision had been taken in Warsaw and could not be changed. He tried to assure me only that the ratification that must follow the signing of the Polish-Soviet protocol would be postponed by the Polish government for a longer time.

On the other hand Cadere informs me from Warsaw that "the postponement of the signing of the Polish-Soviet pact appears to have been won, without my being able to say that they will not sign without us."[99]

This is the impression also [to be] drawn from your telegram No. 164.[100] Cadere believes the Poles fear that the Russians, as a result of an unusually persistent German and Italian diplomatic action, will renounce the signing of the Polish-Russian pact in case of a prolonged delay on the part of Poland.

Respectful considerations,
GAFENCU

DOCUMENT NO. 68

Letter, Cadere *to* Vaida-Voevod

Warsaw No. 2355, 3 July 1932

PILSUDSKI PROMISES ONLY TO RATIFY WITH ROMANIA

STRICTLY CONFIDENTIAL

Mr. Prime Minister,

As I had the honor to telegraph Your Excellency,[101] the audience with Marshal Pilsudski took place today, from 1:00 to 2:00 P.M. at the location of the supreme command of the Polish army. Mr. Beck, undersecretary of state for foreign affairs, was also present. The audience developed a cordial tone.

After I had presented the marshal with the friendly greetings of the new Romanian government, I developed the arguments that militate even in Poland's interests against signing the pact of nonaggression separately. I demonstrated that the only thing with real importance in today's circumstances is the solidarity developed between allies, which in the past, too, has given such felicitous results; that, through lack of an exact answer—apparently because of pressures or deadlines—doubt is created in relations between us; and that the eventuality of a separate signing gives Mr. Litvinov the liberty to sign or not—according to his pleasure— the pact of nonaggression with Romania. Aside from this it encourages intrigues, especially by Germany, which has every interest in these pacts not being concluded.

To sign separately, I added, means to do grave injury to our alliance, especially from the point of view of the moral repercussion on Romanian public opinion and the accentuation of insecurity that has already been produced in European public opinion.

Finally, I affirmed that [since] the government is at this date firmly determined to sign the pact of nonaggression [. . .] Poland could wait so that the signings [would] take place together.

The marshal seemed particularly impressed by the latter argument and told me on his part "not to ask better than signing together. . . ." But, he immediately added, because of us the unity of action has been broken, because the Baltic States had already finalized their pacts. I answered that this was probably due to their desire to show themselves independent . . . to which the marshal ironically remarked, "Especially when they depend, as for example does Latvia, to their last penny on Russia."

The marshal does not believe that Litvinov is inclined to make only a facade of promising and of not signing with Romania, because presently the Soviets want to sign such pacts. For what motives? Either because their internal situation is not too good, or because things appear to deteriorate between them and the Germans, or because in the Far East they are menaced by new events . . . [the] fact is that they wish to sign and that Romania can profit from this disposition.

Concerning the international crisis, the marshal believes, according to the latest news, [that] the situation seems to be becoming clearer. . . . There remain to be clarified the intentions of Germany and the disposition of relations with Russia. And now that the signing of the pacts of nonaggression is imposed . . . at least with the Soviets a step forward is being taken:

> I am happy to know that the present government is determined to sign, because the hesitations of the former foreign minister caused us to mark time for many months. Naturally, as in the pact or in another act, you will receive a formula like the one we have currently hit on, that is, "neither profit from nor impair the actual state of affairs, or about. . . ." But the signing would also be an act of friendship on the part of Romania, which we also appreciate. . . . Perhaps this would end many intrigues. . . .[102]

Finally, the marshal concluded, we will not hurry the signing, which will take place in Moscow, in the days immediately following Mr. Litvinov's return there. "If by then the Romanian government has not decided to give full powers for signing, [then] *we will not ratify in any case except . . . with Romania.*"

The ineffectiveness of these purely formal measures was pointed out to Marshal Pilsudski. He answered that the circumstances are difficult, especially the financial ones. Then I thought it useful to make [an] allusion to the international [economic] situation, which is becoming clearer, thanks in particular to French efforts. . . . Then capital will be found with our friends . . . at which [point] the marshal reminded me of an old Polish proverb that says, "Let us love like brothers, but in business treat them as Jews!"

The marshal believes that on Wednesday he will have exact information from Geneva. Obviously, he is alluding to the action of Mr. Zaleski because both the marshal and Mr. Zaleski want to leave on vacation at the end of the week. The marshal did not know anything precise about the return of Mr. Litvinov to Moscow. It appears that this will take place only when the work of the Disarmament Conference in Geneva is suspended.

During the entire duration of the conversation with the marshal he carefully avoided any indication of [a] deadline, leaving me to understand that Romania has sufficient time to coordinate her actions with Poland's.

* * * *

From the conversations here yesterday (with Messrs. Beck and Patek)[103] and today with the marshal, Poland's tendency, under French prompting, to show herself independent of [events in] Geneva is made all the clearer. This must be why the marshal affirmed that the signing will take place in Moscow.

But really, if a common [course of] action and the effective signing of the pact by Romania [and France] is accomplished in a few days, then I believe Warsaw, too, would opt for signing in Geneva.

Perhaps the real drift of the marshal's policy can also be explained by the urgent necessity of thus forcing a loan? Only so could one explain— up to a point—the attempt to arrive at the signing of the pact even at the risk of an isolated political gesture. Here the interest that Poland has in Soviet orders that appear to have already been promised by Litvinov for the industries of Upper Silesia (for the Königschutte and Laurahutte factories) should be noted.

In the second place, a means is being sought here to avoid Poland's responsibility for not signing the pact of nonaggression concomitantly with Romania. If and when the intermediary action of Mr. Zaleski eventually fails, an honorable exit will be sought, namely . . . that Romania continuously dallied, she alone being responsible in case of damage to the alliance.

The Litvinov proposal, with his promise to sign a pact of nonaggression with Romania, comes at a time when it facilitates an exit from the impasse in which Poland currently finds herself.

From all these considerations one can deduce that although the marshal's attitude is not greatly modified, nonetheless we have before us sufficient time to reach a definite signing of the pact of nonaggression, which would put an end to the different [. . .] and injurious manifestations in the relations between the two countries.

Please receive, Mr. Prime Minister, the assurance of my highest consideration.

V. CADERE

DOCUMENT NO. 69
(Reg. No. 35481 of 5 July 1932)

Decoded telegram, TITULESCU *to* FOREIGN MINISTRY

Lausanne No. 178, 5 July 1932
STRICTLY CONFIDENTIAL—WITH THE REQUEST THAT IT
BE TRANSMITTED TO H. M. THE KING

Since Zaleski came to the Lausanne meeting with MacDonald today, I had a conversation about the pact of nonaggression with him.[104] I asked him to tell me the result of his conversations with Litvinov. Once more Zaleski told me that he has not yet [received] an answer from Litvinov, who returns to Geneva this evening. I could not help but express my surprise to Zaleski that, for fifteen days from the time I gave him and he received the mandate to negotiate with Litvinov, I had not had from him any kind of explanation in one form or another. Zaleski said that in the conversations he had had with Litvinov, the latter had insisted that, in one way or another, it is specified that the Russo-Romanian agreement [should] not prejudge issues between the two states that are still open. I replied: "So, the Soviets have not budged one iota from the position they took at Riga. And although they ask to declare in litigation the possession of Bessarabia, whose integrity Poland is obliged to militarily defend, Poland is ready to sign with them without Romania and has also told the Baltic States about it. Therefore the chances of an agreement with Moscow are destroyed by Poland." Zaleski answered: "It's not at all so. This Friday evening I told Litvinov that we will not sign without Romania." I asked Zaleski if I could transmit his answer as Poland's official answer to the Romanian government. Zaleski answered: "Unfortunately no, since there is also the marshal. But to give the marshal a compromise solution that would reconcile the interests of Poland and the interests of Romania, I wrote him that Poland could sign declaring . . . formally in Moscow that she will never ratify without a Romanian-Russian accord."

I showed Zaleski that signing would be a serious matter even without ratification. And I asked him if at least I could give the Romanian government as [an] official answer that the ratification will never take place if a Russo-Romanian agreement does not intervene. Zaleski answered: "This is my intention. But for the moment from which you ask an official response from me, I must see if the marshal gives the same interpretation as I do." In other words, today Zaleski transposes his so-called divergences with the marshal from the domain of signing to the domain of ratification. I told Zaleski that convincing the Soviets that Poland would never sign without Romania constitutes the only chance of concluding a Romanian-Soviet agreement. But, starting with Marshal Pilsudski's declarations on the occasion of his visit to Bucharest, Poland has done everything to make the Soviets arrive at the opposite conviction, that is, that there is no need to sign with Romania in order to obtain Poland's signature. Thus Poland is responsible for today's situation, which can be altered only by a change of attitude by Poland toward the Soviets. I will see Zaleski again on Thursday in Lausanne.

TITULESCU

DOCUMENT NO. 70

Letter, VAIDA-VOEVOD *to* TITULESCU

Bucharest, n.d.

Thank you for your telegram No. 179.[105] I must tell you that I am in full agreement with you.

In conformity with the understanding between us, we are determined to demonstrate our undivided good faith to bring the negotiations with Russia concerning the Russo-Romanian nonaggression pact to a favorable end as rapidly as possible in order not to weaken the value of the Polish-Romanian alliance before public opinion and in order at the same time to take into account the urgings of the French government, whose [course of] action appears to be to stop the Poles and to push us.

Of course . . . in no case will we consent to sign an agreement with Russia as long as the Soviets ask that we recognize, in one form or another, the existence of [a] litigation about Bessarabia.

With my best friendly greetings,
VAIDA-VOEVOD

DOCUMENT NO. 71

Telegram, GAFENCU *to* CADERE

Bucharest No. 35803, 6 July 1932

I received your telegram and report about your audience with Pilsudski. I took note with satisfaction of the good sentiments expressed by the marshal and of the fact that, it would seem, he better understood our true intentions at this time. However, we regret that at this time we did not receive the assurance that we expect from a friendly and allied government, to wit, an assurance that Poland will not sign before we, too, reach an agreement with Russia. All the objections that we raised on the occasion of the other communications of the Polish government thus remain unmet. We also expressed this regret to Count Szembek, who transmitted to me a telegraphic report about your meeting with the marshal.

Concerning the marshal's declaration that "Poland will never ratify except . . . with Romania," please obtain an official confirmation on the part of the Polish government that this declaration constitutes a formal promise that Poland will not ratify before a Romanian-Russian agreement specified by telegram is reached.[106] You will seek to obtain such a confirmation without your insistences in this regard in any way weakening your resolute efforts to obtain a postponement not only of the ratification but also of the signing of the Polish-Russian pact.

We are informed from Geneva that Litvinov insists on introducing into the pact an allusion to the territorial litigation between us and Russia. We have not yet arrived at the formula about which the Marshal spoke, "The pact does not in any way modify the present situation of the two contracting parties." As you know, the point of view of our government in this matter is well established. We can accept the formula to which the marshal alluded. We will never accept recognition in one or another form of the existence of the litigation over Bessarabia.

GAFENCU

DOCUMENT NO. 72
(Reg. No. 36187 of 8 July 1932)

Decoded telegram, TITULESCU *to* MINISTRY OF FOREIGN AFFAIRS

Lausanne No. 182, 7 July 1932

STRICTLY CONFIDENTIAL—WITH THE REQUEST THAT IT BE
TRANSMITTED TO H. M. THE KING

Following my telegram 181.[107] Today I saw Laboulaye. At the Quai d'Orsay he is especially concerned with the question of the nonaggression pact.[108] He considers that the Soviets' pretension of demanding that we recognize that Bessarabia is a disputed territory is inadmissible. He told me that he had the impression from his conversations with the Soviets' ambassador to Paris that the Russians would not insist on the insertion of this recognition in the treaty, being satisfied with omitting the question of Bessarabia. And, says Laboulaye, the question of Bessarabia is [certainly] not left out by recording it in black on white in the treaty. He is surprised by the Soviets' change of attitude, and does not know to what causes to attribute it. I answered, "Now that the Soviets are convinced that Poland will sign without us, the only question we need consider is how to dissuade the Soviets from this conviction." Laboulaye told me that he would undertake action on two fronts:

1. He will telegraph Warsaw that the Soviet exigencies are inadmissible and that Poland [must not] sign without Romania, especially when Zaleski himself recognizes by the letter he sent to us that the pact of nonaggression supported by Litvinov is in his own opinion inadmissible for us.
2. He will speak with Herriot because he will tell Zaleski on the one hand that Poland cannot sign in such conditions without Romania, and on the other hand he will tell Litvinov when he sees him presently in Geneva that, if the Soviets want to have a pact of nonaggression with France, they must reach an agreement with Romania—and for this they must cease demanding that Romania alone recognize that Bessarabia is a territory subject to litigation.

I thanked Laboulaye for his declarations and we agreed that in his capacity as a responsible official of the Quai d'Orsay he will speak even today with Herriot as Romania's spokesman.

TITULESCU

DOCUMENT NO. 73
(Reg. No. 36251 of 8 July 1932)

Decoded telegram, TITULESCU *to* MINISTRY OF FOREIGN AFFAIRS

Lausanne No. 181, 7 July 1932

STRICTLY CONFIDENTIAL—WITH THE REQUEST THAT IT BE
TRANSMITTED TO H. M. THE KING

As I immediately communicated to the prime minister, yesterday I received by mail from Zaleski the draft pact of nonaggression proposed by Litvinov.

I will limit myself to reproducing a single passage from it:

> ... *the conclusion of the present treaty does not prejudice in any way the position of each of the parties in the territorial and other litigations existing between them, these litigations being omitted and not being in any case affected by the present treaty.*

The judgment on this pact of nonaggression is made by Zaleski himself in a letter he sent to us along with Litvinov's draft in the following terms.

> Dear Friends, Mr. Litvinov came to see me this morning and gave me his draft pact of nonaggression for you. After I had examined it, I declared I would transmit it to you but that I could now state that, in my opinion, it would not be acceptable for you. Signed ZALESKI.

It would be difficult for Romania to have any other opinion of this pact except that of Zaleski. I will see Zaleski and will ask if Poland can really sign with the Soviets [and] without Romania, given that after fifteen days of so-called conversations with Litvinov, the latter has made a proposal that Zaleski himself considers unacceptable for Romania. I say "so-called conversations" because, contrary to the newspaper stories spread by Poland [and in order] to place Zaleski's mediatory action in relief, the latter gives me the impression of a man who wishes more to cover up the responsibility of Poland's signing without Romania saying that she had done all she could, than a man who has made effective efforts to obtain a change in attitude from Litvinov. Otherwise it would be inexplicable that after fifteen days of so-called negotiations with Litvinov, Zaleski had the nerve to send me as the Soviets' proposal exactly the text because of which Romania had broken with the Soviets at Riga. The fact that the Soviets did not even put on a show of changing their reservations concerning Bessarabia, at least in form, is due only to the assurance they have that Poland will sign without Romania.

I will again explain the situation to the representatives of France.[109] More than ever I am reinforced in my conviction about the mistakes committed by Romania concerning the manner and the conditions under which she began the negotiations with the Soviets and which motivated my trip to Bucharest last February. The premonitions that I had then and that I exposed to the king, the government, and the leaders of the parties have unhappily become reality. More than ever I am strengthened in my conviction ... expressed in my telegram No. 137 after the visit of Marshal Pilsudski to Bucharest.[110] I will do everything within my power to at least inform Poland in the last moment about the political mistake that is about to take place and its consequences. But I consider that our duty is also to regard the reality before us with courage and calm. Certainly it is painful to know that the Polish-Romanian front is broken. But what would happen if [to remedy] the pain we agreed to sign a pact in which we declared Bessarabia territory subject to litigation between us and the Soviets. Once the joy of maintaining the Polish-Romanian front is past, this stipulation would hang over the country like a terrible sword of Damocles. Whoever recognizes that he has a litigation over a territory, implicitly also recognizes the obligation to find a solution to this litigation as well—arbitration or plebiscite. Moreover, article II of the Kellogg Pact obliges us to find peaceful solutions for existing litigations. And, Romania's recognition before the Soviets that the possession of Bessarabia is litigious would hasten even more the rhythm of the application of article II, following which recognition we will no longer have a means of defense. . . . Today it is not without interest that we should recall a few facts in particular from the past in this concern.

The international recognition of the union of Bessarabia to the mother country is the work of Prime Minister Vaida-Voevod, who by his action in the winter of 1920 convinced the Great Powers of the necessity of this recognition. When, as a delegate of the government of General Averescu to the Peace Conference, I had to discuss the text of the treaty that consecrated the recognition of the union of Bessarabia to the mother country obtained by Mr. Vaida-Voevod, the allies proposed a totally unacceptable formula by which it was recognized that the Soviets had the right to appeal to the League of Nations against the decision of the Great Powers considering Bessarabia as politically united with Romania. I had to struggle the entire month of May 1920 in London to purge the text proposed by the allies of any substance expressly stipulating that Romania's sovereignty over Bessarabia and its frontiers were liable to the recognized right of appeal by the Soviets. As a result, the text I negotiated and Take Ionescu signed in October 1920 could with good reason sustain that Romania's sovereignty over Bessarabia was recognized by the Great Powers, signatories of the treaty. Unfortunately, Japan has not ratified this treaty, which thus has not been able to enter into force. From the moral point of view it is evidently difficult for England, France, and Italy even in these conditions to sustain that Romania is not sovereign over Bessarabia once they have signed and ratified the treaty. From the legal point of view, these states still would be free to do so because the treaty has not entered into force. This being so, when the Soviets have not recognized the union of Bessarabia with Romania, when the international position of the signatory states is as I described it above, what would become of our situation if we ourselves recognized before the Soviets that the possession of Bessarabia is litigious? Today's frail international situation would become a nonexistent international situation. As long as Romania does not recognize the existence of the litigation over Bessarabia, its defense vis-à-vis the Soviets is the following: "Bessarabia was united with the mother country by virtue of [the process of] self-determination. This was recognized as international fact by England, France, and Italy. We know that the Soviets consider the conditions of self-determination as defective. But there is no judge or international law who examines the conditions in which a self-determination is carried out without the consent of the interested parties. On the other hand, by the Kellogg Pact the Soviets renounced war as an instrument of national policy. We know that the Soviets have pretensions about Bessarabia, but from the moment when we realize that the Soviets have at hand neither international [precedent], which does not exist in this material, nor the way that they have already renounced, we are entitled to maintain that for us the question of the Bessarabian litigation does not exist."

I ask, can Romania keep up this defense any longer if she recognizes the existence of the litigation over Bessarabia by diplomatic treaty? And if Romania can no longer present this defense for the respect of her rights, what other defense can she use in international forums? So, my conclusion remains the same as in the past:

(1) We [should] do everything to inform Poland about the grave political consequences that will inevitably follow their association with the Soviets without Romania, precisely on the question that is the object of our alliance. And [we should do so] with dignity, without pleading or imploring, so as not to transform Poland into our savior exactly when she is about to desert us. (2) We [should be] calm, explaining to Romanian public opinion that the treaty of alliance with Poland remains in force and that we already have the Kellogg Pact with the Soviets and that it is preferable for the country's interests to avoid a new pact from the moment when the price asked of us for signing it is not only the prejudicing of the existing international situation but something more: the prejudicing of our own conception of it.

TITULESCU

DOCUMENT NO. 74
(Reg. No. 36477 of 9 July 1932)

Decoded telegram (copy), TITULESCU *to* MINISTRY OF FOREIGN AFFAIRS

Lausanne No. 183, 9 July 1932
STRICTLY CONFIDENTIAL—WITH THE REQUEST THAT IT BE
TRANSMITTED TO HIS MAJESTY, THE KING

The démarches I have made in the question of the pact of nonaggression have begun to produce results. In a new conversation which I have had with Zaleski, at my insistence, Zaleski authorized me to telegraph you as the firm declaration of Poland that Poland will not ratify the agreement with the Soviets until Romania also has concluded a similar agreement. Here are the circumstances in which I was able to obtain this official declaration from Zaleski. Zaleski came to Lausanne to see Herriot, who spoke in the same terms as Laboulaye had spoken to me. From Herriot's very room, Zaleski telephoned me that he wished to see me immediately. Zaleski began by criticizing the pact of nonaggression proposed by Litvinov and told me that it is unacceptable. Then he insisted on the importance that the concomitant signing of the pact by Poland and Romania would have. I replied that this was also our conclusion, but how will we be able to sign a pact that asks us to recognize Bessarabia as a litigious territory as the price for nonaggression? Zaleski answered that he must convince Litvinov to give up his pretension and added that to this end nothing would be more useful than if I saw Litvinov at Zaleski's. I replied that I do not believe that Litvinov will give up his pretension because he felt certain that Poland [would] sign without us. Zaleski answered that only the day before yesterday he had told Litvinov that Poland will never ratify the pact without an agreement between Romania and the Soviets intervening, and that Litvinov had retorted that in this case Poland's signing had no value. That being so, he did not see why I refused to meet Litvinov. I admit that Zaleski's words made a twofold impression on me. On the one hand I had the impression that Zaleski wants me to see Litvinov so that he can say he has done all that he could and thus morally justify Poland's isolated signing. In fact Zaleski has done nothing but transmit to me, after fifteen days of so-called conversations, the draft that Romania had at Riga. On the other hand, it seems to me that Zaleski, in case I refuse to see Litvinov, wants to have the excuse that we have done nothing to effect a change in the Soviet conviction and as a result we carry the responsibility for the present situation. In order to reconcile these two impressions that I had, and to profit from an eventual meeting with Litvinov, I gave the following answer to Zaleski: "If, conforming to your wish, I meet with Litvinov in your house, I [will] ask you in front of him if it is true you will never ratify the pact with the Soviets if Romania does not also conclude a pact with the Soviets satisfactory [that is] for her. What will you answer?" Zaleski told me: "I will answer in front of Litvinov that Poland will never ratify the treaty with the Soviets so long as an agreement between them and Romania does not intervene." So, I told Zaleski that it would eventually be possible that I would see Litvinov at Zaleski's as the result of a new conversation between Zaleski and Litvinov.

Zaleski informed me that Litvinov did not make the question of Romania's recognition that Bessarabia is a litigious territory a condition "sine qua non," which would call into [question] the utility of my meeting with Litvinov. I want to add that Massigli, on the other hand, was asked by Herriot to put in a word with Litvinov in Geneva in favor of the withdrawal of the Soviets' pretension of asking that we alone declare the existence of a litigation over Bessarabia by diplomatic treaty.[111] It remains for Zaleski and Massigli to telephone me presently. Please take measures to avoid any indiscretions on this question since it is very possible that I will not see Litvinov and, in case I do not see him, Zaleski told me that it is preferable to keep it secret. I did not then shrink from showing Zaleski all the grave consequences that could follow from the engagement Poland had made to the Soviets to sign without us when she had [already] agreed with Romania that the negotiations for the pact of nonaggression be conducted on two bases: the leaving aside of the question of Bessarabia, and the refusal to sign the pact by one of the two states if the other did not conclude a similar pact. Zaleski told me that what, among other [things], determined Marshal Pilsudski to sign without Romania is the fact that after the declaration he made on the occasion of his visit [to Romania], the politicians of Bucharest allegedly said that what the marshal declared was of no consequence because France would impede him from signing alone. This attitude had affected the marshal and at the same time had convinced him to undertake an action that would prove that Poland knew what to do, and not what France wanted. I asked Zaleski to give me the names of the Bucharest politicians who had used such language. Zaleski did not want to give me the names. Then I said: "It must be a plot by elements who want to split Poland from Romania. In any case I am inclined to believe that Poland grounds her actions on the basis of political conceptions and of the just appreciation of her interests and not on gossip." Zaleski answered that he did not wish to say that only this convinced the marshal to sign, but that this factor, founded or unfounded, also entered into the marshal's psychology.

I asked Zaleski:

"May I transmit to the Romanian government on your part as the official and firm declaration of Poland that Poland will never ratify the treaty with the Soviets if an agreement between them and Romania does not intervene?"

Zaleski answered: "Yes. You can today transmit this declaration as official and firm on my part since I have convinced the Marshal. And because I wish to be prudent, that is, because I do not wish it to be said that I have prevented Poland from ratifying the accord with the Soviets even in case of Romania's ill-will, [please] transmit my earlier declaration thusly: Poland will never ratify the pact of nonaggression with the Soviets as long as the Soviets ask that Romania recognize that Bessarabia is a litigious territory."

TITULESCU

DOCUMENT NO. 75
(Reg. No. 38052 of 16 July 1932)

Decoded telegram, CADERE *to* MINISTRY OF FOREIGN AFFAIRS

Warsaw No. 2384, 16 July 1932
VERY URGENT

In a conversation with Beck, he assured me that Poland is making every effort to persuade the Soviets [to reach] an agreement. Thus the chief of the Eastern Political Section was sent to Geneva to replace Zaleski.[112] Minister Patek has instructions to work toward the same end and here he declared to the Soviets' minister, as Zaleski [had] to Litvinov, that in any case Poland will not ratify before the pact with Romania is also concluded.

For a long time, I insisted on the necessity of signing together, to which Beck declared that the Polish government will not sign before the end of the current month, adding that the Soviets are exerting a lot of pressure for the termination of the nonaggression pacts.

The strictly confidential text follows. Please have Gafencu decode it personally.

I observed from the discussion with Beck that he introduces a reservation on the possibility that Poland may eventually ratify independently, "not considering the engagements undertaken as an absolute obligation, but only a means of pressure on the Soviets and as a means of gaining time for the conclusion of the Russo-Romanian pact."

I protested, pointing out that [such] eventual finalization of the pact with the Soviet Republic, as long as the latter imposes the clause of territorial litigation on Romania, is a direct infringement of the Romanian-Polish alliance based on the recognition of our territorial integrity. I declared that such an act on the part of Poland would have consequences of an incalculable gravity especially at a time like the present when the Soviet Republic is evidently directing a diplomatic attack against the allies of Poland. Where will our alliance be tomorrow in face of even graver events? What do you gain as a result of this act in which Poland embarks upon an isolated action in disagreement with the Baltic States, with France, and with Romania? Beck defended himself energetically, declaring that nothing will impair the value of our alliance and the proof is that in the Polish-Russian pact the intangibility of previous treaties is stipulated. This obliged me to say that [because of] the way in which he viewed the problem, I regretted to state that he excessively burdened the mission of Romania's minister in Poland. Visibly impressed, Beck told me that, since he hoped a Russo-Romanian agreement will be reached, there could be no question of such a thing.

Although I consider that the reservation expressed constitutes more the personal opinion of Mr. Beck, I nonetheless believe the question serious, both in relation to your last telegram and in relation to the uncontrolled local rumors according to which Zaleski will leave as ambassador to London, Patek to Paris, and Beck will become the minister of foreign affairs.[113] We would thus lose, without possibility of replacement, two valuable supporters of our point of view.

CADERE

DOCUMENT NO. 76

A. *Letter of transmittal,* CADERE *to* VAIDA-VOEVOD

Warsaw No. 2623, 21 July 1932

WITH AN ANNEX—CONFIDENTIAL

Dear Mr. President of the Council,

In reference to my report No. 2595 of July 19, I have the honor to send Your Excellency the herein enclosed copy of my letter that I sent yesterday to the undersecretary of state at the Ministry of Foreign Affairs, Joseph Beck, regarding the information appearing in the Polish press according to the *Exchange Telegraph* of London in the question of the pacts of nonaggression with the USSR.

V. CADERE

B. *Enclosure, letter of* CADERE *to* BECK (*Polish Undersecretary*)

Warsaw No. 2610, 20 July 1932
ANNEX TO NO. 2623

Dear Mr. Minister,

In reference to the conversation that I had the honor of having with Your Excellency, Friday, the fifteenth of July,[114] I believe it is my duty to call your attention to the information appearing in two Polish newspapers of yesterday evening (*Kurjer Warszawski* and *Kurjer Codzieny*)—citing the *Exchange Telegraph* of London—about the pacts of nonaggression with the USSR according to which "the Polish government is reported to have declared [to Mr. Litvinov] that the Polish-Soviet pact will not be presented for ratification to the Sejm before the winter session in order to give Romania the possibility of concluding its pact with the Soviets."[115]

If one must believe this quite unexpected information—given the actual state of negotiations between Romania and the Soviets—delay by Poland in ratifying the pact of nonaggression would henceforth be expected.

It is, therefore, with surprise that I saw the *Gazeta Polski* itself repeating the aforementioned information, which cannot avoid being interpreted as the [practically] official confirmation of a new attitude of the Polish government in this matter.

Given the preceding, I am sure that Your Excellency wholly shares my opinion that a clarification is necessary in conformity with the conclusions of our last conversations as well as with the spirit of the engagements that were made in Geneva between the representatives of our two countries.

This clarification would avert the supposition that the attitude of the Polish government has during the last days undergone a modification according to which the signature as well as the ratification of the pact would be seen [in a context] of deadlines and independently of the result of the negotiations between Romania and the USSR.

Please accept, Mr. Minister, the assurances of my high consideration.

The Minister of Romania
V. CADERE

DOCUMENT NO. 77
(Reg. No. 38788 of 22 July 1932)

Decoded telegram, CADERE *to* MINISTRY OF FOREIGN AFFAIRS

Warsaw No. 2619, 21 July 1932

STRICTLY CONFIDENTIAL—SENT VIA THE GENERAL STAFF
IN VIEW OF THE URGENCY

The following completes my report:

After the long discussion today with Beck, in which I reiterated strongly all the known arguments, Beck told me that instructions had been given to Patek to sign the Russo-Polish nonaggression pact on Saturday evening although Litvinov is in Geneva until Saturday and probably returns directly to Moscow.

The undersecretary of state of the Ministry of Foreign Affairs informed me that the chief of the Eastern Political Section will remain in Geneva until Saturday afternoon, and although Litvinov is apparently more conciliatory, if until then our agreement with the Soviets has not come about, he has instructions at least to assure the contact of the Soviets with Romania.

At the same time Beck will ask Patek at Foreign Affairs what the real intentions of the Soviets are in the question of the pact with us, the more so as, Beck says, the Republic of the Soviets has no interest in not signing with Romania, also having in mind the clause about honoring previous treaties stipulated expressly in Poland's pact with Soviet Russia.

It seems that Poland's minister in Bucharest will receive instructions to explain to the press this "justification" of Poland's attitude.

CADERE

DOCUMENT NO. 78

Telegram, GAFENCU *to* CADERE

Bucharest No. 38929, 22 July 1932

I received telegram No. 2617 in the absence of the prime minister, who left for Cluj yesterday evening. I am authorized to communicate to you the following instructions decided upon previously in full agreement with the prime minister and Minister Titulescu.[116]

You will only seek to obtain a new audience with Marshal Pilsudski. If this is impossible, you will make the following communication to Mr. Beck, asking him on behalf of the prime minister to send it only to the head of the Polish government and Marshal Pilsudski.

(1) The Romanian government makes a last appeal to the Polish government not to sign the Polish-Russian pact of nonaggression before an agreement between Russia and Romania is reached concerning a Russo-Romanian pact of nonaggression. In the troubled time through which we are passing, the Romanian government believes that it is the duty of both Poland and Romania to prove [their] full solidarity in all circumstances. The early signing of Poland, regardless of the information and assurances that the two governments would disseminate, will be justly commented upon by friends and adversaries, as it has been to date, as a weakening of the Polish-Romanian common front.

The Romanian government, desirous of successfully implementing the united Polish-Romanian policy of strengthening peace on our eastern frontier and desirous of maintaining a full unity of action with Poland, has shown its categorical determination to reach an agreement with Russia that, naturally, does not weaken Romania's present situation. It is Poland's turn to prove the value and importance that she attaches to common action and full Polish-Romanian solidarity.

(2) Aside from these general considerations, the Romanian government has a special and precise motive for considering the early signing of Poland in fact [as] an unfriendly act toward Romania that corresponds neither to the spirit nor to the text of our treaty of alliance. In truth, article I of the treaty of guarantee between Romania and Poland says: "Romania and Poland promise to reciprocally respect and to maintain against any external aggression their actual territorial integrity and their present political independence."

At Geneva the negotiations, which are continuing through the mediation of a representative of the Polish government, are frustrated by Russia's insistence on introducing in the Russo-Romanian pact of nonaggression the express recognition of the existence of a territorial litigation. Of course, Romania cannot explicitly recognize the existence of such a litigation, which places her territorial integrity itself in question, without weakening her present situation. The Polish government has recognized the full justice of the Romanian point of view. Moreover, the Polish foreign minister, in the name of the Polish government, made the official and formal declaration to Mr. Titulescu that "Poland will never ratify her pact of nonaggression with the Soviets as long as the Soviets ask that Romania recognize Bessarabia as a litigious territory." What meaning can Poland's signing have now, when everyone knows that if Romania also cannot [sign] it is because Russia asks, through Polish mediation, to reach an agreement [in which she would] accept a formula contrary to the principle of her present territorial integrity? And what faith can Romania now place in her alliance with Poland, [which is] designed to defend us from any aggression . . . carried out against our actual territorial integrity, when at the first threat that Russia seeks to make against our territorial integrity—and not by arms but by simple formula—Poland clearly abandons us by her early signing?

(3) In case the Polish government does not take into account this last appeal that we address to them, we have already taken measures to prepare our public opinion for Poland's eventual early signing. We have given the press the following information: Poland's signing does not mean a weakening of the Polish-Romanian alliance. The fullest agreement does not cease to exist· between Poland and Romania.

> Poland's signing must not be interpreted as Poland's separation from Romania in the question of the pact of nonaggression because Poland took pains to give Romania an official assurance that she will not ratify the accord with the Soviets until Romania has also concluded a similar accord with the Soviets. Despite [the fact] that between Romania and the Soviets there already exists a Kellogg Pact, by which the Soviets have renounced war, Romania, nonetheless, desires to conclude with the Soviets a pact of nonaggression similar to that of Poland, but respecting her legitimate interests. The assurances of the Polish government are of a nature to justify the belief of the Romanian government that, through negotiations that continue, the end desired by all in the consolidation of the existing peace can be attained.

These declarations, made only with the aim of calming our public opinion and of making foreign commentary less harsh, do not modify in the least the opinions of the Romanian government expressed in points 1 and 2. The Romanian government believes that it is absolutely necessary, in order for the Polish-Romanian alliance not to lose any value in public opinion, that the Polish government make, in its turn, equally precise and categoric declarations particularly concerning the Polish government's decision to connect the ratification of the Polish-Russian pact of nonaggression with the conclusion of a similar pact between Russia and Romania.

GAFENCU

DOCUMENT NO. 79

Diplomatic note (by hand), CADERE *to* BECK

Warsaw, 23 July 1932

The Royal Government of Romania—given the gravity of the present circumstances—believes that it is a duty as much for Romania as for Poland to prove [their] steadfast solidarity in order to dispel . . . any impression of a weakening of their alliance.

A unified attitude is necessary as a witness of that solidarity, and the Royal Government of Romania asks the Government of the Republic not to sign its pact of nonaggression before Romania in her turn has reached an agreement with the Soviets.

In effect, the Royal Government of Romania has shown itself ready to sign a pact of nonaggression with the USSR on the express condition that in any case this pact should neither imply the recognition of a territorial litigation nor constitute a step backward from the Protocol of Moscow of 1929.

The fact that at Geneva the representative of the Soviets has constantly endeavored to impose the clause about a territorial litigation is considered by the Royal Government as an unfriendly act, in total contradiction with article I of the Treaty of Guarantee between Romania and Poland. This act is, at the same time, contrary to the preliminary conditions that made the resumption of negotiations for the pacts of nonaggression possible.

The Royal Government therefore believes that, by its premature signature, the Republic of Poland—friend and ally—should not countenance an action that may be interpreted as contrary to the spirit and to the letter of the Treaty of Guarantee that unites the two countries, especially at a time when the Soviets present, through Poland's intermediary, a formula opposed to the territorial integrity consecrated by article I of the said Treaty.

On the other hand, the Royal Government of Romania believes necessary the confirmation by a categorical declaration by the Government of the Republic of Poland that the ratification of the Polish-Soviet pact of nonaggression will not take place until after the conclusion of the pact between Romania and the Republic of Soviets.

The Royal Government attaches the greatest importance to common action and the full solidarity between the two countries.

It awaits the effective proof of this solidarity by the Polish Government.

DOCUMENT NO. 80

Press release, ROMANIAN MINISTRY OF FOREIGN AFFAIRS

Bucharest, 25 July 1932

In order to put an end to any misinformation concerning the conditions in which the Polish signing has taken place, the Ministry of Foreign Affairs makes the following official communiqué.[117]

Poland's signing must not be interpreted as a separation of Poland from Romania in the question of the pact of nonaggression because Poland has taken pains to give Romania her official assurance that she will not ratify the agreement with the Soviets until Romania has also concluded a similar agreement with the Soviets.

Although the Polish-Romanian alliance . . . remains in force, and despite [the fact] that between Romania and the Soviets there exists the Kellogg Pact by which the Soviets have already renounced war, Romania is nonetheless desirous of concluding with the Soviets a new pact of non-aggression similar to that of Poland, but respecting her legitimate interests.

The assurances of the Polish government are of a nature to justify the belief of the Romanian government that she will be able to attain the goal desired by all in the general interest of the consolidation of the existing peace.

DOCUMENT NO. 81

Letter, GAFENCU *to* CADERE

Bucharest No. 39550, 25 July 1932

Count Szembek came to see me today, July 25, inquiring about the form and terms in which Mr. Zaleski gave us the declaration concerning the ratification.

Although Count Szembek sidestepped making any precise declaration, I had the impression that the Polish government is seeking a way in which to renege in the question of the ratification. In obscure and hesitating terms, Mr. Szembek left me to understand that his government feared that we had somehow misunderstood the engagement made by Poland in the question of the ratification. The Polish government believes that it really promised to postpone the ratification of the Polish-Russian pact for a while in order to give Romania time to reach an understanding with Russia, but that it did not promise to postpone the ratification until the conclusion of the Russo-Romanian pact.

I bluntly answered Count Szembek that it is not a question of a mis-understanding but of a formal and precise obligation that the Polish Foreign Minister had made in the name of his government to Romania. I most energetically added that the Romanian government could not allow Poland to renege on this promise.

Please use just as firm language with Mr. Beck. You will show him that the Romanian government considers the Polish government bound by Mr. Zaleski's declaration.

For the central interest in our relations of alliance it is not possible to rely on the promises and declarations that change from day to day as the interests of the moment may dictate. The fate of our alliance depends on loyalty and on our steadfastness in the reciprocal engagements we make. In this case, the fate of our alliance depends on the loyalty and stead-fastness with which Poland will respect the engagement made concerning ratification.

In its communiqué the Romanian government expressed its defini-tive and irrevocable point of view regarding this question, both on the basis of the precise declarations made by the Polish foreign minister, and on the basis of the faith that it maintains in the Polish-Romanian alliance.

Concerning the communiqué that the Polish government will make, you will ask that this communiqué correspond to ours.

In case you become convinced that any insistence on our part is use-less and that Poland is not able to confirm in a public communiqué the information comprised in our communiqué, you will make it clear that the official declaration of the Polish foreign minister in the question of ratification, [a] declaration that we did not ask for and for which we had no need of confirmation, remains definitive and irrevocable for us.[118]

GAFENCU

DOCUMENT NO. 82
(Reg. No. 41576)

Letter, CADERE *to* VAIDA-VOEVOD

Warsaw No. 2720, 25 July 1932
STRICTLY CONFIDENTIAL—A CONVERSATION WITH
MESSRS. BECK AND SCHAETZEL

Mr. Prime Minister,

I have the honor of informing Your Excellency that today, after the lunch I offered Mr. Beck, the undersecretary of state at the Ministry of

Foreign Affairs, [a lunch] that was also attended by the director of eastern policy, Mr. Schaetzel, who had returned from Geneva this very morning, as well as [by] the first secretary of the legation, G. Davidescu, I had a prolonged conversation with Mr. Beck about the situation created for Romania by the Polish government's decision to sign the pact of nonaggression with the Soviet Republic.

Having inquired of Mr. Schaetzel about the result of his meetings with Litvinov in Geneva, he informed me that the people's commissar of foreign affairs had declared himself disposed to reopen the negotiations with Romania at [the time of] the resumption of the work of the Secretariat of the Disarmament Conference, that is, on September 21. Nevertheless, until this date any other occasion might be used. Thus September 21, the date indicated, would be the latest moment for the resumption of the negotiations.

With all the failures of the past, Mr. Schaetzel still has the hope that before the resumption of the negotiations . . . a formula that reconciles the two theses concerning the known "difference" will be found. [It is his impression that] a definitive renunciation by the Soviets of their demand concerning such a formula [is not to be expected].

On his part Mr. Beck expressed the conviction that after the failure of the Geneva negotiations and after the signing of the Polish-Russian pact, it certainly will not be much more difficult to arrive at an understanding with the Soviets.

In an obviously annoyed tone, Mr. Beck then told me that the declarations given to the Romanian press from [an] official source concerning the engagement made by the Polish government not to present the pact with the Soviets for ratification before a similar pact is concluded between [the USSR] and Romania, has put the Polish government in a very delicate situation about which, for the moment, it does not see what is to be done. He regrets that these declarations were made in a form that corresponded neither to the engagements nor to the intentions of the Polish government.

I pointed out to Mr. Beck that the Bucharest newspapers published the known declarations in a different manner than the Polish press and that the version that seemed to me [to be] the most exact is the one published in *Universul* on July 24.

Mr. Beck then remarked that *Le Temps* of July 24 recorded the communiqué from Bucharest in a form against which he had no objection; however, the form in which the Romanian communiqué was officially transmitted to the Polish press [of Sunday] by RADOR did not correspond with reality because, Mr. Beck added, the Polish government had not promised not to ratify its pact with the Soviets as long as a similar one was not concluded between Romania and the USSR.[119] In reality, although the Polish government—on the basis of constitutional stipulations—could present the pact immediately for ratification to the president of the Republic, it wished, nonetheless, not to undertake this action, but to leave Romania some time to try again to reach an understanding with the Soviet Republic.

I pointed out to Mr. Beck the responsibility that weighs upon the Polish government in the question of engaging in the negotiations, because no Romanian would ever consent to resume the Riga negotiations with the Soviets without having the formal assurance, transmitted by the Polish government itself, that the question of Bessarabia would remain completely left out of these negotiations. In Geneva, it was the Polish representative himself who transmitted to Romania's representative the Soviet formula that represented a new attack against our territorial integrity, and Mr. Zaleski was personally persuaded of the Soviets' bad faith toward us. If the Polish government now accepts such Soviet maneuvers, what will happen when Romania is attacked by the Soviets with more powerful means? This means favoring the Soviets in contradiction to our alliance.

Mr. Beck repeated the assurances that nothing could disturb the integrity of our alliance because article IV of the pact provides sufficient guarantees. Then he revealed the fact that if the question of the pacts was thus introduced, this was the responsibility of the French government (of Mr. Laval), who, because of domestic considerations, was inducing other governments to take the same course.

I then reminded Mr. Beck of the conversation I had with Marshal Pilsudski on July 3—which he witnessed—and in which I obtained two assurances: (1) that the signing of the Polish-Soviet pact would be postponed until after the presumed return of Mr. Litvinov to Moscow, thus, to about July 20; (2) that the ratification of the Polish-Russian pact would only take place simultaneously with our pact with the Soviets; that I warned him even then, without him making any objection, that these points would be telegraphed to Bucharest, after which . . . Mr. Schaetzel [also] made no objection when I told him on July 9 that the Romanian government had taken note of Marshal Pilsudski's declaration.

Mr. Beck in no way denied these things. However, in response he expressed regret that, through the official declaration [that] appeared in the press, "today an attempt was made to force the hand of the Polish government" to obligate itself in a direction it did not wish to take.

I also reminded Mr. Beck of the engagement made by Mr. Zaleski to Mr. Titulescu in Geneva, which he [Mr. Beck] interpreted as a dilatory engagement, confirming what was expressed in my telegram of July 15, in my report of July 21, and in [my] letter of July 23.

He was satisfied to tell me that the Polish government is obliged to follow the path begun after the Baltic States had greatly accelerated their action (Finland, especially, was the one that most hastened to ratify). Poland cannot now abandon the Baltic States, which are exposed to the intense political and economic action of the Soviets.

Here Mr. Beck gave precious evidence that sheds true light on the entire question of the pact of nonaggression and of the connection with the Baltic States.

Poland has a treaty of alliance with Romania, which remains valid for any eventuality as a result of article IV of the Polish-Soviet pact of non-aggression. However, she is not bound to the Baltic States by similar treaties.

Thus, Poland, in her desire to secure her left flank, desires at any price as close a connection as possible with the Baltic States. Toward this end she does not hesitate to foster as conscious a spirit of independence as possible in these countries, since, in case of conflict [with the USSR], the Baltic States would play the role of a "Belgium of the Eastern front."

In other words, Mr. Beck is reduced to the following: Poland is sure of Romania's immediate collaboration in any circumstances, while a similar assurance in the North must be created now. . . . In this way of thinking, our "difference" with the Soviets appears as an actual advantage for Poland, since it is a guarantee to her that Romania will not be able to have another political orientation as long as it is believed that only the Polish-Romanian treaty of alliance guarantees Romania her territorial integrity.

*   *   *   *

Mr. Beck again assured me that in the conference that will take place in Wilno Thursday between Marshal Pilsudski, Mr. Prystor, president of the Council of Ministers, and himself, the object of my communication of Saturday the twenty-third will be discussed and that then he will give me the definitive response of the Polish government.[120]

From today's conversation as from our other recent meetings, I have gained the impression that Poland not only will extricate herself from responsibility in the question of the resumption of our negotiations with the Soviets, but also that, after the separate negotiations with the Soviets, contrary to her initial assurances to negotiate only concomitantly with us, and after the separate signing of the pact as well as after the interpretation that she seeks to give the recent engagements, Poland's independent ratification should not surprise us.

* * * *

Just as Messrs. Beck and Schaetzel were leaving the Legation grounds, I received the telephone communication of the PAT Agency announcing that the Polish-Soviet pact was signed in Moscow at three o'clock.[121]

VICTOR CADERE

DOCUMENT NO. 83

Diplomatic note (by hand), CADERE *to* SCHAETZEL *(Polish Director of Eastern Policy)*

Warsaw, 30 July 1932

By order of his government, the minister of Romania has the honor of informing Your Excellency [Schaetzel] that the official declaration of His Excellency, Mr. Auguste Zaleski, minister of foreign affairs of Poland—[a] declaration by the terms of which Poland will not proceed to the ratification of the pact of nonaggression with the Soviet Republic as long as the Soviets maintain their pretension concerning "the territorial litigation"—is considered by the Royal Romanian Government as definitive and irrevocable.[122]

The Final Phase,
August to October 1932

DOCUMENT NO. 84
(Reg. No. 41402 of 4 August 1932)

Decoded telegram, CESIANU *to* MINISTRY OF FOREIGN AFFAIRS

Paris No. 1260, 3 August 1932

STRICTLY CONFIDENTIAL—FOR THE PRIME MINISTER

Referring to your telegram No. 40980, [which] arrived yesterday evening.[123]

Late this afternoon I had a long meeting with Herriot. I faithfully maintained the Romanian government's point of view, also reviewing the history of the facts because I have followed the question assiduously from its origin, that is, from [last] May, and in addition I have recently had some explanations and details from Minister Titulescu about what [was] discussed in Switzerland.

Herriot gave specific attention to my démarche; then he said:

"I think Romania will have to decide in one way or another. To want or not to want to conclude the nonaggression pact are two attitudes each of which can be sustained with their arguments; but [we must] decide in a not overly prolonged period because clear situations are the best.

"I say [so] as a convinced friend of Romania. The system of procrastinating to gain time is not at all good.

"For France the nonaggression pact with the Soviets does not imply a guarantee of the Rhine frontier but at most a relative calm in the colonies.

"Surely, Romania knows better than anyone what she has to do. As her friend, and within the complex of East European politics—especially when Poland and the Baltic countries have signed pacts of nonaggression—I believe it would be best if Romania did the same. However, I do not wish to push her into this. It is only a piece of advice."

I replied:

"You know, of course, what ruined the Riga negotiations."

"I know," Herriot answered. "However, Romania has not the slightest illusion that the Soviets will ever recognize the annexation of Bessarabia.

"Dovgalevski told me so as did Litvinov repeatedly and he wrote me himself in this vein." (Herriot read me some passages and other sentences from the Franco-Soviet dossier.)

"I reread," said Herriot, "even this very morning the act by which the allies of the Great War recognized Romania's Bessarabia; but today we also have the League of Nations." (I showed surprise.)

To my persistent request to make a friendly but powerfully insistent intervention in Warsaw to convince [Poland] not to ratify, to point out the gravity of Warsaw's intended action, and to show bewilderment about the nonrecognition there of the engagement made by Zaleski in Lausanne, Herriot said: "The ambassador of France being absent from Warsaw, I will call on Poland's ambassador and I will insist.[124]

"But even if I succeed with the Polish government, how long a respite will this be? And I cannot say that I will succeed since the marshal is stubborn, as is Colonel Beck. He also has some sympathy for puritanical movements [such] as the Soviet theories.

"The [possible] disservice to Poland is the prolonged delay in making a definite decision and [the risk] of a discovery like the secret correspondence of General Averescu with the Italian government, known today by all the chancelleries, and of the obligations that resulted."[125]

I answered that there is no likelihood of Warsaw not listening to French advice when it is given with special emphasis.

Herriot answered, "I hope [so], but how long will she take it into account?

"However little value a pact with the Soviets can have, and even if such a pact does not mean the assurance that aggression has been ruled out, the value of the pact is that . . . given that the succession of pacts has been embarked upon, it can assure you of more certain support and aid even on the part of others than allies . . . than you would have had, perhaps, without that pact.

"In concluding a pact with Romania, the Soviets are disposed to guarantee that no territorial litigation be resolved by arms [and] not to attack the frontier of Bessarabia."

I pointed out, "But for us a territorial litigation does not exist." And I asked, "Do you believe the Soviets would ever say anything about Bessarabia that suited us?"

He answered me: "Perhaps not. But a satisfactory formula could be found, and if you wish we will find it together.

"If Romania makes up its mind to resume discussion of the non-aggression pact, do not lose too much more time."

I asked: "Should we take a negative attitude, what will France do? Would she or would she not conclude a pact with the Soviets?"

Herriot answered, "Although the Soviets urge us to take a position, we will not answer positively [but will] wait for you."

I replied, "Would such an attitude on France's part be definitive?"

Herriot answered, "I cannot answer today, and as a matter of fact the dossier concerning the eventual Franco-Soviet pact of nonaggression has not yet been studied by [the] government."

CESIANU

DOCUMENT NO. 85

Romanian draft of Treaty of Nonaggression between Romania and the USSR

The Central Executive Committee of the Union of Soviet Socialist Republics on the one hand and His Majesty the King of Romania on the other hand;

Animated by a desire to consolidate the peace, having the firm conviction that reinforcement of the peaceful relations existing between the two Contracting Parties corresponds to their interests and constitutes an important element in the work of maintaining universal peace;

Loyal to the international obligations that they have previously assumed and declaring that the obligations of the present treaty would not be able to either modify or impair them, inasmuch as these obligations contain no element tending toward aggression;

Have resolved to conclude the present Treaty of Nonaggression, having as its end the completion of the Treaty of Renunciation of War signed in Paris on August 27, 1928, placed into force by the Protocol signed in Moscow on February 9, 1929, and to this end have designated as their plenipotentiaries, to wit:

The Central Executive Committee of the USSR————.

His Majesty the King of Romania ————.

Who, after being communicated their full powers, found in good and due form, have agreed to the following stipulations:

I.

The High Contracting Parties again solemnly affirm the validity and importance of the obligations they assumed in virtue of the Treaty of

Renunciation of War (Kellogg-Briand) signed on August 27, 1928, and placed into force by the Protocol of Moscow signed on February 9, 1929.

II.

The two High Contracting Parties agree to consider as contrary to the obligations foreseen in the aforementioned treaties any aggression separately or jointly with other powers on land, on the sea, or in the air, as well as any act of violence threatening the political independence, the inviolability, and the integrity of territory even if such acts are committed without declarations of war and avoiding all its possible consequences.

III.

In case of one of the Contracting Parties becoming the object of an aggression on the part of a third State or of a group of third States, the other Contracting Party promises to observe neutrality during the entire duration of the conflict.

In case one of the High Contracting Parties resorts to an aggression against a third State, the other Contracting Party will be free to deprive it of the benefit of the present Treaty.

IV.

The present Treaty will be ratified as soon as possible and the instruments of ratification exchanged in Geneva. It will enter into force the day of this exchange.

PROTOCOL OF SIGNATURE

The High Contracting Parties agree that the present Treaty will not in any case be susceptible of being interpreted in such a way that it might ever have as [a] consequence the restriction or extinction of the obligations derived from the Treaty signed in Paris on August 27, 1928.

DOCUMENT NO. 86

News dispatch, Romanian Telegraph Agency (Orient-RADOR)

Bucharest, 16 August 1932

DECLARATIONS MADE BY PRIME MINISTER VAIDA-VOEVOD
IN THE CHAMBER OF DEPUTIES SESSION OF 16 AUGUST 1932

Today, responding to interpellations on foreign policy made by [Ion] Inculeț and Georges Brătianu concerning Poland's signature of her pact of nonaggression,[126] Prime Minister Vaida declared: "It is an international custom respected by all governments and by all states not to discuss an ongoing diplomatic action in public debate. I will, therefore, limit myself to giving the following reply to Messrs. Inculeț and Brătianu: 'In its communiqué issued on the day following Poland's signature of her pact of nonaggression, the Romanian government underlined its strict policy and loyal alliance toward Poland as well as its resolutely peaceful policy toward Russia.[127] At the Genoa Conference of 1922, Ion Brătianu, then chief of the Romanian government, affirmed Romania's desire to conclude a pact of nonaggression with Russia. All the succeeding Romanian governments since then have been prepared to prove their absolutely peaceful intentions toward Russia. In February 1929, the government of Mr. Iuliu Maniu succeeded in giving a concrete form to these intentions by signing the Litvinov Protocol in Moscow, which put into force early the Kellogg Pact between Russia and all her western neighbors. The stipulations against war contained in the Kellogg Pact thereafter received explanations and precious clarifications thanks to the efforts of the League of Nations. A few days after that Mr. Stimson, secretary of state of the United States, made a resounding declaration from which emerged the absolute conviction, entirely shared by Romania, that the Kellogg Pact not only had the character of a declaration of good intentions, but also that it is a treaty of obligation. Besides, the signatories of the Litvinov Protocol and, primarily, the representatives of the Soviet government underlined the fact that, given that the pact signed in Moscow had as its aim the safeguarding of peace in a definite geographical sector running from the Baltic Sea to the Black Sea, it had the character and importance of a true pact of nonaggression. Today Romania is still prepared to conclude a new pact of nonaggression with the Soviets similar to the Polish pact in its respect for our legitimate interests. The assurances of allied governments justify our hope that, by a common and united action, the goal so desired by all might be attained in the general interest of the consolidation of the existing peace.' "

DOCUMENT NO. 87

Intradepartmental memo no. 1 by GAFENCU

Constanța, 29 August 1932
CONVERSATIONS WITH COLONEL BECK, UNDERSECRETARY OF STATE,
AND THE POLISH MINISTRY OF FOREIGN AFFAIRS

We passed on to discussion of the nonaggression pacts.

Colonel Beck reviewed the history of the Polish-Russian negotiations. He stressed the fact that the initiative for these negotiations came from France, who twice asked Poland to prepare a pact of nonaggression with Russia similar to the one that [she] herself was desirous of concluding with the Soviets. In July 1931 Poland answered France that she saw no inconvenience if France alone were to conclude such a pact expressly safeguarding the obligations of the Franco-Polish alliance. Only as a result of new French prodding, and after the Franco-Soviet draft pact had been finished and initialed, did the Polish government decide to begin negotiations with Russia and advised Romania to do the same. The Polish-Russian negotiations were concluded and [the pact] initialed during the winter, but the signing was postponed in order to give Romania time to reach an understanding with Russia. Poland thus only considered her negotiations with Russia and the signing of the pact as a good piece of diplomatic administration, the result of favorable international circumstances, and not as the beginning of a new political orientation, much less [as] the shifting of the Polish political axis toward the East. Such an action cannot in the least weaken the solid and permanent basis of Polish foreign policy, which is and will always be our present system of alliances—in the first place, the indestructible one that binds Poland to Romania. Poland was thus surprised when she witnessed the commotion that her signature stirred up in Romania and the unusually agitated commentaries of the Romanian press.

I answered that the agitated state of Romanian public opinion proved how deeply we valued the Polish alliance and the importance we attached to it. In any event of international significance we undergo a reaction that proves that for us the Polish alliance is not some text that we are naturally prepared to respect as Poland will also respect it, but that it represents still more—a common constant action to which we owe the most happy results. I recall the results obtained by common action that led to the signing of the Litvinov Protocol. It is an action we followed [independently] of suggestions received from the West and sometimes even against these suggestions. We should never have departed from the complete solidarity that characterized this action and its results. Perhaps France, which did not realize the importance the Litvinov Protocol has for us, urged us to depart from it not realizing that it would thus weaken our situation vis-à-vis Russia [and] concluding, instead of a common and unified pact, parallel pacts of nonaggression. However, it is surprising that Poland, which knew all the benefits of the success obtained by the Polish-Romanian diplomatic collaboration, accepted a policy that is destined to separate us—in any case to weaken the bond between us. Thus, I believe that the reaction of Romanian public opinion was a healthy reaction that draws everyone's attention to the danger of permitting united Polish-Romanian action to weaken. And this reaction is especially natural as it occurred at a time when Romania proved that she was determined out of friendship for *Poland* to follow the trail Poland had broken. Poland's signature, postponed at Romania's request, intervened brusquely and unexpectedly just when in Geneva a representative of the Polish Foreign Ministry was endeavoring to obtain Russia's consent for Mr. Titulescu's conciliatory formula.[128] By hastening her signature, Poland encouraged Bolshevik resistance and brought about the rupture of negotiations that could have led to a happy result. And the misunderstanding that, on the day of Poland's signing, separated the Russian from the Romanian thesis was Russia's unjustified pretension of introducing recognition of the Bessarabian litigation in the pact of nonaggression with Romania—a recognition that would weaken the principle of our territorial integrity, [a] principle that, by article 1 of our treaty of alliance with Poland we are mutually obliged to defend by [force of] arms. Here are enough motives [to] justify the anxiety of the press and our public opinion concerning the future of the Polish-Romanian alliance.

Without responding to my counterargument, Colonel Beck talked to us about the information received from Russia. For internal and external motives—the financial crisis in Russia, the threats in the Far East, [and] the weakening of the Russian-German friendship and complicity—Russia is now ready to sign pacts of nonaggression with her western neighbors. It is absolutely necessary to profit from this opportunity. Russia's signature has no great value. Nevertheless, when placed upon an act of nonaggression it contributes to the quieting and relieving of international anxieties. The Polish government is convinced that Russia is disposed to conclude a pact with Romania as well. Perhaps until now Romania's efforts have not been determined enough. Poland does not presume to give us advice. However, she declares herself ready, through the mediation of Mr. Patek, the best expert on Soviet Russia, to discover today what are Moscow's intentions concerning a Russian-Romanian pact and to facilitate as much as possible the preparation of such a pact.

I answered that we were determined to reach an agreement with Russia that, naturally, did not weaken Romania's situation. The proof of this determination is the last formula proposed by Mr. Titulescu, to wit, a pact of nonaggression that contains nothing more than a solemn reiteration of the Kellogg Pact, with the qualifications added to this pact by the League of Nations reinforced by a reciprocal pledge of neutrality in case of aggression. We do not see how such a formula can be rejected by Russia if Russia is well disposed. It is the reiteration of an understanding concluded two [*sic*] years ago and already carrying Russia's signature, [an] agreement strengthened in Russia's favor by a pledge of neutrality and by the fact that, instead of a collective signature, this engagement will only carry the signatures of Russia and Romania. On the other hand, if Russia proves her bad faith by rejecting this formula, we do not understand why Poland separates herself from us, finalizing the signature that she has placed on her pact of nonaggression with Russia.

As far as we are concerned, we are ready, as the prime minister declared in Parliament,[129] to profit from the so-called good inclinations of Russia and to conclude a pact of nonaggression with her. We believe that in order to arrive at the conclusion [of a pact] with Russia we must observe two conditions:

1. That we prove we are not raising any unjustified pretension and that the pact we desire to sign conforms with the spirit and the text of all other pacts of nonaggression;
2. That we convince Russia that the value of concluding pacts of nonaggression with her neighbors would be greater than the value of separating these neighbors.

The first condition depends on us alone. We have abundantly proved our good will and our good faith. The second condition depends on Poland as well. We must present ourselves as a well-united bloc toward Russia. If not, we will be playing the Bolshevik diplomatic game. And Romania is determined not to carry this game any further.

We terminated the discussion with these words, deciding to resume [our talks] the next day in Bucharest.

[GAFENCU]

DOCUMENT NO. 88

Intradepartmental memo no. 2 by GAFENCU

N.p., n.d.

VISIT OF MR. BECK AT THE ROYAL MINISTRY
OF FOREIGN AFFAIRS

In continuation of the discussions occasioned by the visit of Mr. Beck, meetings resulted at Minister Gafencu's house on August 31 and then at the Polish Legation on September 1—meetings that Messrs. Beck, Count

Szembek, Gafencu, and Victor Cadere attended. Discussing diverse formulae recently presented, especially the proposals of Minister Schaetzel and Mr. Titulescu's draft, Mr. Beck said that what is important to follow up now is finding the most suitable technical means to reach the signing of a Romanian-Russian pact [and] that to this end the instructions he gave to Mr. Schaetzel in Geneva were: "That the minimum that must be obtained from the Soviet representatives was the possibility of resuming these discussions through the good offices of Polish representatives wherever he could until the opening of the League of Nations session, at which time the discussions would continue in Geneva." In its role as mediator, the Polish government firmly pledges to place at the Romanian government's disposition all the means at its disposal to facilitate the Russo-Romanian understanding. That, in this vein, as soon as he returns to Warsaw, he will be informed of the current dispositions of [his] Soviet colleagues.

However, concerning a firm promise that the fate of the Polish-Russian pact [should depend] absolutely on the signing of a Romanian-Russian pact of nonaggression, he could not undertake any kind of obligation in the name of the Polish government. Concerning the declarations that Mr. Zaleski allegedly made to Mr. Titulescu, he believes that the problem was a "misunderstanding," since these declarations were made by Mr. Zaleski to Mr. Litvinov in order to exercise pressure in view of the signing of a pact with Romania. [This was an] attitude that he himself had taken with the Soviet representative in Warsaw when, being asked by the latter about the date of ratification, Mr. Beck declared, "This is entirely up to you. Hurry up and reach an agreement with Romania."

As a result, concluded Mr. Beck, Mr. Zaleski's declarations could not in any case be interpreted as conveying a pledge to the Romanian government. At the same time, it is morally impossible [for] the Polish government to renege on the question of her pact of nonaggression only because of the meanings of such words as difference, litigation, etc., that some interpretations attributed to them. [The Polish-Soviet pact] represented the result of the political direction of an entire people preoccupied with its own difficulties.

To this Mr. Gafencu answered in the following way: No misunderstanding exists concerning the formal and precise promise made by Mr. Zaleski in the name of his government to Mr. Titulescu tying Poland's ratification to the conclusion of a Russian-Romanian understanding. It is correct that Mr. Zaleski made a declaration to Mr. Titulescu in the sense explained by Colonel Beck. Three days later, however, Mr. Zaleski made a new declaration concerning the ratification and this declaration was made in categorical terms that need no explanation, no interpretation, and no commentary.

Passing then to the proposals of Colonel Beck, Mr. Gafencu said the following: In the situation in which we find ourselves, we propose for the friendly and allied Polish government more than the role of mediator. If we agree on a minimal formula, the Polish government would promise in exchange to impose this formula as a result of concerted action, and as a demonstration of the alliance between the two countries. This would make the finalization of the Polish-Russian pact conditional on the success of the signing of this minimal Romanian-Russian pact. Concerning the formula that gives the most satisfaction to both parties, we have at hand the Titulescu proposal, which has the advantage of being a development of the Kellogg Pact, accepted and signed by the Soviets. Along with the pact already existing between us and them, [by] accepting the Titulescu formula the Soviets also gain:

a. The convention of neutrality
b. The isolated signing of Romania
c. A special protocol of signature by which "the contracting parties agree that the pact of nonaggression cannot be, in any case, interpreted in such a way as to ever have as [a] consequence the restriction or widening of the engagements resulting from the Kellogg Pact."

By this procedure a Russian-Romanian pact that the Romanian government sincerely desires to sign could be reached very soon. Not out of consideration that the country's security or other questions under discussion would gain something by this signature, but in order to pursue a common action with the allies, thus providing proof of the most complete solidarity, even though the point of departure of our allies in these "suprapacts" *is questionable.*

In the case that the Polish government obtains the consent of the Soviets on the basis of the above proposal, [a] proposal that must be presented to the Soviets not as a Romanian proposal but as a Polish formula, then the Romanian government is ready in twenty-four hours to sign this protocol of nonaggression wherever, for example in Geneva, Vienna, Constantinople, etc. If not, that is if the Soviet government raises objections to the Titulescu draft and asks modifications of this draft or a return to the Litvinov-Schaetzel draft, *then the Romanian government sees no inconvenience in the Polish government,* by its own initiative and on its own responsibility, seeking to discover *the Soviet point of view for preparing the conversations that would be resumed on September 22 in Geneva.*

In this case, however, Mr. Gafencu insists on the following two points:

1. It is necessary that the soundings in Moscow not lead to the impossibility of resuming the negotiations in Geneva or somehow prejudice Romania's situation and her liberty of action and decision when the conversations begin again in Geneva.
2. The Romanian government continues to have strong reservations about the last formula of Mr. Schaetzel, which does not satisfy the thesis sustained by Mr. Titulescu in Geneva; the formula of Mr. Schaetzel reading, in the preamble after paragraph 4: "stating that the present treaty can prejudice nothing in the relations between the two contracting parties beyond nonaggression"; and in article I: "as well as all attempts to settle by violence all differences between the two contracting parties."

Mr. Beck recognizes that the Titulescu formula is acceptable. All the same he believes that a discussion centered on this formula could have two inconveniences:

a. That being a completely new formula it could again give birth to a Soviet counterproposal, and so the discussion could become interminable;
b. That the word "difference" must not be made an occasion by the Romanian government for categorical nonacceptance [of a pact] with the Soviets. He further suggests on this occasion that continuation of the discussions might somehow benefit from a direct meeting of a Romanian representative with a Soviet one. Mr. Gafencu said that this was *entirely impossible* and that the hypothesis of direct meetings *must be completely excluded.*

After these discussions it was agreed that:

(1) The Polish government will present as its formula the nonaggression pact stemming from the Kellogg Pact in the Titulescu version and that if this pact is accepted, the Romanian government will immediately proceed to sign it;

(2) That in any case, conforming to what [was] agreed in the last session in Geneva, the Polish government will continue its mediator's role between Romania and the Soviets, putting every means of pressure at its disposal on Moscow with a view to reaching the signing of a Russian-Romanian pact of nonaggression.

[GAFENCU]

DOCUMENT NO. 89

Diplomatic note (by hand), CRETZIANU *to* HAUTECLOQUE

Bucharest, 2 September 1932

(1) The Romanian government warmly thanks the president of the French Council [of Ministers] for the solicitude he displays in favor of a prompt conclusion of the Romanian-Soviet nonaggression pact.[130]

The Romanian government assures Mr. Herriot and the French government that it will spare no effort in order to arrive most rapidly at an accord with the USSR that corresponds to the most elementary exigencies of its security and its interests.

(2) The French government appears to base the support it intends to give the Romanian government to succeed in the negotiations with the USSR on three conditions:

> *a.* Resumption of the Soviet negotiations with the briefest delay, that is, before the foreseen date of September 21
> *b.* Renunciation of any demand for direct or indirect recognition by the USSR of the annexation of Bessarabia
> *c.* Acceptance of a formula that expressly relates, as the government of the USSR demands, to the existing litigious question.

The Romanian government's point of view concerning these three conditions is the following:

(*a*) Romania just agreed with the Polish government, through the intervention of Colonel Beck, undersecretary of state for foreign affairs of Poland, about the immediate resumption of the Polish-Soviet conversations concerning the Romanian-Soviet pact of nonaggression. Mr. Patek, Poland's minister in Moscow, will immediately propose to the government of the USSR a draft [of a] Russo-Romanian pact simplified to the point of eliminating any possible opposition on the part of the USSR. This draft, whose terms the Romanian government has communicated to France's chargé d'affaires in Bucharest, restricts itself to repeating the stipulations of the Kellogg Pact, solemnly affirming once more the value and importance of the obligations contained in this pact.

An explicatory article contains the qualifications given to the sense and the extent of the Kellogg Pact in Geneva.

The draft stipulates, moreover, a neutrality clause in case one of the contracting parties becomes the object of aggression on the part of a third state. In a protocol of signature, the high contracting parties agree that the treaty cannot in any case be interpreted in such a way that it can ever have as a consequence the restriction or extension of the obligations contracted in Paris on August 27, 1928.

The Romanian government believes that the Soviet government cannot refuse a draft that contains nothing more in favor of Romania than is already contained in the Kellogg Pact, placed into force in advance in Moscow by the Litvinov Protocol, but that, in exchange, contains a neutrality clause and a protocol of signature in favor of the government of the USSR.

In case the USSR should reject this draft right away by demanding its modification or by wishing to return to the former text that was used as a basis of discussions at Riga and Geneva, the Polish government will keep the Romanian government informed of the Russian objections and will strive to prepare the grounds of agreement for the resumption of negotiations on September 22.

(b) Romania never asked, either at Riga or at Geneva, for the recognition by the USSR, either directly or indirectly, of the annexation of Bessarabia. She will also refrain from doing so in any new negotiation.

On the contrary, Romania opposed at Riga and at Geneva the transformation of the Russian-Romanian pact of nonaggression into a pact of recognition of an existing territorial litigation. Romania does not recognize the existence of any litigation that endangers her territorial integrity. By signing and ratifying the Treaty of Paris of 1920 on Bessarabia, France has solemnly confirmed the Romanian point of view. Romania cannot deviate from an attitude that is at the very foundation of its policy of security, political independence, and territorial integrity. It is certainly not her ally, France, a signatory to the Treaty of Paris, who can advise her to abandon this policy by recognizing that Bessarabia is a territory in litigation.

In conclusion, the Romanian government believes it has anticipated the desire of the French government by allowing the Polish government to try immediately to resolve the question of the Russian-Romanian pact. The Romanian government believes that if, at the request of Mr. Patek, to whom belongs henceforth the initiative of the conversations in Moscow on the Russian-Romanian pact, the French Embassy lends the determined and energetic support of France's high authority to its Polish colleague, [then] the simplified draft that Mr. Patek will propose to the USSR will be accepted by this power, and that the USSR and Romania will be able to exchange signatures with the briefest delay.

The Romanian government expects an answer from Moscow via the intermediation of Warsaw with the briefest delay. In the case that this response is affirmative, as it hopes, the question raised by the telegram of the president of the French Council [of Ministers] will be immediately resolved.

In the case that the Polish government informs the Romanian government of new objections by the USSR, the Romanian government intends to send to Paris a special delegate to begin without delay the negotiations desired by Mr. Herriot.

DOCUMENT NO. 90

Telegram to French Legation in Bucharest

Paris, 5 September 1932

The intervention prescribed for you with the Romanian government had above all the aim of deciding it to resume negotiations before September 20. Our insistence on this point should be clearly maintained.

As for the formula suggested as [a] point of departure for [the] eventual basis of negotiations, it should necessarily take into account the necessities by which the two parties are inevitably faced. This indication thus provided served to facilitate the Romanian government's task and clearly to enlighten it on the limit of the possibilities that it will encounter on the Russian side. If the Romanian government sincerely believes [that it] can agree with the government of the USSR on a more advantageous incorporation, [then] we will be very happy to receive assurance of it. But you should on this occasion point out to [the Romanian government], in order for it not to mistake the solicitude to which our suggestion bears witness:

1. That the mention judged by it [as] unacceptable did not relate in particular, as your telegram indicates (as a result undoubtedly of a coding error) [to] "the existing territorial litigation," but generally [to] all existing territorial or other litigious questions, and that it might be possible to ask for suppression of the word "territorial" during the course of negotiations;
2. That this mention, excluded from the pact itself and shifted to a simple protocol, could still benefit from the corrective of the final declaration foreseen at the time of signing.

In any case, you will inform Mr. Gafencu that, conforming to his request, we have urgently invited our ambassador in Moscow to support Mr. Patek's démarche to the government of the USSR to hasten and facilitate resumption of the Romanian-Soviet negotiations.

DOCUMENT NO. 91

Intradepartmental memo by CRETZIANU

Bucharest, 9 September 1932

THE ROMANIAN-SOVIET NONAGGRESSION PACT

Count Szembek, the minister of Poland, telephoned me at eight this evening and asked me to pay him a visit [since he wished] to speak with me on an urgent question.

During the meeting that followed, Poland's minister read me passages from the telegram he had received just then from Mr. Beck, Polish undersecretary of state of foreign affairs, informing him of the following:

(1) Mr. Beck had taken advantage of the delay of Mr. Patek's return to his post to personally give him all the necessary instructions, in view of the negotiations that were to begin in Moscow, conforming to what was decided during the meetings in Bucharest.[131]

(2) Mr. Beck knew from the Polish Embassy in Paris about the démarche made by the French government to the Romanian [government] with a view to hastening resumption of the Romanian-Soviet negotiations relative to the conclusion of a pact of nonaggression. Mr. Beck was very surprised by the new formula suggested by Mr. Herriot.[132] That formula seems to him more unfavorable to Romania than the Titulescu draft, than the Schaetzel draft, and even than the latest Litvinov proposals.

The Polish undersecretary of state is also anxious that Mr. Herriot not communicate his formula to the Soviet ambassador in Paris as well.[133] In such a hypothesis Mr. Patek will find himself faced by an understandable Soviet intransigence during the negotiations which would follow in Moscow.

Mr. Beck has instructed the Embassy in Paris to obtain information in this regard.

I answered Mr. Szembek that I will transmit the aforementioned to Mr. Gafencu, and that I would ask him to keep us informed as to the answer he receives from Paris concerning the communication eventually made by Mr. Herriot to the Soviet ambassador.[134] I added that we could not believe, until contrary verification, that such a communication was made. In any case, in face of the promise made by Mr. Herriot that France's ambassador in Moscow will support Mr. Patek's action, we believe that absolutely no change has intervened concerning what was decided on the occasion of Mr. Beck's visit to Bucharest. Therefore we hope that, once he has arrived in Moscow, Mr. Patek will begin talks with

Litvinov on the basis of Mr. Titulescu's draft, and that those talks will have a favorable result.

The Polish minister confirmed that the plan of action settled on in Bucharest will not suffer any modification. However, should the Soviets be informed of the text of the Herriot formula, he fears that the success of Mr. Patek's negotiations would be compromised beforehand.

AL. CRETZIANU

DOCUMENT NO. 92

Telegram, CADERE *to* GAFENCU

Warsaw No. 3339, 15 September 1932

CONVERSATION ON THE HUGHES DEVICE

Patek telegraphs that this morning he had a new meeting with Litvinov, who has unexpectedly decided to leave Moscow this very evening and pass through Warsaw.[135] Litvinov expressed the desire to meet with us at Bialystock or Warsaw, from which point we could begin discussions. The eventual contact would continue in Berlin through the Polish Legation. Litvinov further formulated two wishes:

1. [That] the Romanian delegates have sufficiently full powers;
2. [That] in principle he would wish to make the Riga draft the basis of the discussions.

If no positive result were reached in Berlin, Litvinov could make contact with the Polish foreign minister in Geneva, and the conferences with the Romanian delegates could take place either in Geneva or in another appropriate place.

Patek asks that this time, too, it be kept in strictest secrecy, and would express, with all reservations, the following personal opinion: "He believes that, in face of the attitude of France and Poland, Litvinov is disposed to sign the pact with Romania, seeking, however, to assure himself of the best possible position."

Taking into account the new situation and Litvinov's passing through Warsaw tomorrow, Friday, at ten in the evening, there would [be] sufficient time to realize an agreement in principle. Until now I have not been able to settle on the technical conditions of the meeting, but it is probable that it will take place between Warsaw and Posnan, eventually being able to continue to Berlin. It would be possible formally to give Litvinov the satisfaction of taking as [a] point of departure *various Polish proposals* without specifying which ones. Of course, I would only accept Titulescu's draft, that is, either the pact itself without the protocol of signature, or the pact completed with the already known formula No. 1.[136] For this hypothesis, if the Romanian government wishes on this occasion to go further than simple direct confirmation of its intentions relative to the pact, it would be useful if I have the full powers necessary, thus having the possibility of an immediate action that would have a decided value.

I await your instructions.

CADERE

ANSWER OF MINISTER GAFENCU

The prime minister has agreed that in the case that Litvinov asks to meet you, you [should] place yourself at his disposal. You will therefore take all measures in order to meet Litvinov in Poland without going beyond the borders of that country. We consider your trip in Germany accompanied by Litvinov as inopportune, if only for the reason that it could not be kept an absolute secret. You will show Litvinov that because of technical considerations and lack of time, the Romanian government was not able to authorize you to negotiate with him on the basis of more ample powers. The Romanian government, discovering Litvinov's desire, has urgently directed you to remain at his disposal during transit through Poland in order to confirm to him the Romanian government's desire to reach an agreement with Russia, and in order to be able to better explain by direct contact the problem that interests us. If the prime minister agrees, I will transmit the authorization to initial only Titulescu's draft by a telegram "in the clear"—an authorization that you will be able to show Litvinov during the conversations. *Concerning the way in which you will discuss the different drafts with Litvinov, it remains to your discretion to begin with the draft that suits you, interesting yourself at this time in the best formulae which Litvinov would accept, continuing, however, to push the discussion toward the Titulescu draft, the only one that you can accept.* On this occasion you will point out the superiority of this draft, which contains no equivocation, since it says only what must be said and is impossible to exploit in any way through erroneous interpretation. That is precisely why it does not justify any reservation on his part that would weaken the value of the spirit of relaxation of the pact. You will manifest interest in signing only this simplified draft without any new interventions of new intermediaries. Such an understanding would be the beginning of a policy of relaxation, which we desire. *If Litvinov asks that we establish a direct and permanent contact between our states as he once asked through Davila in Moscow, you must answer that we agree and ask him which among our legations would appear more suitable to make this contact, of course unofficial, with the corresponding Russian legation.* On this occasion you [will] make *an allusion to our economic interests,* among which [are] many similar ones in the basin of the Black Sea.

Before Beck and his government [you will] insist that you will make contact with Litvinov because, as Patek reported, he asked it, and that you speak with Litvinov in order to prove that you do not flee from direct contact and we are ready to facilitate by all means an immediate agreement on our simplified proposal, but not to negotiate in the quality of authorized negotiator. This is in case Patek and Beck take the initiative of your meeting with Litvinov in order to pass the responsibility [for] the negotiations and of their eventual failure on to you.

Please inform [us] if you have understood.

GAFENCU

DOCUMENT NO. 93

Letter (copy), CADERE *to* VAIDA-VOEVOD

Warsaw, 17 September 1932
CONVERSATION WITH LITVINOV—CONFIDENTIAL

Mr. Prime Minister,

I have the honor to inform Your Excellency that, on the basis of the instructions communicated to me by Nos. 48709 and 48764 of September 16, I had with Mr. Litvinov the conversation desired by him during his passage toward Geneva.[137]

The meeting took place between Bialystok and Warsaw because I appreciated, in agreement with Mr. Beck, that the possibility of indiscretion, especially on the part of journalists, is more reduced and the arrangement was more convenient since the conversation would take place between the hours of seven and ten in the evening.

I was accompanied to Bialystok by [Mr. H. Zaniewski, a] counselor from the Polish Ministry of Foreign Affairs and G. Davidescu. (Mr. Zaniewski has for two years fulfilled the function of first secretary of Poland's Legation in Moscow.)

Upon the arrival of the train from the Soviet border at the Bialystok station, I boarded the sleeping compartment that was reserved for me next to the compartment in which the Soviet commissar of foreign affairs and Mrs. Litvinov were traveling.

I was told that Mr. Litvinov was at dinner in the salon car of the foreign minister of Persia, Furugi-Khan, who during his trip to Geneva will stop in Warsaw for a day as the guest of Mr. Zaleski.[138] I was told the dinner would probably last another twenty to twenty-five minutes. Even so, informed of my presence, three minutes later Mr. Litvinov without other formalities rose from the table and was led into my compartment by Zaniewski. Smiling, he extended his hand to me saying, "Good evening, Mr. Cadere." I answered similarly, "Good evening, Mr. Litvinov," during which time the gentlemen who had accompanied me withdrew into another compartment leaving us alone.

After a few banal phrases of courtesy about his trip, the conversation was turned toward the end that preoccupied us both. It lasted for two and one-half hours, being interrupted five minutes before the arrival in Warsaw.

*   *   *   *

I told Mr. Litvinov that in conformity with the desire expressed to Mr. Patek in Moscow—brought to the knowledge of the Romanian government—I received instructions to give him information concerning the projected pact of nonaggression. I immediately added that I was authorized to declare to him on this occasion that the Romanian government is firmly and sincerely determined on its part to do what is possible in order to arrive at the realization of the pact. The Romanian government believes that, taking as a basis the last text proposed by the Polish government, it would be possible to reach a complete agreement, this text representing a formula of compromise that eliminates the complication of the pact.

Taking note of my declaration concerning the intentions of the Romanian government in the question of the pact, Mr. Litvinov formulated the following objections:

1. This draft had already been presented to him in Geneva by Mr. Schaetzel, who told him that this text was a Romanian proposal(?).

2. That basically this draft represented something new and that as a result it demanded a delayed discussion, [it] being more practical to complete the Riga draft.

I reminded him that, from what I knew, he had renounced discussion of this draft in a discussion with Mr. Zaleski. Mr. Litvinov replied that he had not made a categoric declaration in this sense to Mr. Zaleski, and that it is easier for the Soviet government to discuss an old draft in which, in conformity with the procès-verbaux signed by the delegates of both countries, the articles are ones that have already been accepted.

After a series of arguments I invoked in favor of the draft presented by Mr. Patek, Mr. Litvinov accepted the idea of examining the common points of the Riga draft.

Perceiving from that moment that there was no reason to make use of the authority that was given to me by Your Excellency's telegram No. 48709, I told Mr. Litvinov that I remained at his disposal for information about the sense in which the Romanian government conceived this draft, and not in the role of negotiator.

Mr. Litvinov expressed regret that I could not accompany him to Berlin where we could continue our conversation and eventually arrive at the signing.

I answered that, to my regret, there were technical reasons that made it impossible for me to accept his suggestion.

It then remained established that the negotiations would be resumed in Geneva through the mediation of the Polish government. Mr. Litvinov insisted, however, with extensive explanations, on the reasons for which he considered that a direct contact in a location close to Geneva would be preferable.

After prolonged discussion, I could state the following:

(1) Mr. Litvinov accepts the preamble of the pact in the form in which it is found in the Patek-Titulescu draft, expressly renouncing paragraph 4 of the Riga draft, "Stating that. . . ."

(2) In article I of the Riga draft, he renounces the part that begins with the words "as well as any attempt," referring to the territorial litigations.

(3) In exchange, Mr. Litvinov could not accept the editing of article I of the Patek-Titulescu draft, which changes the basis of the discussions. Mr. Litvinov told me what he desired was a direct pact of nonaggression, not a pact that simply refers to a previous treaty.

By this Mr. Litvinov repeated in fact the observations made on the occasion of the signing of the Pact of Moscow of February 9, 1929.

Furthermore, Mr. Litvinov pointed out that if Romania insisted at any price on the Schaetzel-Patek-Titulescu proposal—that is, on a reiteration of the Kellogg Pact—he would be obliged to again take into discussion the entire pact, article by article, which would lead us to new and long conferences. Otherwise, he believes that in [a] very short time it would be possible to arrive at the signing.

Then, article I from the editing of the last draft that was presented to him by Mr. Patek also had the disadvantage that it would refer to a pact *without a real international value*. Moreover, because it omitted previous litigations, he would be obliged, if he accepted such an act, to declare that the USSR had a free hand relative to the liquidation, as she saw fit, of all the older litigations between her and Romania. Anyhow, as the Union's government was firmly determined not to resort in any case to violent means to liquidate these questions, he believes that the categoric affirmation between the two contracting parties that they definitely renounce aggression to liquidate whatever differences between them [. . .] is much more advantageous and in the interests of both countries.

I replied that the new pact is the legalization of a pact already existing between us and has precisely the advantage, through its simple formulae, of avoiding any equivocation or greater interpretation than nonaggression.

Mr. Litvinov again referred to the fact that such formulae have been already definitely accepted by the plenipotentiaries of both countries.

(4) He believes that article II of the Patek-Titulescu pact would be acceptable if it were edited into a formula somewhat more congruent with the text already discussed (paragraph 2, article I).

(5) Article III of the Patek-Titulescu draft (article II of the Riga draft) would remain valid, but he would want to formulate the obligation of the previous denunciation of the treaty as was expressed at Riga, as containing more categoric expression.

(6) On article III of the Riga treaty, however, he considers that it would be useful to continue the discussions.

(7) However, he asks absolutely that article IV of the Riga draft be made part of the new text.

He considers [. . .] this article as providing evident proof of the sincere intentions of the Romanian government concerning the fundamental obligation: nonaggression.

(8) Concerning the duration of the pact, Mr. Litvinov believes that it is not necessary to resume the discussions, since a common point of view was reached already at Riga—a point of view that, moreover, represents a clause foreseen also in the other pacts of nonaggression recently signed.

(9) Concerning the protocol of signature, Mr. Litvinov's opinion is that a broader formula should be adopted without giving me precise [details]. However, he did allude to an intervention on the part of France, who, along with Poland, has been a mediator between Romania and the USSR in the question of the pact—[a] proposal that was rejected by the Romanian government. I replied that I had no knowledge about such a French proposal on this question.[139]

However, I insisted on immediately clarifying that he himself during the discussions between us renounced definitively the terms "territorial litigations" and "existing."[140] Mr. Litvinov confirmed [this] to me adding, however, that in the case of a prompt agreement he could not renounce the expression, "the differences between the two Parties."

In summary, the case would appear to be as follows:

1. Mr. Litvinov accepts the discussion of the pact on the basis of the discussions at Riga with some additions and modifications, accepting the preamble of the Titulescu-Patek text;
2. He accepts the exclusion of the words "territorial or other litigations" and "existing";
3. He seeks to reopen a discussion, the proportions of which cannot be foreseen, concerning the protocol of signature;
4. He wishes to continue the discussion as directly as possible in a location near Geneva and he believes that it would be necessary for our representatives to be accorded as full powers as possible.

My impression is that Mr. Litvinov is animated by good general dispositions concerning the pact, and that he has shown his inclination to arrive at an understanding with Romania as soon as possible.

Our conversation terminated with a series of views about the general political situation, which will be the object of a separate report.

CADERE

DOCUMENT NO. 94

Letter, VAIDA-VOEVOD [?] *to* CADERE

Bucharest, 21 September 1932

Dear Mr. Minister,

I wish to herein confirm to you that you are authorized to make contact with Mr. Litvinov to negotiate and initial a pact of nonaggression. In your negotiations, you will take the following points into consideration:

(1) You will exercise all your persistence in order to get Mr. Litvinov to accept, in its entirety and without any addition, the Patek (Titulescu) draft. You will bring to the defense of this draft all the arguments contained in our past telegraphic and oral instructions.

For your edification, I repeat to you that the unusual value of the

Patek (Titulescu) draft lies in the interpretive character of articles I and II. These articles strengthen the Kellogg Pact, the permanent basis of our peaceful relations with Russia. Once this basis [is] strengthened through the interpretations contained in articles I and II, even if the pact were denounced by the Russians, our legal position before them would remain firm.

(2) Only if you gain the conviction that any agreement on the basis of the Patek (Titulescu) draft, and particularly on the basis of the first two articles of this pact, is impossible, will you take into consideration the old text of Riga. This, however, only under the following conditions.

> *a.* If the Russians declare that the decisions made at Riga cannot be antagonistic to either of the two parties as Mr. Litvinov allowed in front of Mr. Zaleski.
>
> *b.* If you clarify previously the difficulties which arise concerning article IV and the Protocol of Signature. Concerning these two articles you will refer to the formulae prepared in our enclosed draft and which constitute [the] maximum of concessions which we can accept.
>
> You will not accept any other formula which exceeds, in details injurious to our interests which are known to you, the formulae [we] established together.
>
> You will keep us informed of all the Russian objections and counter-proposals.

(3) If the two conditions noted above in points *a* and *b* are fully satisfied, you will be able to accept an agreement on the basis of the Riga draft, in conformity to the text and hypothesis contained in the enclosed draft which constitute the maximum of our concessions.

TREATY OF NONAGGRESSION BETWEEN THE USSR AND ROMANIA

The Central Executive Committee of the Union of Soviet Socialist Republics on the one hand, and His Majesty the King of Romania on the other;

Animated by the desire to consolidate the peace, having the firm conviction that the reinforcement of the peaceful relations existing between the two Contracting Parties corresponds to their interests and constitutes an important element in the edifice of the maintenance of universal peace;

Faithful to the international engagements they have previously assumed, and declaring that the obligations stipulated by the present treaty can neither modify nor impair them, insofar as these engagements contain no element tending toward aggression;

(*In case of the suppression of Litvinov's article IV*) Conscious that none of these engagements can constitute an obstacle to the peaceful development of their mutual relations and are not found in contradiction with the present Treaty, and equally determined not to conclude in the future anything in contradiction with the present Treaty;

Have resolved to conclude the present Treaty of Nonaggression, having as its goal the completion of the Treaty of Renunciation of War, signed in Paris on August 27, 1928, put into force by the Protocol signed in Moscow on February 9, 1929, and to this end have designated as their Plenipotentiaries, to wit:

The Central Executive Committee of the USSR ———.

His Majesty the King of Romania ———.

who, after being communicated their full powers, found in good and due form, have agreed on the following dispositions.

I.

Each of the High Contracting Parties, stating that it has renounced war as an instrument of national policy in international relations, promises not to undertake any aggression separately as well as jointly with other powers on land, on the sea, or in the air, and not to resort in any case to war against the other Contracting Party.

Considered as an act contrary to the engagement foreseen in the preceding paragraph will be any act of violence endangering the integrity and the inviolability of the territory or the political independence of the other Contracting Party

(*completed with Protocol of Signature* a) even if such acts were committed without declaration of war and avoiding all its possible consequences.

(*completed with Protocol of Signature* b) as well as any attempt to solve by violence any difference between the two Contracting Parties even if such acts were committed without a declaration of war and avoiding all its possible consequences.

II.

In case one of the Contracting Parties were to become the object of an aggression on the part of a third State or group of third States, the other Contracting Party promises to observe neutrality during the duration of the conflict.

In case one of the Contracting Parties indulges in an act of violence against a third State, the other Contracting Party will be free to denounce the present treaty without previous warning.

III.

Each of the Contracting Parties promises not to permit on its territory either the sojourn or the activity of organizations having as their object armed struggle against the other Party, or of organizations or persons arrogating the role of government or of representing all or part of its territory, *nor to permit that certain organizations already existing on the territory of one or the other of the two powers employ themselves in whatever manner in provoking or in fostering political disorders or social troubles on the territory of the other.*

IV.

(In case mention were not to be made in the Preamble)

Each of the High Contracting Parties, conscious that no previously assumed international obligation is an obstacle to the peaceful development of their mutual relations and does not stand in contradiction to the present Treaty of Nonaggression, promises equally not to conclude anything in the future in contradiction with the present Treaty of Nonaggression.

V.

The present Treaty is concluded for the duration of three years. If one of the Contracting Parties does not denounce it six months before the end of the period of three years, the validity of the Treaty will automatically be prolonged for a new period of two years.

VI.

The present Treaty will be ratified as soon as possible and the instruments of ratification will be exchanged at. . . .

It will enter into force the day of that exchange.

PROTOCOL OF SIGNATURE

(*a*) The High Contracting Parties agree that the present Treaty cannot be interpreted in any way as ever having as a consequence the restriction or extinction of the obligations derived from the Treaty signed in Paris on August 26, 1928.

The present Treaty, which involves the obligation of each of the High Contracting Parties to

(*b*) The High Contracting Parties agree that the present Treaty will not be able to be interpreted in any way as having as a consequence the restriction or extinction of the obligations derived from the Treaty signed in Paris on August 26, 1928.

The High Contracting Parties also agree that the present Treaty aims only at nonaggression and

abstain from any aggression
against the other, will be
interpreted in the sense that no
litigious question can ever restrict
the said obligations and will never
be able to furnish one or the
other of the High Contracting
Parties with a motive to indulge
in whatever place in acts that
would be contrary to the
obligation of nonaggression
imposed by the present Treaty.
The High Contracting Parties
also agree that the present Treaty
aims only at nonaggression and
cannot be interpreted to any
other end.

cannot be interpreted to any
other end.

DOCUMENT NO. 95

Telegram (copy), Vaida-Voevod *to* Titulescu

Bucharest No. 50647, 26 September 1932

I very much regret that you were not able to decode my telegram No. 50259 in Vienna and I hasten to repeat it. Moreover, I regret that in your absence I was obliged to complete the [Romanian] delegation [to the League of Nations], charging Mr. Madgearu to hold the place of first delegate until your arrival.[141] May I also assume that, having taken up presidency of the Romanian delegation in Geneva, you [will] be willing to attend to our request addressed to the League of Nations?[142] We need your valuable assistance in order to succeed [in] an action begun as a result of your diligence, also documented in full agreement with you by a telegraphic appeal written by you and signed by me. You will find the information with the experts; the acts [that] were drawn up and delivered to me, I will send to you.

Concerning the question of the nonaggression pact, I have authorized Mr. Cadere to inform you about the meeting that, at the persistent request of Mr. Litvinov, I authorized him to have. Moreover, I have authorized him to explain to you the reasons for which I believe that the Litvinov-Cadere meeting must have its sequel only in Geneva in order to clear up the question of the nonaggression pact as rapidly as possible. We want to give our allies indisputable proof, which we would not have been able to give if we had rejected Mr. Litvinov's request, that we would expend every effort until the end in order to reach an agreement with the Russians. If we had refused the meeting requested by Mr. Litvinov, we would have stirred up the impression that we were drawing away from our allies on the Russian question. Our latest proof of goodwill absolves us from the responsibility for such consequences.

I have authorized Mr. Cadere to show you that the only basis on which we would accept an agreement with the Russians is a draft that takes into account the criticism you made of the last Litvinov draft presented by Mr. Zaleski. Our allies have been informed that we are committed to this basis for agreement.

In case we do not reach an immediate conclusion, we will interrupt the negotiations as a result of the last Litvinov-Patek talks in Moscow. In addition we will have a strengthened position vis-à-vis [our] allies. On the other hand, if we confirm the assurances given to us by the French and Poles that the Russians were more inclined to sign, I believe that the conclusion of the pact of nonaggression with Russia could lead to a relaxation, a strengthening in our relations with the allies, and a consolidation that our country needs in its international position.

Therefore, again please take upon yourself the duty of reestablishing this latest contact, either directly or through our allies, with the Russians in Geneva. Cadere will be at your disposal and you will be able to use him to establish contact if you believe it is not suitable that you establish it.

Considering that the telegraphic line passes through Austria and Hungary and the conversations are intercepted, please stay in contact with the Ministry for the exchange of ideas and information by coded telegrams. Moreover, please be willing to directly address me on any situation [about which] you had any dissatisfaction. Through indirect interventions, either telephonic or by means of communiqués, through the press, I have arrived at the awkward situation that differences of views lacking importance and easy to explain are invested by foreigners [with the] character of litigations that absolutely do not exist.

In order to again offer you the undivided possibility of being able to work without any official inconvenience from the government, please authorize me to tell His Majesty the King that I renounce the presidency of the Council of Ministers as well as the portfolio of the Ministry of Foreign Affairs and that you accept these high functions.

Concerning your idea about an eventual exchange of letters between the French and Russian governments, I have pursued this idea almost to its realization and France's legation informs us that its realization would be possible.[143]

> With my best regards.
> ALEXANDER VAIDA-VOEVOD

DOCUMENT NO. 96
(Reg. No. 51418 of 29 September 1932)

Decoded telegram (copy), CADERE *to* VAIDA-VOEVOD

Geneva No. 5, 28 September 1932

After today's meeting, I have the honor to transmit to Your Excellency the following points of agreement established with Litvinov.

The preamble is accepted in the Titulescu version, with an eventual insertion about which I will speak further on.

Article I is accepted in your version, with the final part under letter A.

Article II is unchanged.

Article III is accepted in the following version: "Each of the Contracting Parties promises not to allow on its territory either the sojourn or the activity of any organization having as its object armed struggle against the other party or that of employing itself by whatever means to provoke, etc. . . ." The end follows as in your text. However, Litvinov reserved the right to completely eliminate this article, which he considers as without use in the versions given below. I held to writing [it] in this way in order to avoid especially the expression "persons who arrogate to themselves the role of government or of representatives of the totality of or of part of the territory," considering this part as being able to give rise to dangerous interpretations.

Article IV is accepted in your version, adding on the last line the words "the spirit of" between "with" and "present." It would be possible to reconsider this addition if the newly introduced word[s] appear dangerous.

Article V is unchanged.

For Article VI, we reached agreement in principle that the exchange of ratifications would take place in Turkey.

The Titulescu version of [the] protocol of signature is accepted.

From here begin the disagreements, since Litvinov asked that the words referring to "territorial litigations and differences of interest" be added.

After prolonged discussion, Litvinov offered as [his] final concession to eliminate the words "territorial litigations," to accept the protocol of signature only with the Titulescu version, and proposed to insert into the preamble as [a] new paragraph after paragraph 3 of your instructions the following formula: "stating that the conclusion of the present Treaty does not bear any prejudice to the position of each of the parties in the differences existing between them."

I replied to Mr. Litvinov that I did not see any possibility of us accepting [it]. The only thing I could do was to telegraph my government [about] the point at which we had arrived, arranging a new meeting with him for Saturday.

I decided against sending the special courier to Bucharest, and ask you to be willing to give me instructions in good time.

I have also informed Madgearu, who asked me to send you the following telegram:

"As it is possible for me to meet with Herriot now, I ask for the government's instructions [as to] what I [should] answer in case I am asked about this question, and if eventually I [should] ask for new assistance other than that refused."

CADERE

DOCUMENT NO. 97
(Reg. No. 51437 of 29 September 1932)

Decoded telegram (copy), CADERE *to* MINISTRY OF FOREIGN AFFAIRS

Geneva No. 6, 29 September 1932

After the official conversation of today I had a totally personal exchange of views with Litvinov.

Asking him *how he expected to regulate the "differences" between us, he responded: "This could be made the object of special conferences in which all the pending questions could be discussed because you also have pretensions against us as we have against you."* He views this possibility as a result of the first step of [the] rapprochement [that would be] realized by conclusion of the pact of nonaggression. He showed a special interest in economic ties as well as in eventual economic agreements with [an] international character that could be to the profit of both countries.

Lunch was then taken together as guests of Mr. Schaetzel.

CADERE

DOCUMENT NO. 98

Intradepartmental memo by GAFENCU

Bucharest, 2 October 1932

Mr. Cadere completed his telegram No. 12 by a telephone conversation that he had with me at one o'clock at night. He told me that he is convinced the Russians will not renounce in one form or another the mentioning of the existence of differences. He believes, however, after the assurances given to him by the French, that through a new intervention they are prepared to make, Litvinov will allow the words "any existing or future differences" to be replaced by those of "all past, present, or future differences" (that is the formula proposed by Mr. Nicolae Iorga). It could be possible, moreover, says Mr. Cadere, that the formula requested by Litvinov be replaced by the words "any yet unregulated question (that is, the words used by Take Ionescu in the full powers given to Mr. Filality to negotiate with the Russians in Warsaw in 1921).[144]

I answered Mr. Cadere that, in conformance with all our previous instructions, the word "existing" cannot be accepted by us. I authorized him to carry forward the struggle with our allies to obtain Litvinov's acceptance of our formulae A and B without any modification.

Concerning the suggestion of the French, I told him that I in turn will ask for instructions from the prime minister.

So that is how the situation is now presented on the eve of the last days of negotiations in Geneva.

The Russians have passed from their initial point in Riga, in which they asked for the recognition of an "existing territorial litigation concerning Bessarabia," to the request to indirectly mention [it] in a formula we proposed—in order to guarantee our security through strict application of the obligations of nonaggression—to an addition that joins the words "all differences," contained in our formulae, to the words "existing or future." If these words could be replaced, as the French assure us, with the Iorga formula or the words used by Take Ionescu, I believe, in full conscience, that we can take such a formula into consideration.

Its characteristics are as follows:

(1) The pact will no longer contain any explicit Russian reservation concerning differences. The last Russian resistance concerning such an explicit reservation, that is, Litvinov's formula of "not prejudicing the positions taken [on] existing differences," was totally rejected by our delegates in Geneva.

(2) We thus find ourselves before the text we proposed with the two

variations A and B, [a] text that was submitted for the distinguished approval of His Majesty the King and that was brought to the knowledge of the party leaders, of which some, Marshal Averescu and I. G. Duca, categorically approved it, and others took note of it without formulating any reservations or criticism.[145]

(3) Litvinov accepts this text in its entirety, either with the addition of formula A, or with that of formula B. However, he asks incidentally for an addition, in the formulae that, as I said, have the direct aim of strengthening our security (see formula A—Hautecloque), in the protocol of signature or formula B, that is, the eventual paragraph 3 of article I. This addition would have the content of the Iorga formula ("past, present, or future"), or of the formula used by Take Ionescu ("still unregulated questions").

(4) The fact that we used "all differences" or "any difference" in our formulae A and B cannot in any case be interpreted as recognition of the reservation about which the Russians are thinking. The term "difference" is used in our formulae in order to define and make precise the obligations of nonaggression. It is thus used in the same sense and even with possibly more effect and in a broader sense than in the Kellogg Pact, in which the word "difference" is mentioned in the broader sense both in article I and in article II. . . .

(5) Concerning the two formulae suggested to Cadere by the French to be inserted in our formulae A and B, both of which succeed in attenuating the meaning that the Russians would give to the word "existing." The first formula, that of Mr. Iorga, has, particularly in French, the meaning of generalizing the differences of which there could be question, and it puts no accent on the existence of present differences. Take Ionescu's formula has the disadvantage of insisting on the existence of questions still unregulated. It has, on the other hand, undoubted advantages: first, of replacing the word "difference" with that of "question," that is, of greatly lessening [their] importance; and, secondly and especially, it is a formula already used vis-à-vis the Russians and is covered by the incontestable authority of Take Ionescu.

Therefore, I believe that in the case that we do not succeed in passing on to our formulae pure and simple, we can accept one of the two formulae suggested by the French, leaving [it] to their discretion to obtain what would seem possible. The Take Ionescu formula is preferable; and from among our two formulae A and B, we must place all our insistence that the formulae suggested by the French be inserted preferably in formula A (rather) than in formula B.

[penciled] GAFENCU

DOCUMENT NO. 99

Telegram, VAIDA-VOEVOD *to* CADERE

Bucharest No. 52056, 3 October 1932

As a result of our telephone conversation, by which you brought me up to date on the last stage of your negotiations, I confirm by this telegram what I said to you on the telephone. You will exhaust every effort to obtain Litvinov's acceptance of the first paragraph of formula A (Hautecloque) without any modification or addition. I insisted to our allies that they lend you all their support in this effort. We have a particular interest that the formula be accepted exactly in the form in which we gave it to you. Concerning paragraph 2 of the Hautecloque formula, you will make every effort [to see] that the text we gave to you be replaced by Mr. Maniu's text, to wit:

"The pact does not aim at anything but the assurance of the existing peace through the reciprocal obligation of nonaggression." I accept, in case of need, the Russian addition, "and has no other aim."

You are authorized to sign only the draft of the pact with formula A unmodified in paragraph 1 and modified in the sense of the Maniu proposal in paragraph 2.

If Litvinov insists [that] article II remain in its old form, you will not use this as a motivation for breaking off [the negotiations] and, moreover, you have the authority to sign.

At the same time, I authorize you, but only in the extreme case when you have determined that our resistance is useless and could lead to compromising the negotiations, to sign the draft pact with formula A modified either in the sense of Mr. Maniu's proposal, "any difference of whatever nature," or the Iorga formula, "any past, present, or future difference"; or, finally, the formula with the words used by Take Ionescu, "any still unregulated question."

With my best regards,
ALÉX. VAIDA-VOEVOD

DOCUMENT NO. 100
(Reg. No. 52142 of 4 October 1932)

Decoded telegram, CADERE *to* VAIDA-VOEVOD

Geneva No. 13, 4 October 1932

At this evening's meeting with Litvinov the texts on which we agreed were reviewed and approved.[146] Concerning the protocol of signature,

Litvinov asked for immediate signing with the acceptance of "existing differences," which I refused. Examining then the suggestions relative to your new proposals, Litvinov requests, in any case, a short time for communicating with Moscow but at the same time he sought to return to the prejudicial questions. Being unable to establish anything definitive concerning the protocol, we agree to meet tomorrow or eventually on October 10 in order not to create the impression that the negotiations were broken off. I then had a conference with Zaleski, Massigli, and Schaetzel to whom I gave the text . . . that is formula A improved with the prime minister's final text. It was agreed that both would make a collective démarche to Litvinov and declare that they are ready within the shortest time to respectively sign and ratify if the USSR signs with Romania without the word "existing." The démarche will be made tomorrow morning if Massigli receives permission from Herriot.

CADERE

DOCUMENT NO. 101

Memo, CADERE *to* MINISTRY OF FOREIGN AFFAIRS

Geneva, 4 October 1932

Mr. Massigli communicated the following to Minister Madgearu concerning his latest démarches to Mr. Litvinov:

On October 3, Mr. Massigli told Mr. Litvinov that the Romanian government refuses decidedly to accept the word "existing" regarding the differences mentioned in the draft of the protocol of signature. Mr. Massigli pressed Mr. Litvinov to renounce the word "existing." Mr. Litvinov energetically refused, adding that he would break off the negotiations with Romania on the occasion of the next meeting with Minister Cadere, which would take place in two days. On this occasion the Soviet commissar of foreign affairs asked Mr. Massigli when the French signing would take place. Mr. Massigli replied that he would request the necessary information from the Quai d'Orsay.

On October 4, at noon Mr. Massigli informed Mr. Litvinov, on the basis of instructions given by Mr. Herriot, that the French government considered that the Romanian government had arrived at the limit of possible concessions. Concerning the signing of the Franco-Soviet

Treaty, the French government had decided to proceed to the said signing after the signing of the Romanian-Soviet Treaty had taken place.

Mr. Massigli believes that the fact that the Romanian-Russian negotiations have not been broken off was due to this intervention of the French government. Mr. Massigli believes, as [does] Mr. Madgearu, that the threat made by Mr. Litvinov to Mr. Cadere during their last meeting to make a polemic declaration in the press concerning the negotiations with Romania is a "bluff."

Minister Madgearu believes that the Romanian government must maintain itself with determination and calm on the basis of its last proposal (formula A, unmodified), intervening with our allies the French and the Poles to sustain this formula with the greatest energy.

If he receives *formal* instructions in this sense from the Romanian government, Minister Madgearu, accompanied by Mr. Cadere and assisted by Mr. Cesianu, will make the proper démarche to Mr. Herriot.

Mr. Madgearu believes that we must not rely very much on the result of the interventions made in Bucharest with France's and Poland's ministers, who do not always have a decided influence on their governments, and who frequently give us optimistic information about the intentions of those governments that does not correspond to reality.

DOCUMENT NO. 102
(Reg. No. 52233 of 5 October 1932)

Decoded telegram, CADERE *to* VAIDA-VOEVOD

Geneva No. 14, 5 October 1932

Today I had a meeting with Litvinov. Despite the démarches made by Massigli and Schaetzel, I discerned no amelioration in the Russian pretensions, so I did not believe it necessary to insist on anything like the new concessions for which Litvinov wishes to have permission from Moscow [and] once again to return to the prejudicial questions. In these conditions, the discussion about the protocol of signature remains open. We agreed that we could resume the negotiations after October 10 in Geneva, or even earlier in Paris (the latter solution seems to me to be improbable).

Today Litvinov declared to me that he had received instructions from

Moscow to respond to the known interview.[147] He had not done so, however, in order not to break off the negotiations and in the belief that we would reach an agreement. I answered that each one is free concerning the declarations he wishes to make, but that we could not arrive at an agreement except within the limits of the proposals I made, proposals that represent the maximum Romanian concessions. Litvinov said that the Soviet government has also yielded: at the Riga negotiations they had renounced talking about Bessarabia, about territorial litigations; they had accepted our pretensions in the new version of the protocol of signature. Why did not the Romanian government yield in the question of "existing differences"?

I replied that this pretension of his subverts all the value of the pact and does not prove any real desire for détente on the part of the Soviets.

In summary, I have noted in the last two meetings that Litvinov's resistance has grown. Discussion within the framework of the nonaggression pact being strictly speaking exhausted, his arguments since have recently aimed at explanations of a political nature.

I note that the praiseworthy efforts expended here by [our] allies have not led to the expected results, and that Litvinov is influenced evidently by currents hostile to our allies.

Among the elements of your decision relative to the fate of the negotiations, I believe it necessary to consider:

1. The interruption of a few days might be salutary, demonstrating not too great a haste on our part;
2. There must be an absolute agreement with our allies on a definitive text [to be] accepted by Litvinov before contact with him is resumed;
3. The possibility [exists] of resuming the discussions with the Soviets after the treaty's eventual signing;
4. Discontinuance [will] lead to Litvinov's declarations to the press.

As I said to you on the telephone, Cretzianu left for Bucharest this evening bringing the texts definitively fixed. Davidescu, after eight days of leave, [will] return to Warsaw. I leave for Paris, where I [will] await Your Excellency's instructions.

Madgearu says that he will also go [to Paris] for financial questions and eventually for a common démarche to Herriot.

CADERE

DOCUMENT NO. 103
(Reg. No. 53107 of 8 October 1932)

Decoded telegram, CESIANU *to* MINISTRY OF FOREIGN AFFAIRS

Paris No. 1312, 7 October 1932

CONFIDENTIAL

The Quai d'Orsay, with which I made contact today, told me regarding France's letter to [the] Soviets that it considered it inopportune,[148] since the Soviets, in the case that they replied to France's letter, would make formal reservations that would definitely not be to Romania's benefit. It added that France's minister in Bucharest, also speaking about this fact, had informed Paris that Their Excellencies Vaida-Voevod, Mironescu, and Gafencu had found that France's anxiety about the inopportuneness of the letter was justified. Nonetheless, [when] I insisted [the Quai] told me that, in conclusion, this point of view was not the last, since the prime minister also has to judge and to decide, and that in any case the Quai d'Orsay will wait to declare itself [until] the final result of the talks with Litvinov, that is, until the resumption of the talks in Geneva after October 10.

CESIANU

Notes

Every effort was expended to verify the factual content of each of the documents by comparing them with the contents of other archival and published documentary sources. These sources are cited in abbreviated form conforming to the following list.

ALPA   Academy of the Romanian Socialist Republic, Manuscript Section, Palace Archives. Cited as in the catalog.

BPPR   *Bulletin périodique de la presse roumaine.* A Quai d'Orsay house organ.

DBFP   *Documents on British Foreign Policy.*

DDF   *Documents diplomatiques français.*

DiM   *Documents and materials on the history of Soviet-Polish relations.*

DVP   *Documents of the USSR's foreign policy.*

FO   Foreign Office correspondence housed in the Public Records Office, London. Cited as in the catalog (see below).

NTCPN   Nicholas Titulescu Collection, Archives of the Hoover Institution, five dossiers labelled "USSR Peace Negotiations 1931–1932," found in boxes 14 and 15 of the collection. Cited with a number that represents the order in which the document is found in the dossiers.

SARH   State Archives of the Socialist Republic of Romania, Royal House Collection. Cited with a dossier number and year, as in the catalog.

The published British, French, Soviet, Polish, and American documents are cited with a volume number, page number(s), and, as a courtesy to the reader, document number, date, and (where appropriate) specifics of the document. More complete information on these volumes is cited in the bibliography. The system used by the Public Records Office, because of its apparent complexity, deserves an extra word or two of explanation. It depends on a system of code numbers and letters.

Thus, in note 48 of the foreword, the citation FO 371 C585/270/37 refers to Foreign Office (FO), political correspondence (371), Eastern Europe (C), chronological order of receipt by year (585), problem area (270), and country (37)—in this case, Romania.

Preface

1. Many of these documents have been verified by the author's research in the Arhivele Statului [State Archives], Bucharest, and the Manuscript Collection of the Library of the Academy of the Romanian Socialist Republic.

2. A copy of the former speech may be found in the Hoover Institution Archives under the author's name.

3. See part one, article one of the *Treaty of Peace with Rumania* (n.p., 1947), p. 2, and the commentaries in the two volumes of *Roumania at the Peace Conference* (Paris: n.p., 1946), written by Grigore Gafencu and others.

4. See Stephen Fischer-Galati, *Twentieth Century Rumania* (New York and London: Columbia University Press, 1970), pp. 159, 178–79; Kenneth Jowitt, *Revolutionary Breakthroughs and National Development: The Case of Romania, 1944–1965* (Berkeley and Los Angeles: University of California Press, 1971), pp. 206–9, 221; David Floyd, *Rumania, Russia's Dissident Ally* (New York: Praeger, 1965), 112–17; and the statement itself, "Declaraţia cu privire la poziţia Partidului Muncitoresc Romîn în problemelor mişcări comuniste şi muncitoreşti internaţionale adoptată de plenara largită a C.C. al P.M.R. din aprilie 1964" (Bucharest: Editura politică, 1964).

5. Andrei Oţetea, ed., *Karl Marx: Insemnari despre Români, manuscrise inedite* (Bucharest: Editura politică, 1964), the major portion of which appears as U.S. Joint Publications Research Service, *Report* No. 30394, 3 June 1965. For an excellent summary, see Dionise Ghermani, "Revirement doctrinal," in George Cioranesco et al., *Aspects des relations russo-roumaines* (Paris: Minard, 1967), pp. 218–26, hereafter cited as "Cioranesco et al."

6. For the West, see Gy. Jozsa, "Marx-Engels et les roumains," *Documentation sur l'Europe Centrale* 10 (1972): 310–26; Alexander Suga, "Bessarabien—noch immer umstritten?" *Osteuropa* 21 (May 1971): 316–23; Hans Hartl, "Bessarabien," *Südosteuropa Mitteilungen* 15 (February 1975): 61–71; for Russia, see the articles by Suga and Hartl (the Soviet reaction was most marked in the Moldavian SSR, especially in Kishinev's two leading dailies, *Comunistul Moldovei* and *Moldova Sochialiste*).

7. E.g., Nicolae Ceauşescu, *Romania on the Way of Completing Socialist Construction,* vol. 1 (Bucharest: Meridiane Publishing House, 1969), p. 351, speech of 7 May 1966; idem, *Romania on the Way of Building Up the Multilaterally Developed Socialist Society,* vol. 7 (Bucharest: Meridiane Publishing House, 1973), pp. 508–9, speech of 19 July 1972.

8. Ion M. Oprea, *Nicolae Titulescu* (Bucharest: Editura ştiinţifică, 1966), the essence of which was translated into English as *Nicolae Titulescu's Diplomatic Activity* (Bucharest: Publishing House of the Academy of the Socialist Republic of Romania, 1968). It should be noted that, as of the mid-1960s, not only had

Titulescu been completely rehabilitated, but he had also been designated as a predecessor of contemporary Romania's independent statesmen. Two other books of note are: George Macovescu, ed., *Nicolae Titulescu: Documente diplomatice* (Bucharest: Editura politică, 1967); and Robert Deutsch, ed., *Nicolae Titulescu discursuri* (Bucharest: Editura ştiinţifică, 1967). Macovescu was Romania's foreign minister from October 1972 to March 1978.

9. I. M. Oprea, *O etapă rodnică din istoria relaţiilor româno-sovietice 1928– 1936* (Bucharest: Editura politică, 1967).

10. Suga, "Bessarabien," p. 322.

11. ĪÂ. M. Kopanskiĭ and I. E. Levit, *Sovetsko-Rumynskie otnoshenīâ 1929– 1934 g. (ot podpisanīâ Moskovogo protokola do ustanovlenīâ diplomaticheskikh otnoshenīĭ)* (Moscow: Izdatel'stvo "Nauka," 1971).

12. Komissīâ po izdanīû diplomaticheskikh dokumentov, *Dokumenty vneshnei politiki S.S.S.R.* (Moscow: Izdatel'stvo politicheskoĭ literatury, 1957–), hereafter cited as *DVP*. Some Soviet documents have also been published in English, e.g., Jane T. Degras, ed., *Soviet Documents on Foreign Policy* (New York: Oxford University Press, 1951–), hereafter cited as "Degras"; and Xenia J. Eudin and Robert M. Slusser, eds., *Soviet Foreign Policy 1928–1934, Documents and Materials* (University Park, Pa., and London: Pennsylvania State University Press, 1966).

13. The Hoover Institution Archives, Nicolae Titulescu Collection, box 14. For Titulescu's Soviet policy, see Miron Constantinescu and Vasile Liveanu, "Remarks on Nicolae Titulescu's Actions for a Rapprochement between Romania and the U.S.S.R." in their *Problems of History and Social Theory* (Bucharest: Publishing House of the Academy of the Socialist Republic of Romania, 1970), pp. 129–70.

Introduction

1. The foregoing is based primarily on Romanian sources: Grigore Filliti's account in Cioranesco et al. pp. 60–88; Alexandru Boldur, *Basarabia românească* (Bucharest: Tipografia Carpaţi, Petre Barbulescu, 1943), pp. 127–35; George I. Brătianu, *La Bessarabie: Droits nationaux et historiques* (Bucharest: Institut d'histoire universelle "N. Iorga," 1943), pp. 130–42. Not surprisingly, Soviet and Sovietophile historiography is quite different, e.g., Louis Fischer, *The Soviets in World Affairs* (New York: Vintage Books, 1951), pp. 50–51.

2. Filliti in Cioranesco et al., pp. 94–96; Stefan St. Grauer, *Les relations entre la Roumanie et l'U.R.S.S. depuis le traité de Versailles* (Paris: Pedone, 1936), pp. 27, 29–30, hereafter cited as "Grauer"; Hoover Institution Archives, Krupensky Collection, especially boxes 1–3.

3. Filliti in Cioranesco et al.; Grauer, pp. 36–47. Romania's actions at the peace conference are adequately analyzed by Sherman D. Spector, *Rumania at the Peace Conference: A Study of the Diplomacy of Ion I. C. Bratianu* (New York: Bookman Associates, 1962). The Bessarabian Convention never legally came into force because Japan never ratified it.

4. Romanian sources (Filliti in Cioranesco et al., p. 97, and Grauer, p. 32) claim that Litvinov personally acknowledged Bessarabia's right to self-deter-

mination and Russia's obligation to return the treasure ($80 million). It was later confiscated because of Romania's "occupation" of Bessarabia.

5. Romanian Minister Davila wrote to the American secretary of state in 1933 that Karakhan had told the Romanian delegate Filality: "We know that Bessarabia will remain yours, as we do not want to, or cannot, take it back, but you must pay the price for our recognition of your title to Bessarabia, an act which will weigh heavily in the balance later on." *Foreign Relations of the United States, Diplomatic Papers 1933,* vol. 2, *The British Commonwealth, Europe, Near East and Africa* (Washington, D.C.: U.S. Government Printing Office, 1949), p. 664, Davila to the secretary of state, 29 March 1933. Fischer, *Soviets in World Affairs,* p. 375, claims that Karakhan's suggestion was the work of Trotsky and was later dropped because of strong Ukrainian opposition.

6. Filliti in Cioranesco et al., pp. 112–15; Grauer, pp. 76–87; Fischer, *Soviets in World Affairs,* pp. 375–76; "Déclarations faites par la délégation roumaine à la conférence russo-roumaine de Vienne, 27 mars–2 avril 1924" (Bucharest, n.d.), a copy of which the author studied at the Library of the Academy of the Romanian Socialist Republic; and *DVP,* 7:164–69 (no. 87) and ibid., pp. 171–75 (no. 90), "Declarations of the Soviet Delegation at the Meetings of the Soviet-Romanian Conference in Vienna, March 28, 1924, and April 2, 1924."

7. E. g., Khristian G. Rakovskiĭ, *Roumania and Bessarabia* (London: W. P. Coates, 1925); N. Titulescu, "Two Neighbors of Russia and Their Policies, I: Roumania and Bessarabia," *The Nineteenth Century and After,* 95 (June 1924): 791–803.

8. Grauer, pp. 93–97; N. Titulescu, "România şi Franţa" [Romania and France], a manuscript no. 27829 in the Central State Library, Library for Foreign Literature, Bucharest (written in 1937).

9. Filliti, pp. 124–25; Oprea, *Etapă rodinică,* pp. 28–29.

10. Eudin and Slusser, *Soviet Foreign Policy,* vol. 1, p. 168.

11. Chantal Beaucourt, "L'Union Sovietique et la Roumanie," in *Les frontières européennes de l'U.R.S.S. 1917–1941,* ed. Jean-Baptiste Duroselle (Paris: Colin, 1957), pp. 294–95, citing *Pravda* of 26 January 1930.

12. Bohdan Budurowycz, *Polish-Soviet Relations 1932–1939* (New York and London: Columbia University Press, 1963), pp. 6–7, hereafter cited as "Budurowycz."

13. Ibid., pp. 9–10; Josef Korbel, *Poland Between East and West: Soviet and German Diplomacy Toward Poland 1919–1933* (Princeton, N.J.: Princeton University Press, 1963), p. 266.

14. William Scott, *Alliance Against Hitler: The Origins of the Franco-Soviet Pact* (Durham N.C.: Duke University Press, 1962), pp. 10–11; Max Beloff, *The Foreign Policy of Soviet Russia 1929–1941,* vol. 1, *1929–1936* (London, New York, and Toronto: Oxford University Press, 1947), p. 20.

15. Jules Laroche, *La Pologne de Pilsudski: Souvenirs d'une ambassade 1926–1935* (Paris: Flammarion, 1953), p. 104, hereafter cited as "Laroche"; Korbel, *Poland between East and West,* p. 267.

16. *Documents on British Foreign Policy,* 2d ser. 7:217, Ovey (Moscow) to Foreign Secretary Henderson, 21 July 1931 (no. 141), hereafter cited as *DBFP;* ibid., 7:217 (no. 142), Strang (Moscow) to Henderson, 10 August 1931.

17. A. Zatorsky et al., eds., *Dokumenty i materialy po istorii sovetsko-polskikh otnosheniĭ*, vol. 5, *maĭ 1926—dekabr 1932 g.* (Moscow: Izdatel'stvo "Nauka," 1967), pp. 491—92 (document no. 296), record of a conversation with Patek signed "L. Karakhan" (hereafter cited as *DiM*).

18. Ibid., pp. 292—94 (no. 297).

19. Budurowycz, pp. 10—11; Korbel, *Poland between East and West*, p. 268; *DBFP*, 7:218—20 (no. 144).

20. Budurowycz, pp. 11—12; Jan Librach, *The Rise of the Soviet Empire: A Study of Soviet Foreign Policy* (New York: Frederick A. Praeger Publishers, 1964), p. 62.

21. *DVP*, 14:640 (no. 338), Litvinov's notes on the conversation. A footnote reveals that "left open" was later replaced with "left aside" ("laissé à part" in French, "ostavlennyĭ v storone" in Russian). This wording was the source of considerable controversy (document 42). See also *DiM*, p. 504 (no. 305) for the same notes. Patek's version, on which document 7 is based, is *DiM*, pp. 506—8 (no. 306).

22. Hoover Institution Archives, Nicolas Titulescu Collection, USSR Peace Negotiations, 1931—1932, boxes 14—15, sixteenth document in order of appearance (hereafter cited as *NTCPN/* order of appearance).

23. *NTCPN/27*, Cesianu (Paris) to the Foreign Ministry, 26 November 1931, on a conversation with Berthelot, who, Cesianu later reported, thought the moment was particularly auspicious for Romanian-Soviet negotiations given Soviet anxiety about the Far East. Ibid./33, excerpts from Cesianu to the Foreign Ministry, 2 December 1931. Prime Minister Iorga recorded that France had been negotiating in Romania's name for some time: see Iorga, *Memorii*, vol. 6, *Incercarea guvernării peste partide (1931—32),* (Bucharest: Datina româneas-că, 1939), p. 171 (entry for September 1, 1931).

24. *DVP*, 14:688 (no. 361), Surits (Ankara) to the People's Commissariat, 2 December 1931; *NTCPN/43*, Sturdza to the Foreign Ministry, 5 December 1931; *DVP*, 14:699 (no. 366), Svidersky (Riga) to the People's Commissariat, 8 December 1931.

25. A sentiment shared by Iorga and by Pilsudski. See F. C. Nano, *The Foreign Policy of Romania 1918—1939* (New York: Mid-European Studies Center, n.d.), p. 198; and Laroche, p. 106.

26. E.g., Iorga, *Memorii*, vol. 6, p. 255 (11 December 1931).

27. Oprea, *Nicolae Titulescu*, p. 134.

28. Michel Sturdza, *The Suicide of Europe: Memoirs of Prince Michel Sturdza, Former Foreign Minister of Rumania* (Boston and Los Angeles: Western Islands Publishers, 1968), p. 45, hereafter cited as "Sturdza." Sturdza was foreign minister in the Iron Guard government of 1940—41, and his memoirs reveal him as an unrepentant follower of Corneliu Zilea-Codreanu, the "captain" of Romanian fascism.

29. Ibid., p. 50.

30. *NTCPN/80*, Carp (Constantinople) to the Foreign Ministry, 4 January 1932; ibid./83, Sturdza to the Foreign Ministry, 4 January 1932; *DiM*, p. 491 (no. 296), record of a conversation with Patek signed L. Karakhan, 4 August 1931.

31. *NTCPN*/91, Sturdza to the Foreign Ministry, 5 January 1932; ibid./93, Sturdza to the Foreign Ministry, 5 January 1932.

32. See also Iorga, *Memorii*, vol. 6, pp. 273–74 (5 January 1932).

33. E.g., Romulus Seişanu's lead article in *Universul* (Bucharest), 1 January 1932, p. 1 (Seişanu was the leading commentator on foreign affairs); *Bulletin périodique de la presse roumaine* (Paris), no. 103 (30 November 1931–16 January 1932): 2–3 (hereafter cited as *BPPR*).

34. Sturdza usually sent two reports of each session to Bucharest. Document 28 is his "verbatim" report and is much longer than his short report (i.e., *NTCPN*/99, Sturdza to the Foreign Ministry, 8 January 1932). For a slightly different version see Sturdza, p. 50. For Stomonyakov's referral see *DVP*, 15:15 (no. 4), Stomonyakov to the People's Commissariat, 7 January 1932.

35. *DVP*, 15:15 (no. 5), Litvinov to Stomonyakov, 7 January 1932; ibid., 18–19 (no. 10), Litvinov to Stomonyakov, 10 January 1932.

36. As per Ghika's explicit instructions. *NTCPN*/101, Ghika (Warsaw) to Sturdza, 8 January 1932.

37. *La Roumanie Nouvelle* (Bucharest), 8 (December 1931–January 1932): 2796–98.

38. Ibid.; *Universul*, 10 January 1932, p. 11; Laroche, p. 106.

39. *BPPR*, 103 (30 November 1931–16 January 1932): 3; *Universul*, 13 January 1932, p. 1.

40. *DVP*, 15:21 (no. 14), Litvinov to Stomonyakov, 12 January 1932.

41. A condition repeated to a British diplomat in Moscow. *DBFP*, 7:228 (no. 147), Ovey to Foreign Secretary Simon, 14 January 1932.

42. Ibid., 229–30 (no. 149), Ovey to Simon, 19 January 1932; Budurowycz, p. 12.

43. *NTCPN*/133, Sturdza to the Foreign Ministry, 18 January 1932, in which Sturdza complained that the French and Poles had leaked the proposal to the Soviets.

44. *DVP*, 15:43–44 (no. 30), Stomonyakov to the People's Commissariat, 20 January 1932.

45. Sturdza, pp. 52–53, charged that Titulescu later gave the contents of the letter to Pertinax (Andre Géraud) of *L'Echo de Paris* in order to discredit him. A major portion of Sturdza's memoirs is devoted to an attack on Titulescu, which contrasts with the admiring supplications directed at him by Sturdza in the hope of advancing himself in the foreign service. See NTC/box 13, four letters from Sturdza to Titulescu.

46. In fact, substantial agreement was reached on the noncontroversial parts of the pact. Only the preamble, article I, paragraph 2, and the articles on conciliation and interdependence were not agreed upon. See *NTCPN*/147, Sturdza to the Foreign Ministry, 20 January 1932; ibid./175, Sturdza to Prime Minister Iorga, 12 February 1932. See also *NTCPN*/165, the Juridical Council's opinion of the negotiations' results, the basis for which, *NTCPN*/164, is also found in the Palace Archives in the manuscript section of the Library of the Academy of the Romanian Socialist Republic, LVIII/varia 11, as "Rezultatul negocierilor noastre cu sovietele la Riga," (hereafter cited as *ALPA*, for Academy Library Palace Archives).

47. Document 42, which appears out of chronological order in *NTCPN*, sheds some light on the apparent cause of the basic misunderstanding: two widely differing interpretations of the Patek-Litvinov conversation of 14 November 1931.

48. Public Records Office (London), Foreign Office Correspondence Files 371, C585/270/37, Palairet (Bucharest) to Simon, 13 January 1932 (hereafter cited as *FO* 371). For method of citation, see headnote to notes.

49. Ibid., C645/645/37, Palairet to Simon, 20 January 1932; *BPPR*, 103 (30 November 1931–16 January 1932): 2–3; *Universul*, 16 January 1932, p. 9.

50. *DVP*, 15:57–59 (no. 41); in English in Degras, pp. 522–23.

51. Budurowycz, p. 13, citing Josef Beck's *Final Report* (New York: R. Speller, 1957), p. 10.

52. See also *NTCPN*/154, Bilciurescu to Iorga, 27 January 1932; Iorga, *Memorii*, vol. 6, p. 299 (28 January 1932).

53. The Geneva proposal was also presented to Litvinov, *DiM*, p. 523 (no. 314), Litvinov's record of a conversation with Patek, 23 January 1932. The Poles also urged concessions on Sturdza in Riga (*NTCPN*/147, Sturdza to the Foreign Ministry, 23 January 1932), and on Cesianu in Paris (ibid./157, Cesianu to the Foreign Ministry, 30 January 1932).

54. Scott, *Alliance Against Hitler*, p. 36. Tardieu's anti-Sovietism was known to and appreciated by the Romanians. E.g., *NTCPN*/167, Ghika (Geneva) to the Foreign Ministry, 4 February 1932.

55. *NTCPN*/166, Ghika to the Foreign Ministry, 6 February 1932; ibid./171, Ghika to the Foreign Ministry, 8 February 1932; ibid./172, Ghika to the Foreign Ministry, 9 February 1932.

56. Ibid./167, note by Arion on a conversation with Szembek, 9 February 1932./177, note by Arion on a conversation with Dembinski, n.d. Szembek also put pressure on Iorga (*Memorii*, vol. 6, p. 299, 28 January 1932), and delivered a note from Beck to the same effect (ibid., p. 314, 14 February 1932). For Beck in Warsaw, see *NTCPN*/178, Bilciurescu to the Foreign Ministry, 20 February 1932.

57. *Universul*, 25 November 1932, p. 7, Titulescu's speech to the Romanian Chamber. Iorga's reaction was to try to resign even before Titulescu's arrival in Bucharest, but King Carol would not allow it. Iorga, *Memorii*, vol. 6, p. 311 (11 February 1932); *FO* 371, C1582/448/37, Palairet to Simon, 19 February 1932.

58. Iorga, *Memorii*, vol. 6, p. 317 (16 February 1932).

59. *Universul*, 23 February 1932, p. 5, and 16 February 1932, p. 1; see also *FO* 371, C1939/448/37, Sargent [the Foreign Office's expert on Romanian affairs] to Palairet, 12 April 1932, on a conversation with Titulescu.

60. *NTCPN*/178, Bilciurescu to the Foreign Ministry, 20 February 1932; Iorga, *Memorii*, vol. 6, pp. 328–29 (24 February 1932).

61. *DVP*, 15:140–41 (no. 95), Litvinov to the People's Commissariat, 26 February 1932, on a conversation with Zaleski. Another stimulus for Romanian recalcitrance was Estonia's delay in concluding her pact with the USSR. See *NTCPN*/180, Ghika (Geneva) to the Foreign Ministry, 23 February 1932; *FO* 371, C 2229/645/37, Palairet to Simon, 14 March 1932.

62. Litvinov did state his views to *Dziennik Poznanski*. *NTCPN*/188, Bilciurescu to the Foreign Ministry, 11 March 1932; *DVP*, 15:172 (no. 116), Litvinov
(Geneva) to Stomonyakov, 7 March 1932. Document 51, like several others
in *NTCPN*, is also found in dossier 85/1932, pp. 5–8, of the Royal House
Collection in the State Archives in Bucharest (hereafter cited as *SARH* 85/1932).

63. *NTCPN*/182–86. Of special interest are no. 184, Titulescu to the
Foreign Ministry, 6 March 1932 (*SARH* 85/1932, p. 9); no. 185, Titulescu to the
Foreign Ministry, 9 March 1932 (*SARH* 85/1932, pp. 11–12, and, interestingly,
Nicolae Titulescu: Documente diplomatice, pp. 403–4); and no. 186, Titulescu to the
Foreign Ministry, 14 March 1932 (*SARH* 85/1932, pp. 17–19).

64. *NTCPN*/189, Titulescu to the Foreign Ministry, 18 March 1932 (SARH
85/1932, pp. 35–36). Like Zaleski, Tardieu was a close friend of Titulescu.

65. Budurowycz, p. 15. The incident involved a Soviet charge that Polish
diplomats were responsible for the attempted assassination of the counselor of
the German Embassy in Moscow. The impression of Soviet second thoughts,
especially insofar as Romania and Estonia were concerned, was given to a British
diplomat by Litvinov. *DBFP*, 7:237 (no. 152), Ovey to Simon, 28 March 1932
(no. 152).

66. *NTCPN*/199, Sturdza to the Foreign Ministry, 9 April 1932.

67. Ghika immediately informed the interested legations and Titulescu
about the interview; see *NTCPN*/203, Ghika to the Warsaw, Paris, and Riga
legations, and Titulescu, 14 April 1932.

68. *La Roumanie Nouvelle*, 8 (April 1932): 2907; document 62, in this book;
DVP, 15:274–75 (no. 183), Stomonyakov to Antonov-Ovseyenko, 22 April 1932.

69. A threat Titulescu often made, but never implemented. See *NTCPN*/
256, Titulescu (Geneva) to the Foreign Ministry, 29 June 1932; Walter Bacon,
"Nicolae Titulescu and Romanian Foreign Policy 1933–1934" (Ph.D. dissertation, University of Denver, 1975), pp. 58, 58–59, 183.

70. *Le Mois* (Paris), 17 (1 May–1 June 1932): 22–33; ibid., 18(1 June–
1 July 1932): 38–44. In Romania, Herriot's victory was seen as a victory for
those who favored closer Franco-Soviet ties and thus was greeted with considerable anxiety; see *La Roumanie Nouvelle*, 8 (May 1932): 2932.

71. The crisis, which had been developing for some time, was exacerbated
by the public disclosure of a report of a commission of League of Nations'
financial experts headed by the French economist Charles Rist. The report
indicated the Iorga government's financial ineptitude. *FO* 371, C4152/92/37,
Palairet to Simon, 7 June 1932; Henri Prost, *Destin de la Roumanie* (1918–1954)
(Paris: Berger-Levrault, 1954), pp. 59–60.

72. *Universul* (Extra), 31 May 1932; Iorga, *Memorii*, vol. 6, pp. 408–9 (31
May 1932).

73. Prost, *Destin de la Roumanie*, pp. 60–61; *La Roumanie Nouvelle*, 8 (June
1932): 2935; *Universul*, 2–5 June 1932, passim.

74. Since Vaida was both prime minister and foreign minister, Gafencu was
in day-to-day control of the Foreign Ministry. *Foreign Relations of the United
States, Diplomatic Papers 1932* (Washington, D.C.: U.S. Government Printing
Office, 1947), vol. 2, pp. 511–12, document 932, Sussdorf (Bucharest) to the
Secretary of State, 17 August 1932.

75. *NTCPN*/233, Davidescu (Warsaw) to the Foreign Ministry, 11 June 1932; ibid./234, Sturdza to the Foreign Ministry, 12 June 1932.

76. As per instructions; ibid./246, Gafencu to Cadere, 22 June 1932 (also in *ALPA*).

77. *NTCPN*/250, Cadere to Gafencu, 25 June 1932.

78. Ibid./255, Gafencu to Titulescu, 30 June 1932.

79. Ibid./276, Vaida to Titulescu, 13 July 1932; ibid./277, Vaida to Titulescu, 14 July 1932; ibid./279, Titulescu to the Foreign Ministry, 15 July 1932; and ibid./281, Titulescu to the Foreign Ministry, 17 July 1932.

80. *Universul*, 29 July 1932, p. 1. Szembek emphasized Poland's "continued" loyalty to the Romanian alliance, adding: "In April [Poland] delayed the signing [of the pact] in the hope that Romania could reach a similar agreement. Now she has signed the pact, but will postpone ratification."

81. Ibid., 16 June 1932, p. 11, 18 June 1932, p. 7, and 19 June 1932, p. 1.

82. *NTCPN*/247, Titulescu (Lausanne) to the Foreign Ministry, 22 June 1932. Zaleski saw Litvinov the following day. *DVP*, 15:380 (no. 259), Litvinov to the People's Commissariat, 23 June 1932.

83. *DVP*, 15:382 (no. 266), Krestinsky to Litvinov, 28 June 1932; ibid., p. 393 (no. 268), Litvinov to the People's Commissariat, 30 June 1932.

84. Ibid., pp. 395−99 (no. 273), Litvinov to the People's Commissariat, 5 July 1932, including Litvinov's draft pact, pp. 396−99. The draft is also in *NTCPN*/289.

85. Vaida approved the proposed meeting. *NTCPN*/273, Vaida to Titulescu, 9 July 1932.

86. Ibid./281, Titulescu to the Foreign Ministry, 17 July 1932 (*SARH* 85/1932, pp. 220−22). Litvinov was disposed to reopen the negotiations in September (document 82).

87. For Zaleski's last unsuccessful effort see *DVP*, 15:405−6 (no. 285), Litvinov to the People's Commissariat, 14 July 1932.

88. Ibid., p. 404 (no. 284), Litvinov to the People's Commissariat, 10 July 1932; ibid., pp. 410−11 (no. 289), Litvinov to the People's Commissariat, 16 July 1932.

89. *BPPR*, 107(24 June−28 July 1932): 1−2.

90. *Documents diplomatiques français 1932−1939*, 1re série (*1932−1935*), vol. 1 (Paris: Imprimerie Nationale, 1964), p. 64, document 64, Puaux (Bucharest) to Herriot, 26 July 1932 (hereafter cited as *DDF*); *BPPR*, 108(29 July−17 October 1932): 1.

91. *DDF*, 1:103−4 (no. 66), Puaux to Herriot, 27 July 1932; *Universul*, 28 July 1932, p. 1; Scott, *Alliance Against Hitler*, p. 58.

92. *DVP*, 15:440−41 (no. 301), Dovgalevsky to the People's Commissariat, 25 July 1932. See also Dovgalevsky's version of the Romanian-Soviet talks in a letter to Herriot, ibid., pp. 441−42 (no. 302), 27 July 1932, also in *DDF*, 1:105 (no. 67).

93. *DDF*, 1:149−51 (no. 90), Bressy (Warsaw) to Herriot, 6 August 1932; ibid., pp. 159−60 (no. 94), Bressy to Herriot, 10 August 1932; *DiM*, pp. 536−38 (no. 324), Klapovsky (Paris) to Zaleski, 13 August 1932; *NTCPN*/325,

Davidescu (Warsaw) to the Foreign Ministry, 9 August 1932; ibid./330, David-escu to the Foreign Ministry, 11 August 1932.

94. The National-Peasants had secured a parliamentary majority through the usual not-quite-democratic methods in the July elections (Prost, *Destin de la Roumanie*, p. 61), but in August Vaida was forced to resign when Iuliu Maniu reclaimed the presidency of the party; see *Politics and Political Parties in Roumania* (London: International Reference Library, 1936), pp. 79–80. Maniu, however, refused to form a government because of the Crown's overly great influence; see Nicolae Iorga, *Memorii*, vol. 7, *Sinuciderea partidelor 1932–1938* (Bucharest: Datina românească, 1939), 19 (11 August 1932); *FO* 371, C7263/448/37, Randall (Foreign Office) to Simon, 26 August 1932.

95. The draft had already been presented to Litvinov by Schaetzel in Geneva in July; see *DDF*, 1:91 (no. 56), Massigli (Geneva) to the Ministry of Foreign Affairs, 23 July 1932.

96. *NTCPN*/343, intradepartmental memo, unsigned but clearly by Gafen-cu, undated but probably of 31 August 1932, on a telephone conversation with Titulescu, who was in Bad Gastein (Austria).

97. *DVP*, 15:462–63 (no. 314), Dovgalevsky to the People's Commissariat, 10 August 1932; ibid., p. 481 (no. 329), Litvinov to Dovgalevsky, 20 August 1932; ibid., p. 499 (no. 343), Dovgalevsky to the People's Commissariat, 30 August 1932.

98. *DDF*, 1:245–47 (no. 134), Herriot to Puaux, 1 September 1932; *NTCPN*/344.

99. *NTCPN*/355, intradepartmental memo by Cretzianu, 6 September 1932. Not only were the Soviets told about the démarche (*DVP*, 15:502–3 [no. 345], Rosenberg (Paris) to the People's Commissariat, 2 September 1932), but also about Romania's response (ibid., pp. 513–15 [no. 355], Rosenberg to the People's Commissariat, 6 September 1932). The Romanians, however, did not know this; see *NTCPN*/361, intradepartmental memo by Cretzianu, 8 Septem-ber 1932.

100. *NTCPN*/362, aide-mémoire by Gafencu on the Bad Gastein meeting, 9 September 1932; ibid./363, aide-mémoire by Gafencu for Cesianu, 9 Septem-ber 1932.

101. Ibid./370, Cadere to the Foreign Ministry, 14 September 1932; *DVP*, 15:526–27 (no. 361), Litvinov's notes on the meeting with Patek, 13 September 1932.

102. *NTCPN*/372, Cadere to the Foreign Ministry, 14 September 1932; *DVP*, 15:530–31 (no. 364), Litvinov's notes on a meeting with Patek and a letter to Patek, 14 September 1932.

103. *DDF*, 1:318–19 (no. 176), Dejean (Moscow) to Herriot, 14 September 1932; *DVP*, 15:532 (no. 365), Litvinov's notes on a meeting with Dejean, 14 September 1932.

104. *DDF*, 1:345–46 (no. 192), Herriot to Puaux, 18 September 1932.

105. Ibid., p. 353 (no. 196), Puaux to Herriot, 20 September 1932; *NTCPN*/ 383, Gafencu to the Paris Legation, 19 September 1932.

106. *NTCPN*/383; ibid./387, intradepartmental memo unsigned but by Gafencu, 22 September 1932 (penciled), on a conversation with Puaux; *DDF*, 1:374–75 (no. 207), Puaux to Herriot, 23 September 1932.

107. *NTCPN*/396, Foreign Ministry communiqué, 25 September 1932, denying a divergence of opinion with Titulescu. *Universul*, 26 September 1932, p. 11, like most other Romanian newspapers, ridiculed the communiqué as false and the government's sending of Cadere to Geneva as contrary to national interests.

108. *SARH* 158/1932 (also in the Hoover Institution Archives under the author's name). This dossier, which contains a wealth of information about Titulescu's resignation and the resulting political crisis, is comprised of news releases from Titulescu's news and propaganda mill, Sud-Est Agence Télégraphique; see also *Universul*, 26 September–19 October 1932, passim; *La Roumanie Nouvelle*, 8 (September 1932 and October 1932): 3017, 3049–52.

109. *NTCPN*/401, Cadere (Geneva) to the Foreign Ministry, 27 September 1932.

110. For the French intervention, see *DVP*, 15:546 (no. 383), Rosenberg to the People's Commissariat, 29 September 1932; ibid., p. 547 (no. 384), Litvinov (Geneva) to Rosenberg, 29 September 1932; *NTCPN*/407, Cadere (Madgearu, temporary first delegate to the League) to the Foreign Ministry, 29 September 1932; ibid./409, Cadere (Madgearu) to the Foreign Ministry, by telephone, 30 September 1930; ibid./411, Cadere (Madgearu) to the Foreign Ministry, 30 September 1932. For the Polish intervention, see *NTCPN*/412, Cadere to the Foreign Ministry, 30 September 1932.

111. *DVP*, 15:554–55 (no. 389), Litvinov to Stalin (!), 3 October 1932 (author's emphasis). Ibid., p. 558 (no. 391), Karakhan to Litvinov, 4 October 1932.

112. Later (4 December 1932) Cadere wrote Titulescu that he had never accepted "differences" modified with anything, but that the Soviets had agreed to "existing" or "present or future." Grauer, pp. 124–25. When the author of the present work asked Cadere about this contradiction in June 1972, Cadere replied that I would have to make my own judgment as to whose version was the truth.

113. *NTCPN*/437, Litvinov's exposé of the Romanian-Soviet talks, 15 October 1932; also in Degras, pp. 543–46. See also *DDF*, 1:491–93 (no. 251), Payart (Moscow) to Herriot, 19 October 1932.

114. *DDF*, 1:429–30 (no. 238), Léger's notes on a conversation with Titulescu, 11 October 1932; ibid., pp. 433–35 (no. 241), Herriot to Puaux, 13 October 1932. The message Titulescu gave the French was essentially the same one he gave the Romanian parliament on 23 and 24 November 1932. A copy of the former speech from *Universul*, 25 November 1932, pp. 7–8, is in the Hoover Institution Archives under the author's name.

115. *DDF*, 1:681 (no. 314), communication from the Embassy of the USSR in Paris, 9 November 1932; also in Degras, p. 547.

116. Bacon, "Titulescu and Romanian Foreign Policy," pp. 75–90, 141–51, 277–78.

Documents

DOCUMENT NO. 1: *Submitted to Minister Ghika* [Dimitri Ghika, foreign minister in the cabinet of Prof. Nicolae Iorga], *the minister of war* [Gen. Stefanescu-Amza], *and the chief of the General Staff* [Gen. Samsonovici] *in conference that took place at the Foreign Ministry, June 5, 1931* [marginal note in Titulescu's handwriting]. Mihai Arion was director of eastern political affairs in the Ministry of Foreign Affairs at Bucharest.

    1. Count Ian Szembek.

    2. Since the Soviet-Polish border was mutually recognized and the Soviet-Romanian border was not.

Document No. 2: Enclosed with document no. 1.

Document No. 3.

    3. *NTCPN*/6, 7, and 8.

Document No. 4: *Received from Minister Szembek July 31, 1931, for submission to Minister Ghika upon his return from vacation. I believe that it would be right to give our text to the Polish Legation because Mr. Szembek told me that Poland will soon begin negotiations with the USSR on the basis of the Polish text of July 31, 1931* [manuscript note by Mihai Arion].

Document No. 5: *The text of the Romanian draft given to Count Szembek by the minister of foreign affairs, August 25, 1931* [original headnote].

    4. *Reservations formulated on the occasion of Romania's accession to the voluntary clause of article 36 of the statute of the Permanent Court of International Justice* [original manuscript note].

    5. *Conforming to article V, Lithuania having subsequently acceded, as did Estonia, Latvia, Persia, and Turkey, to the Protocol of Moscow* [original manuscript note].

    6. *Formula employed in article VI of the Treaty of Guarantee concluded between Romania and Poland* [original manuscript note].

Document No. 6: Alexander Cretzianu was a prominent member of the Romanian diplomatic corps. At that time, he was stationed at the Romanian Foreign Office.

    7. *NTCPN*/11.

    8. *NTCPN*/14.

    9. Auguste Zaleski was Poland's Foreign Minister.

Document No. 7: Grigore Bilciurescu was Romania's minister to Poland.

    10. *NTCPN*/20.

    11. See *DiM*, pp. 502–5 (no. 305) and/or *DVP*, 14:647–50 (no. 338) for Litvinov's notes on the meeting.

    12. See document 2, articles V and VI.

    13. *NTCPN*/16.

    14. There is no further information in *NTCPN* about the source.

Document No. 8.

    15. Because the final procès-verbal would touch upon the cause of failure—Bessarabia.

Document No. 9: *Copy: of* [a dispatch] *from the Ministry of Foreign Affairs (Eastern Political Director) of November 28, 1931, to our Legation in Warsaw* [original heading]. Drawn up by the Eastern Political Affairs Office for Ghika's signature.

16. Document 7.

17. *NTCPN*/27, Cesianu to the Foreign Ministry, 26 November 1931.

DOCUMENT No. 10: *Telegram decoded at 11 o'clock from the Legation in Warsaw no. 4026, dated December 4, 8 o'clock 1931* [original heading].

18. *NTCPN*/35, Bilciurescu to the Foreign Ministry, 3 December 1931.

19. Tadeusz Schaetzel.

20. As prime minister in March 1918, General Averescu had promised to progressively withdraw Romanian troops from Bessarabia. See *DVP* 1:210−11 (no. 90), 5−9 March 1918; and Filliti in *Aspects de relations russo-roumaines*, pp. 80−81.

DOCUMENT No. 11.

21. Document 10.

22. Jules Laroche.

DOCUMENT No. 12: *Telegram decoded at 9 o'clock from the Legation in Ankara, no. 2053, dated December 6, 1931, 7 P.M.* [original heading]. *Communicated to H.M. the King. Sent to Min. Arion* [original routing notes]. Ion Carp was Romanian minister in Ankara.

23. Romanian Minister Carp first talked with Turkish Foreign Minister Tewfik Rusdi Bey on 30 November (*NTCPN*/42, Carp to the Foreign Ministry, 5 December 1931). Acting on Ghika's instructions, Carp told Rusdi that he had orders to sound out Soviet Ambassador Y. Z. Surits on the possibility of Soviet-Romanian talks. On 2 December Rusdi confirmed the Soviets' inclination to negotiate if the initiative came from Romania. On November 30 Rusdi said that he was under the impression that the Soviets wished to nullify the Polish-Romanian alliance, replacing it with a [tripartite] pact of mutual assistance aimed at the aggressor. At the second meeting, Rusdi did not repeat his impression. *NTCPN*/42 is not reproduced because of its length and the amount of extraneous material it contains. For the Soviet side, see *DVP*, 14:688 (no. 361), Surits to People's Commissariat, 2 December 1931.

DOCUMENT No. 13.

24. *NTCPN*/47, Carp to the Foreign Ministry, 8 December 1931, on a second conversation with Surits, who suggested Ankara as the site for Soviet-Romanian negotiations.

DOCUMENT No. 14: Constantin Cesianu was Romania's minister to France.

25. For no. 68453, see *NTCPN*/26, Ghika to the Paris Legation, 26 November 1931; for no. 70298, see *NTCPN*/41, Ghika to the Paris Legation, 5 December 1931.

26. For Riga, see *NTCPN*/22, Ghika to the Riga Legation, 26 November 1931; ibid./49, Sturdza (Riga) to the Foreign Ministry, 8 December 1931. See also ibid./29, 30, 43, and 44 for other Ghika-Sturdza exchanges. For Ankara, see documents 12 and 13.

27. See document 12, note. 22.

DOCUMENT No. 15.

28. For no. 4099, see *NTCPN*/51, Bilciurescu to the Foreign Ministry,

9 December 1931; for no. 4108, see *NTCPN*/52, Bilciurescu to the Foreign Ministry, 10 December 1931.

29. By way of Dovgalevsky, *DVP*, 14:703 (no. 369), Litvinov to Dovgalevsky, 10 December 1931.

DOCUMENT No. 16: *Telegram decoded at 9 A.M. from the Legation in London no. 3127, dated December 12, 7:01 P.M. 1931* [original heading]. Nicolae Titulescu was Romanian minister to the Court of St. James and delegate to the League of Nations.

30. Quite obviously, Titulescu was annoyed by the government's failure to inform him and to ask his advice. Since the mid-1920s he had been consulted on every major foreign-policy decision.

DOCUMENT No. 17.

31. *On December 17 the translated text had not yet been received by the Foreign Ministry* [original manuscript note].

32. *NTCPN*/51, Bilciurescu to the Foreign Ministry, 9 December 1931.

DOCUMENT No. 18.

33. The dispatch referred to as no. 67648 is probably either *NTCPN*/61 or 62, although the number is wrong. In the former (18 December 1931), Ghika instructs Bilciurescu to ask Antonov-Ovseyenko about the Soviet choice for the site for negotiations, while in the second (19 December 1931) Ghika says that the Soviets had rejected Warsaw and instructs Bilciurescu to suggest Riga. For no. 4214, see *NTCPN*/63, Bilciurescu to the Foreign Ministry, 18 December 1931, reporting that the Soviets had rejected Warsaw and had proposed Moscow, a choice seconded by Laroche.

34. The first time having been in February 1929 for the signing of the Litvinov Protocol.

35. "Estonia" on the document, but Latvia is the country referred to.

DOCUMENT No. 19: *Communicated to H.M. the King* [original heading]. C. Zanescu was Romania's chargé d'affaires in Italy.

36. The political director of the Italian Foreign Ministry was Raffaele Guariglia; the Italian ambassador in Moscow was Bernardo Attolico.

37. Ghika, a former Romanian minister to Italy, initiated this flow of information from Rome; see *NTCPN*/28, Ghika to the Rome Legation, 27 November 1931.

DOCUMENT No. 20: *Telegram decoded at 4 P.M. from Mr. Minister Carp in Constantinople, no. 2212 dated December 30, 12:45 P.M.,1931* [original heading]. *Communicated to H.M. the King* [original routing note].

38. *DVP*, 14:739−40 (no. 394), Surits to the People's Commissariat, 27 December 1931.

DOCUMENT No. 21

39. Document 20.

40. *The text of this telegram was written by Minister Ghika on the original telegram No. 2212 from Carp. The original was given to Minister Arion* [original manuscript note].

DOCUMENT No. 22: Mihai R. Sturdza was Romanian chargé d'affaires in Riga.

41. Document 19.

42. Document 23.

DOCUMENT No. 23: This was the "Riga Draft," i.e., the revised draft sent to Sturdza in Riga along with document no. 22.

DOCUMENT No. 24: For these events, see Iorga, *Memorii*, vol. 6, p. 275 (entry for January 5, 1932).

43. Document 23.

DOCUMENT No. 25: *Coded and sent at 7:00 P.M. [A]rion. The text of this telegram was written by the* [foreign] *minister* [.] [T]*he original* [is in the possession of] *Minister Arion* [original manuscript notes].

DOCUMENT No. 26.

44. Document 27.

45. The French colleague was Jean Tripier, the Polish Miroslav Arciszewski.

DOCUMENT No. 27: The Soviet text given to Sturdza at Riga.

DOCUMENT No. 28.

46. See Sturdza, p. 50; *NTCPN*/99, Sturdza to the Foreign Ministry, 8 January 1932.

47. *DVP*, 15:15 (no. 4), Stomonyakov to the People's Commissariat, 7 January 1932.

DOCUMENT No. 29: Sent from Riga at midnight and decoded in Bucharest at 9:45 A.M. (information from original document). *Sent to H.M. the King* [original routing note].

48. See also *NTCPN*/110, Sturdza to the Foreign Ministry, 11 January 1932.

49. *DVP*, 15:15 (no. 5), Litvinov to Stomonyakov, 7 January 1932; ibid., pp. 18−19 (no. 10), Litvinov to Stomonyakov, 10 January 1932.

DOCUMENT No. 30: *The text of this telegram was sent with no. 1603 of January 12, 1932* [original headnote].

50. Document 29.

DOCUMENT No. 31.

51. Document 29.

DOCUMENT No. 32: Decoded in Bucharest at 9:30 P.M. (information from original document).

DOCUMENT No. 33: Sent from Riga at 6:00 A.M. and decoded in Bucharest at noon (information from original document).

52. *DVP*, 15:21 (no. 14), Litvinov to Stomonyakov, 12 January 1932.

DOCUMENT No. 34.

53. Document 33.

54. Document 30.

DOCUMENT No. 35: Sent from Warsaw at 10:30 P.M. on January 15 and decoded in Bucharest at 1:00 P.M. on January 16 (information from original document).

55. *NTCPN*/112, Ghika to the Warsaw Legation, 13 January 1932.

DOCUMENT No. 36: Sent from Riga at 2:00 A.M. and decoded in Bucharest at 4:00 P.M. (information from original document).

DOCUMENT No. 37: Sent from Riga at 10:20 P.M. on January 16 and decoded in Bucharest at 11:00 A.M. on January 17 (information from original document).

56. Document 34.

DOCUMENT No. 38: Sent from Warsaw at 6:45 P.M. on January 16 and decoded in Bucharest at noon on January 17 (information from original document).

57. *NTCPN*/118, Ghika to the Warsaw Legation, 15 January 1932.

DOCUMENT No. 39: Sent from Paris at 8:00 P.M. on January 18 and decoded in Bucharest at 11:00 A.M. on January 19 (information from original document). The "no. 2479" referred to here may be identified as *NTCPN*/119, Ghika to the Paris Legation, January 15, 1932, instructing Cesianu to inform Berthelot of the Riga negotiations' progress. This was followed by *NTCPN*/122, Ghika to the Paris Legation, n.d., stating Romania's juridical objections to various Soviet texts.

DOCUMENT No. 40.

58. *NTCPN*/133,134, Sturdza to the Foreign Ministry, 18 January 1932.

59. The Romanian word "pretenţiune" occurs frequently in the Romanian documents and has been rendered as "pretension" rather than "claim" in order to emphasize the unfounded nature of Soviet assertions of their rights over Bessarabia. The post-World War II less latinate "pretenţie" is the contemporary spelling.

60. *DVP*, 15:43−44 (no. 30), Stomonyakov to the People's Commissariat, 20 January 1932.

61. Document 40.

DOCUMENT No. 41: See *DVP*, 15:44−45 (no. 31) for Russian version.

62. See Document 40.

DOCUMENT No. 42.

63. *NTCPN*/144, the Foreign Ministry to Bilciurescu, 3 February 1932.

64. *DVP*, 14:649 (no. 338), Litvinov's notes on a meeting with Patek, 14 November 1931.

65. Ibid., note.

66. Degras, 2:522−23.

DOCUMENT No. 44.

67. *Universul*, 22 January 1932, p. 11.

DOCUMENT No. 45.

68. Pierre Laval had replaced Aristide Briand as Foreign Minister on 13 January.

69. Iorga, *Memorii*, vol. 3, p. 299 (28 January 1932).

DOCUMENT No. 48: Sent from Paris at noon on January 31 and decoded in Bucharest at 1:20 P.M. the same day (information from original document).

DOCUMENT No. 49: Manuscript note.

70. The capitals referred to were Vienna in 1924 and Moscow in 1929.

DOCUMENT No. 50: Manuscript note on *NTCPN*/179 identifies telegram no. 9369 as one of February 19 from Prime Minister Iorga to Ghika in Geneva: Iorga asks Ghika to clear up conflicting statements by Beck and Zaleski.

DOCUMENT No. 51.

71. *DiM*, pp. 528−29 (no 318), Stomonyakov to Antonov-Ovseyenko, 5 March 1932; *DVP*, 15:140−41 (no. 95), Litvinov (Geneva) to the People's Commissariat, 26 February 1932.

72. Pilsudski had arrived in Romania. Iorga and Szembek met with the marshal on 2 March, but there was no discussion of the Soviet talks. Iorga, *Memorii*, vol. 6, pp. 333−34 (2 March 1932); *Universul*, 4 March 1932, p. 1.

73. *SARH* 85/1932, pp. 5−8; Iorga, *Memorii*, vol. 6, p. 336 (4 March 1932).

DOCUMENT No. 52: Sent from Geneva at 8:00 P.M. on March 9 and decoded in Bucharest at noon on March 11: extracts (information from original document).

74. The first part of the dispatch (not in the *NTCPN* copy) dealt with the Tardieu Plan for the economic reconstruction of Central Europe, see *SARH* 85/1932, pp. 13−15.

DOCUMENT No. 54: *Delivered with no. 19283 of April 7, 1932* [original headnote].

75. Puaux was probably anticipating a change in French policy following the predicted victory of the Left in the May elections.

DOCUMENT No. 55: For these events, see Iorga, *Memorii*, vol. 6, pp. 374−75 (14 April 1932).

76. Laroche, p. 112, maintains that Pilsudski was never anti-French nor was he ever pro-French, but rather Polish first and foremost.

77. Constantin Argetoianu was minister of finance and interior, and the second most important member of Iorga's government.

78. Romanian newspapers reported almost daily incidents involving Soviet frontier guards killing "kulaks" trying to flee collectivization by fording or swimming the Dniester.

DOCUMENT No. 56: Sent from Paris at 7:50 P.M. on April 18 (information from original document). The no. 20807 referred to in the heading is *NTCPN*/203, Ghika to the Warsaw, Paris, and Riga legations and to Titulescu (Geneva), 14 April 1932, on the meeting with Pilsudski.

DOCUMENT No. 57: *Sent by courier* [original headnote].

79. See note on document 56.

80. Joseph Paul-Boncour was a prominent French politician of the independent Left. In 1932 he was permanent delegate to the League of Nations and later minister of war in the cabinet of Édouard Herriot.

81. See *DVP*, 15:256−57 (no. 174), Dovgalevsky to the People's Commissariat, 19 April 1932.

82. Ibid., p. 274 (no. 183), Stomonyakov to Antonov-Ovseyenko, 22 April 1932.

DOCUMENT No. 58.

83. Document 56.

84. *DVP*, 15:273−74 (no. 183).

85. For French intervention along these lines, see ibid., p. 256 (no. 174).

DOCUMENT No. 59: *Cabinet letter by Mr. Minister Ghika to Mr. Cesianu in Paris* [original headnote].

86. Document 57.

87. *NTCPN*/213, Ghika to Titulescu, April 26, 1932.

DOCUMENT No. 60: Sent from Geneva at 12:50 A.M. on May 5 and decoded in Bucharest at 10:00 A.M. on May 9 (information from original document). This is *SARH* 85/1932, pp. 67–70.

88. A similar appeal was made to Zaleski; see *NTCPN*/223, Titulescu to the Foreign Ministry, 23 May 1932.

DOCUMENT No. 61: Sent from Geneva at 11:15 P.M. on May 26 (information from original document). This is *SARH* 85/1932, pp. 106–7.

89. *DVP,* 15:330–31 (no. 227), Litvinov's record of a conversation with Zaleski, 24 May 1932.

90. Presumably this refers to Patek's idea of not mentioning or referring to Bessarabia in the text, but stipulating in a letter exchanged at the time of signature, "All pending litigious questions between the two countries remain in the state in which they were found at the time of the signing of the pact." See *NTCPN*/240, Cadere (Warsaw) to the Foreign Ministry, 16 June 1932.

DOCUMENT No. 62: Grigore Gafencu was secretary general of the Foreign Ministry in the government of Alexander Vaida-Voevod. The document is also in *ALPA.*

91. Szembek was a little confused. All the pacts had been signed: Finland's on 21 January 1932, Latvia's on 5 February 1932, and Estonia's on 4 May 1932. They were to be *ratified* in June.

DOCUMENT No. 63: Also in *ALPA.*

92. General Janusz Gasiorowski was chief of the Polish General Staff.

93. *NTCPN*/225, Ghika to Titulescu, 30 May 1932.

DOCUMENT No. 64: Victor Cadere had just arrived in Warsaw, replacing Grigore Bilciurescu as Romania's minister to Poland.

94. Franz Von Papen had replaced Heinrich Brüning as chancellor. The Polish-German conflict over Danzig had been sharpened in June 1932 by the ostentatious visit of naval units from both countries to the Free City.

95. Paul Painlevé, French scientist and politician, was air minister in the cabinet headed by Édouard Herriot. The latter was among the most prominent French politicians of the interwar period. He was installed as premier for the third time on June 3, 1932.

DOCUMENT No. 65.

96. *NTCPN*/244, Cadere to the Foreign Ministry, 16 June 1932.

97. Probably referring to *NTCPN*/234, Sturdza to the Foreign Ministry, 12 June 1932.

DOCUMENT No. 66: Filality was a senior Romanian Foreign Service officer, who frequently acted as the senior official when the foreign minister and secretary general were not available. The document is also in *ALPA.*

DOCUMENT No. 67: Titulescu was in Lausanne. The document is also in *ALPA.*

98. Most likely, Major Tadeusz Kobylanski, a specialist in eastern policy assigned to the Bucharest Legation. Major Kobylanski, another soldier turned diplomat like Beck and Szembek, was an expert on East European political problems.

99. *NTCPN*/250, Cadere to Gafencu, 25 June 1932.

100. Ibid./252, Titulescu to the Foreign Ministry, 28 June 1932 (*SARH* 85/1932, p. 132).

DOCUMENT No. 68.

101. *NTCPN*/259, Cadere to the Foreign Ministry, 4 [*sic*] July 1932.

102. I.e., German intrigues; see *NTCPN*/251, Cadere to the Foreign Ministry, 25 June 1932.

103. Ibid./258, Cadere to the Foreign Ministry, 2 July 1932.

DOCUMENT No. 69: Sent from Lausanne at 1:40 A.M. (information from original document).

104. James Ramsay MacDonald was the foremost interwar leader of the British Labour Party. In 1932 he was prime minister and first lord of the treasury in his second government of national union.

DOCUMENT No. 70: Alexander Vaida-Voevod was a leader of the National Peasant Party and both prime and foreign minister of Romania (June–October 1932).

105. *NTCPN*/264, Titulescu to the Foreign Ministry, 5 July 1932 (*SARH* 85/1932, pp. 174–75).

DOCUMENT 71.

106. Repeated in ibid./271, Gafencu to Cadere, 8 July 1932.

DOCUMENT No. 72: *SARH* 85/1932, pp. 189–91.

107. Document 73.

108. André Lefebvre de la Boulaye was a French diplomat. In 1932 he was subdirector of the European Department and of the Office of Commercial and Political Affairs at the Quai d'Orsay.

DOCUMENT No. 73: Sent from Lausanne at 11:30 P.M. on July 7 (information from original document). This is *SARH* 85/1932, pp. 181–88.

109. See document 74.

110. Document 47.

DOCUMENT No. 74: Sent from Lausanne at 1:50 A.M. on July 9 (information from original document). This is *SARH* 85/1932, pp. 192–96.

111. René Massigli was a prominent French diplomat of the interwar period. In 1932 he was France's deputy delegate to the Disarmament Conference and chief of the League of Nations section of the Quai d'Orsay.

DOCUMENT No. 75.

112. Tadeusz Schaetzel.

113. The "last telegram" was *NTCPN*/275, Gafencu to Cadere, 13 July 1932, in which Cadere was fully informed of the Titulescu-Zaleski talks in Lausanne.

DOCUMENT No. 76.

114. Document 75.

115. The Sejm was the Polish parliament.

DOCUMENT No. 78.

116. See *DDF,* 1:81–82 (no. 50), Puaux to Herriot, 22 July 1932.

DOCUMENT No. 80.

117. *Universul,* 27 July 1932, p. 1.

DOCUMENT No. 81.

118. This interview was followed up by another more heated Szembek-Gafencu exchange on 28 July 1932; see *NTCPN*/301, intradepartmental memo by Gafencu, 28 July 1932. See also *DDF,* 1:103–4 (no. 66), Puaux to Herriot, 27 July 1932.

DOCUMENT No. 82.

119. RADOR was the Romanian press agency.

120. Wilno (Vilnyus) was part of Poland at the time.

121. PAT was the Polish news agency.

DOCUMENT No. 83.

122. This note was given to the Polish Foreign Ministry, on explicit instructions from Bucharest. *NTCPN*/300, Gafencu to Cadere, 27 July 1932. A brief history of the pledge may be found in ibid./299, Cadere to the Foreign Ministry, 27 July 1932.

DOCUMENT No. 84.

123. Probably a misprint, in reality referring to no. 40988, *NTCPN*/307, Vaida to Cesianu, 1 August 1932, instructing the latter to make this démarche.

124. See *DDF,* 1:142–43 (no. 84), Herriot to the legations in Warsaw and Bucharest, 3 August 1932.

125. Because the Averescu-Mussolini correspondence was, in fact, secret, we can only guess its content. In 1926 or 1927 Mussolini agreed to ratify the convention concerning Bessarabia in return for Averescu's personal assurances that Romania would look more favorably on Italy's Danubian policy and on Italian economic advantages in Romania. See Filliti in Cioranesco et al., p. 121; Arnold J. Toynbee, *Survey of International Affairs 1926* (London: Oxford University Press and Milford, 1928), pp. 158–59; *I documenti diplomatici italiani,* 7th series, "1922–1935," 5 (7 February–31 December 1927): 39 (no. 38), Durazzo (Bucharest) to Grandi (Rome), 28 February–1 March 1927; ibid.: 64–65 (no. 54), aide-mémoire by Guariglia for Mussolini, n.d. (sometime between 23 February and 7 March 1927).

DOCUMENT No. 85: The text was sent to Cadere with the intention that he would give it to the Poles, who would present it to the Soviets in the guise of a Polish proposal (information from original document).

DOCUMENT No. 86.

126. *NTCPN*/334. The interpellation asked Vaida to clarify what appeared to be a contradiction between the Foreign Ministry's communiqué of 25 July (document 80) and Vaida's statement to a Polish interviewer that he *hoped* the Poles would not ratify their pact. See *NTCPN*/322 and *Universul,* 8 August 1932, p. 1.

127. Ion Inculeţ was the most prominent Bessarabian member of the National Liberal Party. He was his party's Bessarabian "expert" in the Romanian parliament. George I. Brătianu was the leader of the dissident (i.e., Carolist) wing of the Liberal Party as well as a famous scholar who wrote a Bessarabian history.

DOCUMENT No. 87: *Constanţa, Hotel Carol, August 29, 1932. Present: Colonel Beck, Count Szembek, Messrs. Cadere, Tilea and me* [original headnote].

128. Document 85.

129. Document 86.

DOCUMENT No. 89: *Given to Mr. de Hautecloque, chargé d'affaires of France, on September 2, 9:30 P.M. a.c.* [original headnote].

130. *DDF,* 1:245–47 (no. 134), Herriot to Puaux, September 1, 1932.

DOCUMENT No. 90: This French document was either intercepted by the Romanians or given to the Romanian government by the French Legation. No further information is given.

DOCUMENT No. 91.

131. *NTCPN*/354, Davidescu (Warsaw) to the Foreign Ministry, 5 September 1932.

132. *DDF,* 1:245–47 (no. 134).

133. He had. *DVP,* 15:499 (no. 343), Dovgalevsky to the People's Commissariat.

134. *NTCPN*/361, intradepartmental memo by Cretzianu, 8 September 1932.

DOCUMENT No. 92: The telegram was sent from Warsaw at 8:25 P.M., Polish time (information from original document). The "Hughes device" was no doubt a two-way version of the type-printing telegraph patented by the American inventor David Edward Hughes (1831–1900).

135. *DVP,* 15:533–34 (no. 368), Litvinov's notes on a meeting with Patek, 15 September 1932.

DOCUMENT No. 92.

136. Document 93.

DOCUMENT No. 93.

137. The first communication referred to is *NTCPN*/380, Cadere to the Foreign Ministry, 17 September 1932. For nos. 48709 and 48764, see *NTCPN*/378–79, Vaida to Cadere, 16 September 1932; for Litvinov's version, see *DVP,* 15:539–40 (no. 373), Litvinov (Berlin) to the People's Commissariat, 17 September 1932.

138. Muhammad Ali Furughi was a prominent interwar Persian statesman, several times prime minister and foreign minister.

139. The Herriot Formula, point B. See *DDF,* 1:246 (no. 134).

140. Compare to document 102.

DOCUMENT No. 94: Unsigned, but probably by Vaida. The Vaida government decided to accept Litvinov's suggestion of renewed negotiations in or near Geneva. Cadere is hereby assigned to be the Romanian negotiator.

DOCUMENT No. 95: Titulescu was now in London.

141. Virgil Madgearu was a noted Romanian economist and one of the leaders of the National Peasant Party. At the time of his appointment as delegate to the League of Nations, he was minister of commerce and industry in the Vaida government.

142. For financial assistance.

143. See document 103.

DOCUMENT No. 96: Sent from Geneva at 10:35 P.M. on September 28 (information from original document).

DOCUMENT No. 97: Sent from Geneva at 1:00 A.M. on September 29 (information from original document).

DOCUMENT No. 98.

144. *DVP,* 15:550 (no. 386), Litvinov to the People's Commissariat, 1 October 1932.

145. Averescu was leader of the People's Party, Duca of the National Liberal Party.

DOCUMENT No. 99: The telegram is addressed via Davidescu, Cadere's assistant, at the Hotel Richemond (information from original document).

DOCUMENT No. 100: Sent from Geneva at 12:45 A.M. on October 4 (information from original document).

146. *DVP,* 15:554−55 (no. 389), Litvinov to *Stalin,* 3 October 1932 (author's emphasis).

DOCUMENT No. 101: *Communication that was made at the time of Minister Madgearu's departure from Geneva. s.c.* [original manuscript note].

DOCUMENT No. 102: Sent from Geneva at 12:30 A.M. and decoded in Bucharest at 9:30 A.M. (information from original document).

147. Titulescu's Reuters interview, *NTCPN*/413, also in *SARH* 158/1932.

DOCUMENT No. 103: Sent from Paris at 3:56 P.M. on October 7 (information from original document).

148. A rejection that had been decided upon quite a bit earlier. See *DDF,* 1:381−82 (no. 212), Herriot to Puaux and Massigli (Geneva), 24 September 1932.

Bibliography

Archives of the Hoover Institution on War, Revolution and Peace. Titulescu, Krupensky and Bacon Collections. Stanford, California.

Bacon, Walter M., Jr. "Nicolae Titulescu and Romanian Foreign Policy 1933–1934." Ph.D. dissertation, University of Denver, 1975.

Beloff, Max. *The Foreign Policy of Soviet Russia, 1929–1941.* Vol. 1, *1929–1936.* London, New York, Toronto: Oxford University Press, 1947.

Beaucourt, Chantal. "L'Union Sovietique el la Roumanie." In *Les frontières européennes de l'U.R.S.S. 1917–1941,* edited by Jean-Baptiste Duroselle, pp. 293–330. Cahiers de la Fondation Nationale des Sciences Politiques, no. 85. Paris: Librairie Armand Colin, 1957.

Boldur, Alexandru V. *Basarabia românească* [Romanian Bessarabia]. Bucharest: Tipografia Carpaţi, Petre Bărbulescu, 1943.

Brătianu, George I. *La Bessarabie: Droits nationaux et historiques.* Bucharest: Institut d'histoire universelle "N. Iorga," 1943.

Budurowycz, Bohdan B. *Polish-Soviet Relations 1932–1939.* New York and London: Columbia University Press, 1963.

Bulletin périodique de la presse roumaine. Paris, irregularly, 1916–

Ceauşescu, Nicolae. *Romania on the Way of Completing Socialist Construction.* Vol. 1, *Reports, Speeches, Articles, July 1965–September 1966.* Bucharest: Meridiane Publishing House, 1969.

———. *Romania on the Way of Building up the Multilaterally Developed Socialist Society.* Vol. 7, *Reports, Speeches, Articles, March 1972–December 1972.* Bucharest: Meridiane Publishing House, 1973.

Cioranesco, George et al. *Aspects des relations russo-roumaines.* Paris: Minard, 1967.

Constantinescu, Miron, and Liveanu, Vasile. "Remarks on Nicolae Titulescu's Actions for a Rapprochement Between Romania and the U.S.S.R." Translated by Mary Lazarescu. In *Problems of History and Social Theory,* Biblioteca Historica Romaniae studies, no. 30, pp. 129–170. Bucharest: Publishing House of the Academy of the Socialist Republic of Romania, 1970.

Degras, Jane T. *Soviet Documents on Foreign Policy.* Vol. 2, *1925–1933.* New York: Oxford University Press, 1952.

Deutsch, Robert, ed. *Nicolae Titulescu discursuri* [Nicolae Titulescu Speeches]. Bucharest: Editura ştiinţifică, 1967.

Eudin, Xenia Joukoff, and Slusser, Robert M., eds. *Soviet Foreign Policy 1928–1934: Documents and Materials.* Vol. 1. University Park, Pa., and London:

Pennsylvania State University Press, 1966.

Fischer, Louis. *The Soviets in World Affairs: A History of Relations Between the Soviet Union and the Rest of the World, 1917–1929.* Abridged. New York: Vintage Books, 1960.

Fischer-Galati, Stephen. *Twentieth Century Rumania.* New York and London: Columbia University Press, 1970.

Floyd, David. *Rumania, Russia's Dissident Ally.* New York: Praeger, 1965.

France, *Documents diplomatiques français 1932–1939,* 1st ser. (1932–35), vol. 1 *(19 July–14 November 1932).* Paris: Imprimerie Nationale, 1964.

Gafencu, Grigore et al. *Roumania at the Peace Conference.* Paris: n.p., 1946.

Grauer, Stefan St. *Les relations entre la Roumanie et l'U.R.S.S. depuis le traité de Versailles.* Paris: Editions A. Pedone, 1936.

Great Britain, *Documents on British Foreign Policy.* Second series, vol. 7. London: Her Majesty's Stationery Office, 1958.

Great Britain. Public Records Office, Foreign Office Correspondence. London.

Hartl, Hans. "Bessarabien." *Südosteuropa Mitteilungen,* 15:61–71.

Iorga, Nicolae. *Memorii.* Vol. 6, *Incercarea guvernării peste partide (1931–32)* [The attempt of the nonparty government, 1931–32]. Bucharest: "Datina românească," 1939.

———. *Memorii.* Vol. 7, *Sinuciderea partidelor (1932–1938).* [The Suicide of the Parties, 1932–1938] Bucharest: "Datina românească," 1939.

Italy. *I documenti diplomatici italiani,* 7th ser. Vol. 5, *1922–1935.* Instituto poligrafico dello stato, 1967.

Jowitt, Kenneth. *Revolutionary Breakthroughs and National Development: The Case of Romania, 1944–1965.* Berkeley and Los Angeles: University of California Press, 1971.

Jozsa, Gy. "Marx-Engels et les Roumains." *Documentation sur l'Europe Centrale,* 10: 310–26.

Kopanskiĭ, ÎA., and Levit, I. Ė. *Sovetsko-rumynskie otnosheniĭa 1929–1934 g. (ot podpisaniĭa Moskovogo protokola do ustanovleniĭa diplomaticheskikh otnosheniĭ)* [Soviet-Romanian relations 1929–34 (from the signing of the Moscow Protocol to the establishment of diplomatic relations)]. Moscow: Izdatel'stvo "Nauka," 1971.

Korbel, Josef. *Poland Between East and West: Soviet and German Diplomacy toward Poland 1919–1933.* Princeton, N.J.: Princeton University Press, 1963.

Laroche, Jules A. *La Pologne de Pilsudski: souvenirs d'une ambassade 1926–1935.* Paris: Flammarion, 1953.

Librach, Jan. *The Rise of the Soviet Empire: A Study of Soviet Foreign Policy.* New York and Washington, D.C.: Praeger, 1964.

Macovescu, George, ed. *Nicolae Titulescu documente diplomatice.* [Nicolae Titulescu Diplomatic Documents] Bucharest: Editura politică, 1967.

Le Mois Paris, monthly, 1931–

Nano, F. C. "The Foreign Policy of Romania 1918–1939." Incomplete manuscript. Typed. New York: Mid-European Studies Center, n.d.

Oprea, Ion M. *O etapă rodnică din istoria relațiilor diplomatice româno-sovietice*

1928–1936 [A fruitful stage in the history of Romanian-Soviet diplomatic relations 1928–36]. Bucharest: Editura politică, 1967.

———. *Nicolae Titulescu.* Bucharest: Editura ştiinţifică, 1966.

———. *Nicolae Titulescu's Diplomatic Activity.* Translated by Andrei Bantaş. Biblioteca Historica Romaniae studies, no. 22. Bucharest: Publishing House of the Academy of the Socialist Republic of Romania, 1968.

Oţetea, Andrei, ed. *Karl Marx: Însemnări despre Români, manuscrise inedite.* [Karl Marx. Notes about Romanians, unpublished manuscripts] Bucharest: Editura politică, 1964.

Poland and USSR. *Dokumenty i materialy po istorii sovetsko-polskikh otnoshenii* [Documents and materials on the history of Soviet-Polish relations]. Vol. 5 *(May 1926–December 1932).* Moscow: Izdatel'stvo "Nauka," 1967.

Politics and Political Parties in Romania. London: International Reference Library Publishing Company, 1936.

Prost, Henri. *Destin de la Roumanie 1918–1954.* Paris: Editions Berger-Levrault, 1954.

Rakovskiĭ, Khristian G. *Roumania and Bessarabia.* London: W. P. Coates, 1925.

Romania. Central State Library, Library for Foreign Literature, Manuscripts. Bucharest.

Romania. Library of the Academy of the Romanian Socialist Republic, Manuscript Section. Bucharest.

Romania. State Archives, Royal House Collection. Bucharest.

Romanian Workers Party, *Declaraţia cu privire la poziţia Partidului Muncitoresc Romîn în problemele mişcări comuniste şi muncitoreşti internaţionale adoptată de planara largită a C.C. al P.M.R. din aprilie 1964* [Statement concerning the position of the Romanian Workers Party on the problems of the international communist and workers' movement, adopted by the enlarged plenum of the Central Committee of the Romanian Workers Party of April 1964]. Bucharest: Editura politică, 1964.

La Roumanie Nouvelle. Bucharest, monthly, 1924–

Scott, William Evans. *Alliance Against Hitler: The Origins of the Franco-Soviet Pact.* Durham, N.C.: Duke University Press, 1962.

Spector, Sherman D. *Rumania at the Paris Peace Conference: A Study of the Diplomacy of Ioan I. C. Bratianu.* New York: Bookman Associates, Inc., 1962.

Sturdza, Michel. *The Suicide of Europe: Memoirs of Prince Michel Sturdza, Former Foreign Minister of Rumania.* Boston and Los Angeles: Western Islands Publishers, 1968.

Suga, Alexander. "Bessarabien—noch immer umstritten?" *Osteuropa* 21: 316–23.

Titulescu, N. "Two Neighbors of Russia and Their Policies." Part 1, "Roumania and Bessarabia." *The Nineteenth Century and After,* 95: 791–803.

Toynbee, Arnold J., ed. *Survey of International Affairs 1926.* London: Oxford University Press and Humphrey Milford, 1928.

Treaty of Peace with Rumania. n.p.: n.p., 1947.

Universul. Bucharest, daily, 1884–

U.S. *Foreign Relations of the United States: Diplomatic Papers 1933.* Vol. 2, *The*

British Commonwealth, Europe, Near East and Africa. Washington, D.C.: U.S. Government Printing Office, 1949.

USSR, Komissiíà po izdaniíù diplomaticheskikh dokumentov [Commission for the Publishing of Diplomatic Documents]. *Dokumenty vneshnei politiki SSSR* [Documents of the USSR's foreign policy]. Moscow: Izdatel'stvo politicheskoĭ literatury, 1957—   .

Index